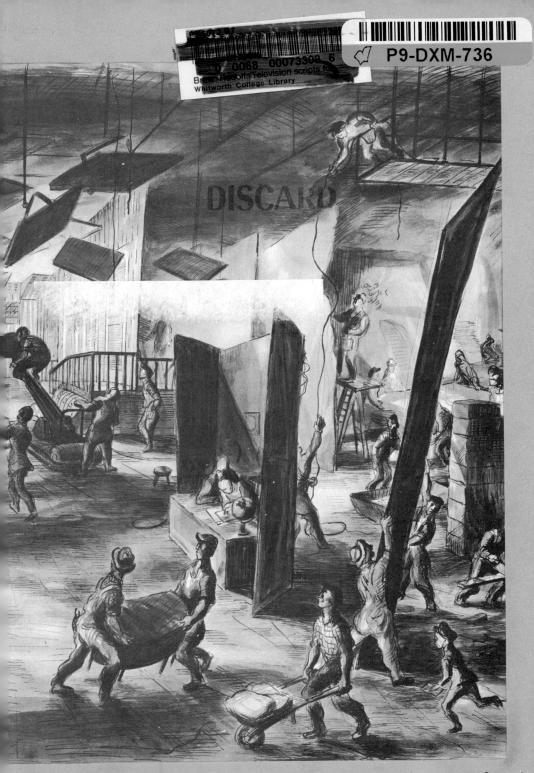

"Giant in a Hurry" by John Groth is reproduced here as an exercise in camera handling. Assume you have a camera which takes in only a small portion of this scene. You can make a frame out of a piece of paper which will show you this camera's field of view. Cut a rectangular hole in the paper 1" high and about 1¼" wide. Now lay this over the picture, and pan your camera around the scene. You can frame good and poor compositions, pan along interesting routes, apply many of the camera principles described in the first two chapters of this book.

TELEVISION SCRIPTS FOR
STAGING AND STUDY

Television Scripts

for Staging

and Study

With a Guide to Creative Camerawork

by Rudy Bretz, Television Consultant;
Instructor in Television, College of the
City of New York; Former Writer-Director,
CBS-TV; Former Production Manager,
Station WPIX, New York

and Edward Stasheff, Associate
Professor of Speech, University of
Michigan; Former Television Supervisor,
Station WNYE; Former Assistant Program
Manager, Station WPIX, New York

Over 50 Charts and Diagrams by Rudy Bretz

A. A. WYN, INC. · NEW YORK

ACKNOWLEDGMENTS

To so many people the authors owe a debt of gratitude for their help in the preparation of this book: To Carol Van Sickle, for hours of excellent typing and re-typing of the complete manuscript; to Bert Gold, for several months of office space cleared out of a busy studio; and to Wini James of the A. A. Wyn staff, for her critical judgment and creative suggestions.

For the script from the *Living Blackboard* series, we are indebted to writers Martha Caccamo and Albert Sayer of Station WNYE; the New York City Board of Education; director Freddie Bartholomew, and Station WPIX which made the series possible. To Professor N. Edd Miller of the University of Michigan, for the debate format, "Public Verdict." To Dr. Franklin Mathewson of the Department of Audio-Visual Instruction of the National Education Association, and Robert Herridge of CBS, for the disussion format, "It's Worth Knowing." Particular thanks to Robert Herridge for his notes on the thinking behind this series of productions, and to Dr. Mathewson for generously offering to help readers who want additional suggestions for more programs of the same type. Thanks go to Robert Foshko, student at the University of Michigan, for his excellent dramatic sketch, "Casting Call," written on assignment for this book, to fill the need for a short vignette which could be produced with an all-male cast.

We are grateful also to James Truex for permission to reproduce his charming sketch, "She Walks in Beauty"; to Ted Collins, on whose program, *The Kate Smith Daytime Hour,* it was first produced, and to Albert McCleery for preparing a marked script with his original camera cues and cuts.

For the script "Control of Climate," we are indebted to the Alfred P. Sloan Foundation and Teleprograms, Inc., and to producer William Hodapp and his associate, Robert Wald, for their helpful cooperation. We want to thank Charles Christensen of the NBC staff who originally directed this program, for preparing a faithful copy of his original script for reproduction. Also we are grateful to Dr. Vincent Schaeffer of the General Electric Company for offering to provide the necessary film materials should a group wish to produce this program.

To producer Carol Irwin and writer Frank Gabrielson, we owe thanks for the script, "The Night the Animals Talked," from the series,

Mama. Special thanks are due Ralph Nelson, the director, who prepared a script for our use and contributed a section describing the particular problems he encountered in the original production.

The script "The Line of Duty" from the NBC *Cameo Theater* series is reproduced through the courtesy of NBC and the writer, Guy de Vry. We want to again thank Albert McCleery for devoting so much time in making this book as complete as possible; his assistant, Ruth Girard, for her part in helping to arrange his time out of a particularly heavy schedule; and his script editor, Ethel Frank, for her help in choosing the script and her editorial assistance on the production notes which accompany it.

We thank CBS and artist John Groth for permission to use his lithograph, "Giant In a Hurry," on the endpapers of this volume. Finally we want to mention again both the National Broadcasting Company and the Columbia Broadcasting System for granting permission to use their material and for providing the necessary illustrations.

RUDY BRETZ
EDWARD STASHEFF

FOREWORD

Since the publication of their earlier book, *The Television Program,* the authors have received many helpful comments from teachers and students who have used the book. In the study of television production, the need has been felt for more scripts which students can analyze and discuss, and produce themselves. In addition, advanced students who have mastered the elementary aspects of production have asked for a more detailed coming-to-grips with the basic problems of directing. Principally, they want a better understanding of the camera as a creative instrument.

This volume has been written to meet these needs. It is intended for students who have gone beyond the general aspects of production and are ready to direct a show. The first part of the book is devoted to an intensive consideration of the choices which the director must make as he plans his camera shots and prepares his script. We are concerned here first with individual shots, special camera effects and pictorial composition, then with these shots when placed in sequence with others. The reader is urged to give careful consideration to Part I before proceeding to the scripts themselves, however tempting they may be.

The scripts range from simple formats to complete half-hour dramas. The student-director is given considerable assistance in the production notes accompanying the earlier scripts. As he goes along, he will receive less and less help and will be expected to make more and more of his own creative decisions. Finally, in Part III, the student-director is given the full script as produced by an accomplished director to study the decisions made by a professional craftsman.

It will also be noted that the scripts are of two types: Those which may be produced and broadcast without special permission or payment of royalty, and those which may not be produced without the consent of the author or his agent and payment of a small fee. In the latter category are *The Night the Animals Talked, The Line of Duty,* and the dramatic vignette, *She Walks in Beauty.* The script from the American Inventory series and the one from It's Worth Knowing do not require payment of royalty fees when broadcast over a local station, but permission must be secured from the appropriate parties. In every case, a clear statement of the royalty situation and the name and address of the person from whom permission must be obtained have been provided on the page preceding each script.

Students using the book during a course will find it valuable, in preparing the scripts in Part II for rehearsal, to mark the shots tentatively in the space provided. While this work should be done individually, the results may be compared in class. One student's decisions may then become the basis of the subsequent production, and the other students will have an opportunity to see the results of those decisions. The instructor will probably find it desirable to mimeograph the scripts to be used as class projects, for ease in handling and correcting and so students may follow the professional practice of copying their markings, as amended and corrected, into clean scripts for the final show.

The scripts in Part III might be utilized for an extended classroom project in the following manner: Any one of the scripts which are shown as produced may be assigned to the student for plotting. The student is to assume that he is a director who is planning his camera shots in the first or "paper" stage of preparation. With the floor plan provided in the book, and a shot-plotter like the one described in Fig. 2, page 20, the student-director sets to work. The floor plans of the individual sets inserted in the body of the scripts are to the standard scale of ¼" to the foot. The student may trace these directly or the instructor may have them mimeographed to the same scale. First the student will plot the position of the mike boom for each set, remembering that this may be moved when time permits and that in some cases more than one boom was used in the original production. Knowing the field of view selected by the original director for each shot, the student can choose a lens and determine where the camera was placed for that shot. Trying various camera positions on the floor plan, the student will soon approximate the original lenses and the original camera deployment. Once he has reconstructed the basic camera positions for each set, the student can go through the script with his shot-plotter, working out each shot as planned by the original director. This process, when completed, can form the basis for an actual production of the script.

The student working alone can follow this technique just as readily as the student in class, though he will not have the benefit of an instructor's criticisms or comparison with fellow students. The individual student may find it desirable to extend the technique we have just described to the scripts in Part II, since he will not have the opportunity to see them in rehearsal. Teachers will devise still other methods with which to use the material and the production information herein.

One technique which the authors have used to advantage with their own classes involves the use of a kinescope recording and a marked script of the same production. Each student is provided with a mimeographed script without the director's markings. The kinescope is run off, one scene at a time. At the end of each scene, the projector is run back to the start of that scene and the instructor dictates the original director's camera markings for that scene. After all students have their copies marked, the scene is projected again. This time the students "call the shots" from their marked scripts, watching the screen "respond" to their directions, and at the end of the scene, the projector is run back to the top of that scene, and this time, one or a succession of selected students may be asked to call the shots individually to check on their skill at shot-calling. When perfection has been reached, the same process is repeated for the next scene, and so on, as long as class-time will permit. This is a particularly valuable and practical laboratory exercise. If the student calls the takes correctly, he has a tremendous feeling of power . . . he feels as skilled as the original director. And if he bungles, the "rehearsal" never snarls up as it would if a bungling director were actually calling the shots on a real camera run-through. The program will not suffer, although the student's ego may.

While this technique may be applied to any program for which the instructor may secure both a kinescope and a marked script, we recommend it particularly in connection with *Control of Climate*, page 189, since *American Inventory* and the Alfred P. Sloan Foundation have been so generous in their desire to spread the techniques they have developed.

Ideally, the student will get the greatest value from any script if he takes some part in its production. Even with dummy cameras, used with considerable success by both the authors with their own students, the cast and crew may face actual production conditions. One simple type of dummy camera consists of an ordinary light camera tripod, mounted on a simple caster dolly. On this tripod there is mounted a 16-mm. camera panning head. In place of a camera, a viewing box such as the Bretzbox (Figure 1) is mounted on the camera attachment screw of the panning head. Detailed instructions on building a Bretzbox are to be found in the appendix to this volume.

The student may pan, dolly, re-position, or change lenses, assured that the framing he sees is exactly what a cameraman would see in the viewfinder of a real camera, given the same position and lens. The chief disadvantage of operating with dummy cameras is to the director, who must depend on the cameraman to tell him whether his shots work. And, of course, the student-director can never see the effect of cutting.

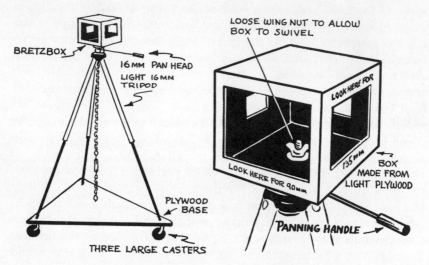

Figure 1. Inexpensive type of dummy camera.

Many professional directors today prefer to rehearse their shows from the floor, looking at their shots through the camera viewfinders. This is a technique which can readily be followed with dummy equipment.

With real equipment available, intensive rehearsal to a point of perfection is almost as valuable as a closed circuit production fed to an audience outside the studio; a closed circuit program is almost as valuable as an actual broadcast. The difference is chiefly psychological.

Producing the program, whether with dummy or real cameras, on closed circuit or on the air, will give all those who work on the show a greater insight into the practical problems of television direction.

RUDY BRETZ
EDWARD STASHEFF

Contents

11

Part III

FULL-LENGTH SCRIPTS

Part I

CREATIVE CAMERA TECHNIQUES

1. Creative Use of Cameras

It is an axiom of the television medium, lovingly described by its practitioners as "organized chaos," that the production of a television program is a joint effort, involving the coordinated activity of a number of specialized craftsmen. Obviously, the more creative and imaginative those people are, the more they are encouraged to contribute individually, the more smoothly they work together, and the better the end-product will be.

In this chapter, we are concerned with one of the most essential factors in creative television production—camerawork. Let us grant that the program begins with the idea, or with the script, if it is a fully scripted program, and that not even the most inspired camera handling can make a silk purse production out of a pig's ear of a script. Yet, given good material in both script and talent, it is camera treatment which must bring that material to the viewer. And it is to encourage fresh, imaginative and original use of cameras that this chapter is written. How can the reader of this section be original if we provide for him several dozen accepted methods of using cameras? Let us recall the motto, "The bricks I used were any man's; the house I built, my own." Here then is a good supply of bricks, and a few general observations on brick-laying.

Who Originates Creative Camera Ideas?

The three craftsmen most involved are the writer, the director and the cameraman. While most directors prefer scripts in which no specific shots are "ordered" by the writer, they do appreciate writing which offers opportunity for imaginative shooting. When a writer thinks in terms of what the camera is viewing, not just of what the microphone is hearing, he is encouraging creative camerawork. When a writer puts action into his script, when he has his camera tell the story, when he provides opportunity for movement and discovery, he is contributing to the whole production's originality.

The director's function is obvious. It is he who must take the writer's ideas and stage them for camera. He must devise action to fit the author's dialogue and stage this action in the most convenient and effective manner for his cameras. The director uses the cameras to show what the author has imagined and to enhance whatever dramatic mood he has conceived, adding his own conception and interpretation through the instruments of his art.

But the actual, literal handling of the camera is done by a cameraman. The best directors look upon the other members of their crews as fellow craftsmen; they do not regard a cameraman as a mere extension of the pan-handle. Cameramen who are encouraged will contribute suggestions; will offer simpler or better ways of obtaining a desired effect; will invent new effects and will practice, frequently on their own time, complicated moves and maneuvers. They ask only the opportunity to originate and to share in the creative process, and the natural recognition of their contribution which they justly deserve.

To repeat: *Who* originates creative camera ideas? The writer, the director and the cameraman all *may* do it. The ideal situation (and the best program) combines the efforts of all three in a fusion of three talents.

When and Where Does the Imaginative Use of the Camera Come into the Production?

At every moment of the production schedule, from the writing of the script to the last second of dress rehearsal, creation is at work. Creative touches may even be added on the air, though this practice is scarcely to be recommended if the smoothest results are to be achieved, and if sufficient rehearsal time is available. To see at what points these opportunities arise, let us examine the ideal rehearsal procedure of a dramatic program.

Stage 1—Paper Planning

Between the moment when the director first looks at the script of a production and the time when the cast is assembled for a first rehearsal, he has planned most of the show in his mind or on paper. Many directors know, at the conclusion of this first stage of camera planning, exactly which cameras are to be used on each shot, where they are to be placed in the studio, and what lenses are to be used. Changes will be made, of course, but the more pre-planning accomplished in this early stage, the better use can be made of the all too short rehearsal periods with cast and with cameras which follow.

First the director must read the script and visualize it. Simply reading through a script is easy—and the director may do this to begin with just to get the idea of the story. Reading a script and *visualizing* it takes time. The director must ask himself on every line "what are they seeing now" and force himself to visualize the picture on a television screen. People who have not had television or film experience may find this particularly difficult. It is natural to visualize as we read—all of us, reading a novel, see the characters in our mind's eye, but not through the eye of a camera. A director with stage background will read the script with a visual picture of actors on a stage. Only experience in the use of cameras will train a director to see close-ups, two-shots, shots which truck or dolly, as he reads the script.

As soon as the director has a clear idea of the kind of production he wants to do, he will go to the set designer and together they will rough out a set. Later, the designer will have a floor plan ready which will show the positions of all sets and furniture accurately and to scale. The director takes this floor plan and uses it as a sort of base map on which to chart his camera placement. The director's most useful instrument at this time is a device called a "shot-plotter." Whether manufactured or homemade, the shot-plotter is basically a protractor on which are marked the horizontal lens angles for the standard camera lenses. A shot-plotter may be a simple triangle, cut from clear plastic, showing the field of view of only one lens; or it may have several sets of lines imprinted on it, representing the angles of several lenses. A certain type of shot-plotter, devised by one of the authors, is adjustable so it may be set for any lens and will show the lens angle of only one lens at a time. Placing the shot-plotter on the floor plan, the director can determine one of three variables involved in each shot: (1) the position of the camera, (2) the lens, and (3) the field of view of the shot. If two of these are known, the shot-plotter will determine the third. Thus, if the director knows the field of view he wants and where he wants to place the camera, he can determine which lens to use. If he knows the lens and the field of view, he can determine where he must place the camera, and if he knows the lens and camera position, he can determine how much of the scene will be in the camera's field of view.

An important part of a good shot-plotter is a measure of the maximum and minimum extensions of the mike boom. Unlike the lens angles, the mike boom extension must be made to scale. (A horizontal angle of 34° will remain 34° no matter what scale the floor plan is drawn to.) Most floor plans are done in a standard ¼-inch to the foot scale, and a standard shot-plotter will show the seven-foot minimum boom extension and the seventeen-foot maximum extension to this scale. The director will generally establish the position of the boom base first, since it takes up considerable room and will determine to some extent the space left for camera movement. The lighting man will often be interested in seeing this floor plan before he plans the lighting, so he can place his lights according to the principal camera angles covering the centers of action.

Figure 2. The Bretz shot-plotter. Made of two pieces of sheet plastic which pivot on a center grommet. Angle between the two inner edges is measured on scale at right, which is calibrated in degrees and specially marked for the standard television lenses.

On some series, the director will work out every show in detail in this manner. Others will require the shot-plotter only on the first show of a series, or whenever a major change is planned. Some directors prefer not to do too much final planning in this paper stage of production, leaving all final decisions until later.

Stage 2—Outside Rehearsal

Rehearsals of these complicated shows always begin outside the studio in a rehearsal hall or some suitable space. The exact size of the studio sets is marked off on the floor; chairs or other furniture are used to simulate sets and props, and the performers get a good idea

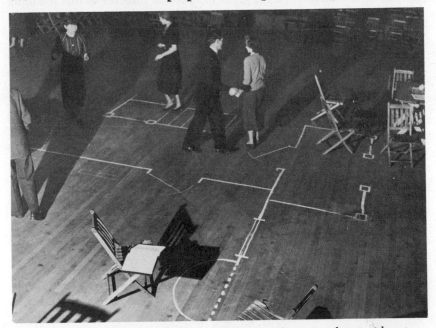

Figure 3. Outside rehearsal of a television dramatic show with sets marked accurately on the floor.

of the space in which they are to work. Here the director will move about, taking the place of one camera and then another, as he views each shot from the position of the camera that will take it. Some directors use an optical viewfinder, which gives them the field of view of the television camera lenses (available on the market at a rather high figure). Other directors will use homemade viewfinders, frame viewers or a simple Bretzbox. (See Appendix for construction.) Many directors, however, frame a picture with their own hands. Some use their arms, some their fingers, but the result is the same—an easier visualization of the picture on the television screen.

Studio rehearsal with facilities is, to a large extent, a period for briefing the cameramen, the floor manager, the stage crew, and the cast, on the many aspects of the show which the director has previously worked out in his mind. If the cameramen have seen the show before rehearsal, much of this time can be saved. Cameramen are authorities on the problems of space and traffic on the studio floor and can spot difficulties of which the director may not have been aware. And finally, the creative mind of the cameraman, and his own powers of visualization, are a great help to the director in this planning

Figure 4. Methods used by various directors to help them visualize a shot within a frame.

stage. If it is at all possible economically, the cameraman should witness an entire rehearsal of a show outside the studio before the first use of cameras on the studio floor. Such an assignment is known at the networks as a "conference day."

Stage 3—Dry-Run

Many directors prefer to use their first hour or so of studio rehearsal for a dry-run. That is, to walk through the show from beginning to end, using no electronic facilities at all, but working with the cameramen and crew on the studio floor. The great value of this dry-run is that all studio personnel get an idea of the show as a unit. Camera blocking, after the next stage, will go much faster because of it. A dry-run is particularly necessary, of course, if the key personnel, the technical director, and the camera crew have not seen the show in outside rehearsal. Without this unified dry-run, the show may remain disconnected in everyone's mind until it actually goes on the air.

Stage 4—Rough Run-Thru

A fourth stage, not always used, is a straight run-thru of the entire show, paying no attention to mistakes, rough places and problems that turn up. This is very valuable for the camera crew, and also for the stagehands who must make scene changes or handle props during the show.

Stage 5—Camera Blocking Work-Thru or Stop-Start

The fifth stage is camera blocking. This takes up the major portion of the rehearsal period. The director works through the show, stopping whenever necessary and working out all the problems as they come up. It is during this period that all the fine details of camerawork are set, and the cast and cameras are coordinated.

Stage 6—Run-Thru

The sixth stage is a run-thru in which the entire show is done as a unit, preferably without stopping. Some directors will run the show as many times as possible; others may rest content with one good run-thru and spend the remaining time working on difficult sequences. More often, there is not time for either procedure, and sometimes a show is worked through so closely to air-time that there is not sufficient time for the dress rehearsal. Most of the small stations, when they put on dramatic shows or other complicated programs, cannot allocate sufficient rehearsal time for all these stages. In such cases, all the steps are eliminated except the paper stage, the outside rehearsal and the work-thru.

Stage 7—Dress Rehearsal

So far, only the actors and the cameras have been involved. With the final dress rehearsal, all the other elements of the show are added to these. Actors don make-up and costume; sound effects, rehearsed separately to the director's satisfaction, are integrated into the show; live musicians arrive from their rehearsal studio; film and slide inserts from the projection room are used now for the first time. Only the ultimate refinements will be added during the dress rehearsal: the tempo of a camera movement, the pace of a dissolve, the slight adjustment of an angle or a grouping for better composition. The director and the cameraman are still trying, right up to air-time, to get just a bit more value out of their planned shots.

Why Does the Director Plan a Shot in a Particular Way?

At this point, we are not concerned with which camera is taking the shot we're discussing, nor where that camera is to be placed in relation to the others. The deployment of cameras on the studio floor, the decisions about the sequence in which we cut from camera to camera come later when we begin to connect the shots to each other. At this moment, we are concerned with a single shot at some given point. In any shot he plans, the director must keep three purposes in mind:

To Show the Subject Clearly

Nothing can infuriate a viewer more than the frustrating experience of not seeing clearly what he believes is happening. The viewer wants to know what is going on, and to see it easily and pleasantly. He is entitled to see the man who is speaking *when he starts to speak*, not seconds later, after the director has succeeded in getting a "suitable" shot.

An overabundance of spectacular effects which leaves the viewer in doubt does not achieve any worthwhile purpose. A tricky angle, an elaborate superimposition, an extreme close-up or long-shot will add to the dramatic effect only if the subject is clearly visible in the first place. Just as a line of doubtful meaning may elicit a "whad'he say?" from the audience, a shot in which the subject or the action is unclear will bring out the much more serious "wha' hoppen'" reaction, which then leads rapidly to "so what."

To Make Good Composition

Showing the action clearly is only the first step. The director and cameraman must show it attractively. Whenever the camera is not in motion, there is an essentially still picture on the screen, and that picture can be well composed or poorly composed. The viewer will understand and follow the meaning if the pictures are explicit, but his pleasure will be intensified by good composition. What is good composition? Volumes have been written on the subject, principally by painters and photographers. Conclusions applied to television are sufficiently important to warrant a separate chapter (3) on this subject. In this preliminary statement, we wish to stress simply that composition is an important factor which the director has in mind when he plans a shot.

Figure 5. Three purposes a shot can fulfill: a. Showing the subject clearly—b. Making a good composition—c. Achieving dramatic effect.

To Achieve Dramatic Effect

Finally, the manner in which the camera is used may add a dramatic quality. Such factors as composition, movement, camera angle, etc., subtly contribute to the viewer's emotional response. A shot may be placid or dynamic; it may give a character importance or insignificance. A big close-up provides dramatic emphasis; an extreme long-shot may dwarf an actor against his background. The important thing is to make sure that the dramatic effect of the shot is in keeping with the dramatic effect of the scene as planned by writer, actor and director.

What Choices Must the Director Make?

In order to achieve these three purposes (clarity, good composition and dramatic effect), the director must decide how much of the subject to show, from what angle to show it, and whether to keep his camera still or in motion. He must also decide which, if any, electronic effects to use in the shot. Let us list and define these four choices, briefly, before discussing the possibilities of each.

Field of View:

The area or the amount of the scene which is shown on the screen. We customarily think of the field of view as providing a long-shot, medium-shot or close-up.

Camera Angle:

The *direction* from which the camera, and therefore the viewer, sees the subject. It may have a profound psychological effect, as we shall discuss on the following pages. The director must decide on his horizontal angle, shooting the scene from head-on (straight in front), from left or right, or from behind. He may also shoot the scene from normal eye level, from a low point of view or from a high vantage point which may even be directly overhead.

Besides the choice of horizontal angle and vertical angle, the director may select a specialized point of view, such as a shot taken through a window or seen in a mirror. He may go so far as to place the camera in what has been called "zero angle," the position of the chief character in the scene. When used thus, the camera is subjective —it becomes the character, and other actors play directly into the lens.

Camera Movement

The movement of the camera, whether it is a simple sweep across the set from left to right (pan), a gradual change of the distance between camera and subject (dolly), or an involved zoom in three dimensions, plays an important part in the effect the director seeks to achieve. While the camera may be still as the subject moves, it may also move with the subject, or it may move while the subject holds still. The director's decision then is whether his camera is to move at all, and if so, to determine which type of movement to use.

Special Camera Effects

The camera and its related equipment make possible a number of effects such as the superimposition of one picture over another, the use of images from two cameras side by side in a "split screen," or the deliberate distortion of the camera's picture. As in all tricky effects, the director must be sure that his decision will add to the value of the shot and not simply distract the audience.

How Does the Director Make These Choices?

Probably no director sits down with the copy of a new script and solemnly tells himself, "First, I must choose my field of view for each shot. Then I must select my camera angle, decide whether I'll move my camera or hold it still, and finally pick out the points at which I'll work in some electronic effects." As in painting a picture, driving a car or swimming, the selective process becomes almost instinctive. The television director stages his action in his own mind as he reads and re-reads his script. As he stages it, he "shoots it" mentally, planning his shots by seeing them in his mind's eye. He may not be aware that he is selecting field of view and camera angle. Rather, he finds himself thinking, "I'll open on an establishing shot from the left, then dolly in toward the stairway as the ·people come down it, arguing. Then, just as they get to the bottom step, I'll hold on a two-shot." In short, the analysis of the myriad choices which an experienced director automatically makes is provided here for the student-director, in order to create in his mind an awareness of what is involved in so seemingly simple a decision as "opening with an establishing shot and then dollying in toward the stairway."

Suppose we turn now to a more detailed discussion of the possibilities available to the director as he makes these basic selections.

Choice of Field of View

The first decision which the director makes, consciously or instinctively, is concerned with how much he wants to show. He must decide whether he wants a single- or a two-shot (one or two people), whether he wants a long-shot, medium-shot, or close-up, and when each of these shots is to begin and end.

In the term "long-shot," "long" refers to the long distance between camera and subject. A long shot is only long, however, in relation to the other shots associated with it. For example, if one is shooting a sequence involving objects on a tabletop, a shot covering the entire table would be regarded as a long-shot. On the other hand, if the sequence of shots covers the entire room, this same table-top shot might be classed as a close-up instead. In the television dramatic show, the long-shot generally shows as much of the set as possible, the close-up includes a head- and shoulders-shot of a single person, and the medium-shot is almost anything in between. A shot which takes in only the head is a "big close-up." Finally, when the camera shows only a portion of the face, this is known as an "extreme close-up."

Many television directors identify the type of shot they want by describing in one word where the lower edge of the frame cuts the actor. This is a fairly exact terminology, since a waist-shot (in which the actor is cut at the waist) will invariably include the same amount of headroom and hence the same field of view every time. Such specific terms as knee-shot, thigh-shot, waist-shot, bust-shot, shoulder-shot, etc., are usually to be preferred over the more general "long-shot," "medium-shot," and "close-up."

The primary purpose of a long-shot is orientation. It is usually necessary for the audience to understand the relationships of the various elements of a scene. The distance from the door to the window may need to be well understood, the relationship of window to fireplace well established, and so on. This is more quickly done by a long-shot than by any other method, although very often a closer shot will perform the same function if it pans across the scene.

The long-shot is necessary sometimes to show the extent of a broad action. Often it must extend beyond the field of action when the space around it is important. At a race-track, as horses are coming down the final stretch, for example, a shot showing only the horses is inadequate. The viewer wants to know how far they are from the finish line. This calls for a much longer shot than the viewer would have wanted earlier in the race.

When the subject is a dancer or a ballet group, the important thing is the movement in space. The audience's desire to see the dancer in detail will give way, as soon as a wider sweep of movement begins, to the desire to see not only the dancer but the pattern he is making in space. The camera must show the space the dancer has just left and the space he is moving into.

The long-shot is frequently necessary to convey the effect of the scenery which the set designer has created. Sets are generally planned in long-shot—sketched out in their entirety, and constructed, painted and dressed as a unit. Portions of the set appearing as background for medium-shots rarely allow the set to put across the values which the designer had planned.

Lastly, the long-shot has a dramatic effect which can sometimes be put to good use. There can be something inherently expressive in the physical size of an object on the television screen. A large object dominates a small one; a person large in the foreground dominates one that is small in the background. A little child wandering and lost could be shown in a close-up, but the shot might not enhance the mood. The feeling of this scene calls for a long shot where the figure is small in relation to its surroundings.

The functional purpose of the close-up shot is obvious; a subject must be large enough on the screen to be clearly seen. Close-ups are particularly important in television not only because of the small size of the average receiver screen, but because of the poor resolution which is displayed. "Resolution" refers to the detail that is visible— the sharpness of focus. Since the average receiver produces a picture which is far from the crisp and sharp image on a motion-picture screen, objects must be larger to be as easily visible. Details in a long-shot are often so fuzzy they cannot be seen. It should be noted, however, that the same lack of detail might be *desirable* in a close-up, and is actually created intentionally by the motion-picture cameraman when he uses glamorizing diffusers and gauzes in front of the lens. Too much detail in a close-up brings out every wrinkle and blemish in the skin.

The close-up is often used for dramatic emphasis. When the attention of the audience is called to a small area of the scene, that particular detail is pointed up and emphasized in a way which would be impossible if it were seen only as one among many objects in a medium-shot. The entire meaning of a scene can be changed by the details which the director may choose to emphasize in close-up shots.

It is important to note here that performers must understand the camera's particular problems in close-up shots, or they may make his work look awkward. They must realize that in a close-up view, even a small movement is greatly magnified on the screen, as are the adjustments which the cameraman is forced to make to keep the moving object correctly framed.

This is particularly true when the close-up is taken by a relatively distant camera with a long lens. It is much more difficult to pan the camera smoothly when a long lens is used, simply because each irregularity is magnified on the screen. The performer, therefore, must be cautioned against any quick movements, and if he is holding an object for very close inspection, he should rest his hand on some solid support, or the slight motions which he is unable to prevent will be exaggerated.

Combination Close-Up and Long-Shot

A very interesting kind of shot frequently used today is the combination of a close-up with a long-shot. One person is close to the camera while another is seen beyond him in the distance. This type of shot lends itself well to interesting composition since there is depth in the scene, the figures of people are of different sizes and different heights. The near person, looming larger and usually higher in the frame, dominates the other. This shot is often used for the dramatic entrance of a dominant new figure: he enters the frame from the side, close to the camera, and very large. To discover the new character in long-shot with the subordinate people large in the foreground might be dramatically wrong. The visual effect might be the reverse of the dramatic feeling and would tend to destroy it.

A valuable use for this shot has been found in the musical show where a singer has a long number and it is desirable to make the song more interesting visually by introducing a dance. If the dancers are seen in the background while the singer continues her song in medium-shot or close-up, the viewer may look back and forth between the two as often as he likes. (Fig. 6)

This combination shot has been seen much more often in television than in motion pictures, even though film cameras with their greater depth of focus would be able to handle it far better. Perhaps the reason is that the combination-shot is valuable for television because

Figure 6. The Combination Long-Shot and Closeup as used in *Your Lucky Strike Hit Parade.*

it is economical of time and cameras. Like the news-story photo, it shows all of the story in one shot. The still photographer, knowing he will get just one picture on the front page of his paper, tries to put as much of the story into his one shot as he possibly can. Not only does he show the injured child, but he tries to get the weeping mother into the same shot. Such a picture will hold interest much longer than one which gives only part of the story. In television, the combination-shot is valuable for another reason. It may replace a sequence of shots back and forth between two people conversing. The viewer is not forced to look only at the person the director selects. Furthermore, there is value in having an actor reveal his feelings to the audience while he is concealing them from the actor to whom his back is turned.

Like anything else, this technique has often been overdone or wrongly used. As a result, it has unfortunately become an accepted convention of television staging for people to converse without looking at each other. All too many conversations feature one of the actors in close-up gazing out past the camera and talking to someone behind his back.

Choice of Camera Angle

The "camera angle" is the *direction* from which the camera views the subject. Re-positioning the camera between shots will alter its lateral angle of view. It may take a full face, three-quarters, or profile view close-up, for example. Raising or lowering the camera will alter the vertical camera angle, creating low and high angle shots. (Camera angle is not to be confused with "lens angle" or "angle of view," two synonymous terms which refer to the field of view shown by the camera, not the direction from which the camera is looking.)

All television cameras are mounted on wheeled dollies and can be quickly re-positioned between shots for a great variety of lateral angles. Changing lateral angle may improve the visibility of a subject by placing it against a better background, or by avoiding foreground objects which might otherwise be in the way. Cameras usually shoot from the fourth, or invisible side of a three-walled set, careful not to position too far to the side lest they shoot out of the set, and, of course, careful not to reveal other cameras or studio equipment. Camera positions must be avoided which line up the performers with objects in the background so that a man standing in front of a circular picture, for example, appears to have a halo around his head.

Figure 7. Reverse Angle Shots.

A shot from the opposite direction to the preceding shot is called a reverse angle. The classic example is a scene involving two people, A and B, in conversation. We see A over B's shoulder and then B over A's. A camera may be placed behind the set for some reverse angles. Special flats are commonly used for background for such shots, set up in the regular camera area and then struck (i.e., removed) again after the shot is over. These are known as "wild walls" or "wild flats." The camera behind the set may be hidden by a picture on the wall which is in reality a sliding panel that can be opened as soon as it is no longer in the shot of the camera on the air.

Vertical Camera Angle

Sometimes nothing but a very high angle "top-shot" will show the subject properly. A square dance, for example, taken from a normal camera height is a hopeless mass of motion; it is only from above that the pattern of movement can be seen. The same is true of small objects on a desk-top, or of action on a football field.

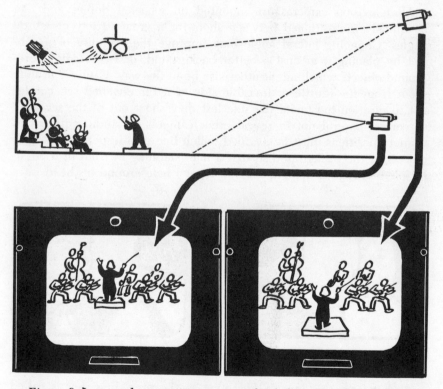

Figure 8. Improved composition as a result of changing vertical angle.

The ends of better composition are often served by proper choice of vertical angle. When the camera is raised to a higher position, foreground objects go lower in the frame. More floor is seen, more of whatever horizontal planes may be present, such as table- or piano-tops, etc. The difference in height between foreground and background figures usually improves the composition when the camera is either lower or higher than eye level.

When the limitations of the budget or the studio prevent the scenery from being built high enough, the cameraman is severely hampered in obtaining good long-shots. When he pulls back to take in a width of, say, 30 feet, he finds that his entire subject matter is then confined to a strip 30-feet wide and usually only 9-feet high.

Since the shape of the television picture requires a height which is three-quarters of the width, the camera in this case must show large floor areas if it is to avoid shooting above the sets. Television designers solve this problem in one way by decorating the floor so that if large areas of it must be seen, they will not be entirely uninteresting. The major problem of good balance in the composition is not solved by this means, however.

Instead, a high camera angle will enable the camera to get better long-shots, or at least make the shots more interesting in design. Although the higher camera illustrated in Figure 8 is shooting with the same lens, the shot it is taking is entirely different. The horizontal planes of the scene cover more area in the picture, and the musicians as seen in the high angle shot are filling a foreground area which in the low shot is occupied by bare floor.

The significance of being able to vary the height of the camera lies mainly in the dramatic effect that the shot can convey. An object seen from below is "looked up to" and the same object seen from above is "looked down upon." Statues are always placed on pedestals so people will have to look up at them and the great men they represent will seem more impressive. A still or movie cameraman is often seen taking low angle shots, down on one knee in the street or lying on his back.

A low angle shot taken from the ringside at a remote pick-up will make the fighters look much more impressive, and some of the most dramatic shots in sports come from low angle cameras.

Just as a low angle will invest a subject with importance, a high angle will produce the opposite effect. This is especially true if the subject is not only seen from above, but is also in long-shot and relatively small in size. A great drawback to many sports pick-ups on television is the lack of anything but high angle shots.

In Paul Nickell's production of "The Medium" on WPTZ in Philadelphia, a high angle long-shot was used for dramatic effect at a point in the show when the medium felt discouraged, lost and unloved. The camera was shooting down through a skylight into the room where the tiny figure of the medium looked very forlorn in the background. The result was dramatically effective.

Choice of Specialized Point of View

Choice of camera angle may also be based on the director's desire to use a specialized point of view. By showing a scene through the eyes of one particular person, the camera can put the viewer in that character's place. If we take the simple example of a man and a child in conversation, we realize that the man naturally sees the child from above; the child sees the man from below. Partially subjective camera positions could convey something of what each feels about the other. Whereas the two-shot could be taken from eye-level, an objective point of view, the close-up of the man might be from a low angle with the camera near the child, and the close-up of the child from above over the man's shoulder. The closer a camera can approach the position of either character, the more subjective the shot becomes. In a totally subjective shot, however, the actor must look directly into the lens of the camera and play to the television viewer as though he were a member of the cast.

Figure 9. Objective and subjective camera angles: a. Completely objective—b. Partially subjective—c. Completely subjective.

It is very difficult to sustain this type of shooting over a very long sequence since the camera must go through a great deal of complex movement. Subjective camera techniques may be used with great effect, however, for short shots at highly dramatic moments. A punch thrown directly into the lens, for example, will make the viewer feel that *he* has been hit. Throughout most of a dramatic show, however, playing to the camera is undesirable. Unless it has been well established that the camera represents a member of the cast, an actor suddenly looking into the lens may call attention to the camera itself and damage the mood of a dramatic show.

Choice of Camera Movement

Let us admit that it is easier to direct a show with cameras which never move while on the air, or which change their positions only between shots. In the early stages of a television course, when student cameramen are inexperienced and not very adept, or in a new station which is breaking in green camera crews, such a procedure may even be advisable—at first. A show produced with static cameras loses much in consequence. The program as seen on the air will lack movement, except by its performers, and may seem slow and fixed. The ingenuity of the director will be taxed as he endeavors to provide a variety of shots by moving his performers into different relations with the cameras, not because the action calls for it, but simply to achieve the feeling of movement. In short, the whole creative level of the program must inevitably suffer when the cameras are frozen in their tracks.

On the other hand, camera movement for its own sake may go too far. Movement that adds nothing to the effectiveness of a shot may be distracting. In general, no camera should move except for a definite purpose, clearly understood by director, cameraman and cast, and subconsciously appreciated by the viewer. Clearly, then, the director's first decisions in this regard are: Whether to move, when to move, whom to move (camera or actor or both). This is not always a matter of simple rules. Often a director will make these decisions instinctively, automatically. He *feels* that a shot is indicated at a certain point in the script, and if pressed, he could probably dig a perfectly rational explanation out of his subconscious. On a more conscious level, he may stop for a moment and decide *how to move* a camera on the air, and it is the reasons for the numerous choices of movement which concern us now.

Whether to move is a matter of taste and judgment, which some directors develop very quickly while others acquire it only through long experience. Briefly and obviously, a camera should be moved only if the movement enhances the value of the shot (1) by showing us something we were not able to see without the movement, or (2) by creating an emotional impact which strengthens the effect which writer and actor are creating.

When to move becomes a corollary of the above; the director moves a camera when he anticipates that the audience will want to see more than is already showing, or when he wants to lead the viewer to another area of the set, or to another subject. In the latter instance, he must provide a plausible motivation for his move, such as following an actor across the set.

Whom to move becomes a matter of personal preference, a choice inevitably based on the nature of the material. Most directors think first of moving their actors. They strive for dramatic effectiveness, good grouping for composition, and natural, realistic action.

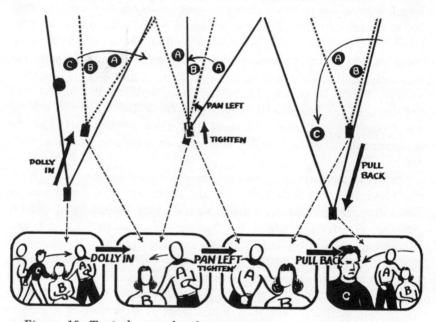

Figure 10. Typical example of camera movement coordinated with actor movement.

A large share of camera movement is devised simply to follow the action of the actors. If a waist-length two-shot is the best field of view to show two people in a conversation, and good staging calls for them to walk together across the set, the camera might best truck or dolly with them, keeping the same length of shot throughout the action, while only the background changes behind them.

The combined movement of actor and camera must be well integrated and well rehearsed. If only limited rehearsal time is available, very little of either can be planned. If the director must "wing a show" ("ad lib" his shots), his safest method is to use static cameras, keeping a wide-angle camera ready with a cover shot at all times in case the action suddenly widens out. It is only when sufficient rehearsal time is available or top cameramen are on the job that a director can so combine actor movement and camera movement that a long-shot becomes a medium-shot, then a close-up, then a full-shot again, smoothly and with constantly balanced composition. Notice in Figure 10 how each camera move is motivated. This is technically all one shot, since only one camera is used; the separate illustrations show stages in the camera movement.

SHOT	MOTIVATING ACTION	CAMERA MOVEMENT
a. Medium-shot (four-shot)	Actor C walks camera right behind A and B and out of the frame. The action is reduced to include only two people, and the audience wants a better view.	Camera dollies in during action of C
b. Two-shot	Actor A walks to other side of B and leans in a little closer.	Camera pans left with action of A and pushes in slightly to hold a tighter shot.
c. Tight two-shot	Actor C comes into frame again from camera right behind A and B, crosses to camera left and comes way down stage.	Camera pulls back as he crosses so as not to lose A and B from the picture.
d. Combination close-up and medium-shot		

This last dolly-back is a motivated move throughout its duration since it is made in coordination with the forward movement of the actor. The shot widens as the action widens. An attempt to pull the camera back to this shot without the actor's movement to motivate the pull-back might easily have called attention to the camera movement. If the last actor, for example, had merely been discovered in the final position after the camera pulled back, there would have been no initial motivation for the camera move. The audience might have felt dragged away from something in which they were very much interested. A cut to this final composition could even have been better than an unmotivated movement of the camera.

Types of Movement from Which the Director May Choose

Panning and Tilting: The simplest way to remove the camera, and one which is possible with even the most meager equipment, is the *Pan.* Panning is simply a matter of moving the camera from left to right or right to left, in a horizontal plane, without moving the camera support. Although panning, literally speaking, is horizontal movement, many stations have begun to think and speak in terms of "panning up" or "panning down." Vertical swiveling of the camera, however, is more properly called *tilting.* Some directors feel that it simplifies matters to use the instruction *Pan* for any movement involving the pan handle. Other directors feel that there is an advantage in using *Pan* for the horizontal movement and *Tilt* for the vertical because the two movements are sufficiently different in operation that the cameraman needs a little advance warning as to which he is called upon to do.

The following types of movement involve moving the whole camera support:

Dollying and Trucking: While smooth dollying is best accomplished with a movable camera mount such as the Panoram Dolly or the Studio Pedestal, an experienced cameraman can get amazingly smooth dolly movement out of a field tripod and three-wheeled dolly. When a director has different types of camera mounts in use on one show, however, he will probably be well advised to plan most of his dolly movement for the pedestal-mounted camera or for the Panoram Dolly if he has one at his disposal.

Dollying means pushing the camera closer to the subject or pulling it farther away. We normally think of dollying as being done on the air, but a director in re-positioning a camera that·is off the air may also use the term.

Again, purists in TV terminology will use the term *dollying* only in relation to a movement toward the subject or away from it. Moving sideways, in a plane roughly parallel to the subject's background, is properly called *trucking.* The camera may move past a line of soldiers, looking into the face of each in turn. Some directors make a distinction between movement toward and movement away from the subject, using "Dolly in" but "Pull back" or "Pull out" rather than "Dolly back or out." As in the case of the terms *pan* and *tilt*, these directors feel that use of the specific term for a specific type of movement saves time, once the distinctions have become habitual through practice, because the cameraman is immediately ready to pull back or push in or haul to left or right as soon as he hears the specific instruction. The beginning director, in all cases, will be well advised to find out the prevailing practice at the station with which he is associated and to follow that practice.

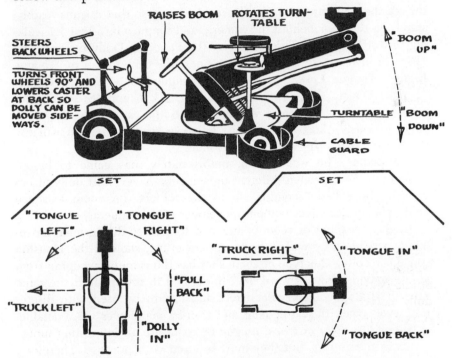

Figure 11. The Houston-Fearless Panoram Dolly and camera movements it makes possible.

Hollywood also uses the term "truck-shot" to mean a "follow-shot," where camera and actors stay the same distance apart, moving in the same direction whatever that may be. "Dollying with" a moving actor would become "trucking with" him according to this definition.

The Arc: A difficult and subtle movement, combining the in-and-out movement of the *dolly* and the sidewise movement of the *truck*, is the *arc*. As its name implies, it is a curved movement of the camera support, calling for constant control of the wheels of the support. Its effect is less obvious than that of either the *truck* or the *dolly*, if it is

done slowly and steadily, and it gives the audience an almost unnoticed but gratifying change of view without the disturbance of a
cut. The arc has sometimes been known as the "trolley-shot," a combination of both names.

Tonguing: With the boom or crane dollies, it is possible to achieve
the arc-shot with another type of motion, *tonguing.* This is basically
a curved movement of the camera. When the Panoram Dolly is placed
at right angles to the set, the tongue or arm which supports the camera
may be swung smoothly to the left or right. When it is cross-wise to
the set, the cameraman often releases the boom so that it spins readily,
stands on the floor behind the camera, and tongues in or out by walking forward or back. The tongue of the Panoram Dolly may also be
raised or lowered, so that we may request the cameraman to "Tongue
Right," "Tongue Left," "Tongue In," "Tongue Out," "Tongue Up" or
"Tongue Down." Some studios prefer "Boom Up" and "Boom Down,"
since they refer to the arm which supports the camera as the *boom.*
And, obviously, those that call the boom or tongue the *arm* will use
the phrase "Arm Up" or "Arm Down."

The Zoom: The word *zoom,* unfortunately, has come to be attached to two somewhat different movements. A very fast dolly-in has
come to be called "zooming" in to the subject. (A zoom lens can
achieve a similar effect without movement of the camera.)

Another meaning of *zoom* is attached to a three-dimensional movement, possible only with a large camera crane, such as the Houston
or Sanner dolly. This type of zoom shot has the camera swooping from
above, moving down toward the subject and in toward it at the same
time. It is a very spectacular effect and one to be used with discretion, even when the equipment and trained manpower are available.

Pan or *tilt; dolly* or *truck; tongue* or *zoom* are all interesting movements in themselves, but they must be used with purpose. Therefore,
let us examine the various ways in which television directors have
learned to use these camera movements.

Purposes in Panning or Tilting

Any camera movement must have a reason for being. When a pan-
shot is complete, it must have accomplished something and fulfilled
a purpose. This purpose may be obvious, or it may be known only to
the director. If it is not apparent to the viewer, at least, at the beginning to motivate the movement, then some other, more apparent,
motivation must be found. As used here, motivation refers to what the

audience wants to see, while purpose refers to what the director wants the audience to see, and *why*.

In general, a pan is a bridge. It starts *here* and ends *there*, and should give us a feeling of completion. Accordingly, directors usually hold the shot until the camera is at rest, so that the viewer will realize the movement has been completed and will not feel that he was snatched off a bridge before he had reached the other side of the river.

Almost all of the purposes to be described hold just as well for the *tilt* as they do for the *pan*. Frequently, the type of movement described is a combination of the two, as when, for example, the camera moves both up and to the right along the back wall of a set before coming to rest upon a key object hanging on the wall.

Here are some of the purposes for which panning and tilting are most frequently done:

Panning to following action. The subject moves across the set, and the camera pans with it. This is by far the most common reason for panning the camera. Movement of the subject is a perfect motivation to pan. The viewer is watching someone, wants to continue to watch that person, and is given just exactly what he wants when the camera keeps the subject in the frame. This results, also, in the smoothest possible viewing, since the position of the subject does not move on the screen. The subject moves, and the camera moves with it, keeping it stationary on the face of the receiver tube. Only the background or surroundings move across the screen; the eye does not have to shift. Sometimes, however, the subject is too small to permit this. A football punt and the high flight of a baseball are both examples in point. Since the moving object is so easily lost in the general blur, the cameraman will do better to pan to the receivers of the ball than try to follow it through the air.

This motivation for panning is so strong, the results so successful, and all other kinds of panning so unreliable, that beginning students in motion-picture camerawork are usually taught never to pan for any other purpose. This is to counteract the typical impulse of the amateur who has a movie camera in his hands for the first time. Since he now has a motion-picture camera, he feels he must invest his pictures with motion; and if the subject doesn't move, at least the camera can. He sweeps the scenery with his camera, as though it were a garden hose. Fortunately, the television cameraman rarely makes this mistake. He does not have to visualize his results; he sees them on the screen before him in finished form. It is a little safer for him to consider, at an earlier point, the other purposes of the pan.

Following reaction. When the camera pans to seek out a new subject which has previously been called to the viewer's attention, it is panning with reaction. If a person looks, or points a gun or a camera at something which is off-screen, motivation is established. The audience wants to see the new subject. Whether this desire is best satisfied with a pan or whether a cut is necessary, only individual circumstances can decide. Usually it is a cut because panning takes too much time.

The reaction pan was most effectively used at a point in a certain show where cutting would have been quite difficult. A group of six people, all murder suspects, were confronted by the detective who shocked them all with the announcement that he knew beyond any doubt the identity of the murderer. Each of the six suspects was afraid the murder would be pinned on himself. This called for six quick close-ups of reaction. Cutting would have required close coordination between camera and switching, so that two cameras would each take three shots, and might have necessitated considerable rehearsal. Since the people were grouped tightly together, however, a single camera was able to cover all six with successive pans from one reaction to the next.

Panning the subjective camera. The subjective camera effectively plays a part in the show. It puts the audience in the actor's place. In this case, the motivations for panning and other camera movement are not necessarily the same as they would be for an objective camera. As long as the shot retains interest throughout, and is constantly showing objects meaningful to the story, it will be accepted. It may go in any direction at any time, and is not dependent on following action or reaction. Whatever the camera may elect to do, so long as some ultimate purpose is served, is accepted as a legitimate motivation. Any camera-consciousness which might develop, as the audience is "dragged" from one subject to another, is translated into actor-consciousness immediately, since camera and actor are identified with each other.

The big problem in handling the subjective camera is to make it do what the viewer himself would do if he were in the same situation. Usually when this technique is used, cutting is avoided, since it is felt that a cut would introduce a cinematic technique and break the continuous effect of a single point of view. This is probably an erroneous theory. The eye really does not pan slowly around a scene the way a camera does. It actually jumps from subject to subject with a shuttering of the eye-lids between "shots" to cut out the blur. Only in rare cases does the eye examine a scene slowly and continuously as the slow panning of a camera might represent.

The Pan for Adjusting Composition

The cameraman may elect to pan his camera for a better balance or design of the picture. Assuming he has composed the picture properly in the first place, he should not have to make any adjustments unless something in the picture moves. When this happens, the adjustment should be made *during* the movement, not after. When the subject itself is in motion, the eye does not notice the slight movement of the camera. The camera movement is obscured by the simultaneous movement of the subject. If the subject should come to rest, however, before the composition is corrected, any further adjustment must be made slowly and imperceptibly. A variety of the pan shot is called for here—a variety which has been called the *ooze* or the *ease* shot. "Ease left" or "ease up" is the director's order.

The Pan for Orientation

The purpose of orientation may lie in the mind of the amateur as he panorams the view. He cannot hold the whole view in one frame, so he pans the camera to include it all. It is not often, however, that such a purpose provides a strong enough *motivation* for a pan. If orientation is necessary, and it cannot be done by a wide-angle shot, a motivation of subject movement is usually necessary. Even in travel films, where the scenery is the theme, and orientation a constant purpose, smooth camerawork generally takes advantage of some sort of subject movement: a car or a train or a rider on horseback, to motivate a pan.

In a dramatic show such motivation is usually provided when an actor crosses the set, the camera panning to follow his movement. However, there are still other ways to motivate this: an orientation pan.

When the characters in a drama enter a new setting, and themselves begin to look around, such an orientation pan is automatically motivated, even though there is no action to follow. The camera becomes, to a certain extent, subjective, showing the audience what the actors are seeing.

A good example of a pure orientation pan is the look-around over the ball park when a remote pick-up has just gone on the air and the game is not yet underway. The audience wants to know where they are, what the place looks like; and this desire is usually satisfied by one or two long pan-shots over the entire park. In this case, the desire for orientation is in itself a motivation for the act of panning.

The Pan of Association

A pan-shot has been described earlier as a bridge. In the pan of association, we concentrate the viewer's attention on the two ends of the bridge and skip quickly over the middle of the span, thus bringing the two terminal objects together in the viewer's mind. For example, we may pan quickly from a phial of poison to a bottle of the antidote, or from a photograph of a student to a photograph of the same young man in uniform.

The Pan of Exploration and Discovery

The exploratory pan is usually made in close-up, the purpose being to conceal from the audience all but one selected detail at a time. It is particularly valuable at the beginning of a sequence or act of a dramatic show. At the opening of the CBS production of *Night Must Fall,* the camera opened with a close-up of the famous hat-box, over which the opening titles were superimposed, then panned down after the titles to show a sign, "Exhibit A." From there the camera moved to a gun, "Exhibit B," and so forth, over several objects, including a model of the house and its environs, then up to the judge, whose voice had been heard summing up the case. When we finally saw the judge, he had come to the end of his summary, and pronounced the death sentence.

This kind of slow exploration of a scene is sometimes very fascinating to watch. In musical or dance shows, an opening 8 or 16 bars of music may be accompanied by a detailed exploration of the set, purely for its decorative value, culminating in a close-up of a vocalist just as he begins to sing. The camera may discover subjects very simply just by panning to include them in the view.

The Build-Up or Cumulative Pan

This kind of pan-shot moves across the scene in such a way that the subject builds up in importance or size or number as the pan progresses. To give an example from motion pictures: The camera may open on a tractor going down a wheat field, pan to three tractors, pan to twenty. Or the camera may reverse its direction, and starting with a long line of tiny tractors, pan to three in the foreground, and culminate with a shot of one gigantic tractor filling the screen.

The Pan for Variety and Change of View

Sometimes a cameraman is left with time to fill, a camera in his hands, and an audience to keep interested. This will happen, for instance, during a brief rainstorm at a baseball game, when the big tarpaulin is stretched over the field and everybody hopefully waits for the rain to stop. The announcer is filling in with color and background information, and the camera is panning around the field for no other purpose than to keep some sort of variety and change of view on the screen. Showmanship is at its lowest ebb. It is only at such a time that panning for variety, or cutting for variety, is of any value. Like anything else, however, it can be done well or it can be done poorly. The cameraman who does it well will pan with deliberation. He will know where he is going, and he will go there smoothly and without hesitation. Having arrived at one goal, he will choose another and a path to reach it, and proceed again with the same deliberation. He will take advantage of any natural motivations that he finds. Any movement of people on the field or in the stands will form a perfect path for him to follow.

He will remember also that there must be continuous interest in the picture, and to this end he will avoid empty spaces where there is nothing to look at. He will instead pan *along* things: along the stands, up a pillar to the upper tier, along the upper tier to the end, down the structure to the top of the bleachers, along to the scoreboard, etc.

There are some things the cameraman should be cautioned not to do, except in the case of unusual motivation. First, he should not pan aimlessly. Having started the camera moving in one direction toward one goal, he should not change his mind and wander off somewhere else. And above all, he should not reverse direction and go back over areas that the audience has already seen.

When a pan-shot begins, the attention of the audience is drawn to the extreme edge of the screen, watching for the new subject that the camera will bring into view. If the cameraman alters the direction of panning, the eye is drawn to another edge of the frame, and so on for each change of direction. The viewer expects each movement of the camera to bring him something new. If the camera goes to the right, then up, then down again, then to the left—without arriving at any particular goal—the frustrated audience will quickly lose confidence in the cameraman, and reject his work. As far as going back over the same route is concerned, the viewer is just not interested. If there is no other way back, the director must come to the rescue with a cut or dissolve, and start another camera on a voyage of exploration.

Panning and Composition

While the whole of Chapter 2 is devoted to pictorial composition, it may be wise to stress at this point that camera panning is very closely related to composition of the frame. Panning is, in a sense, composition in movement. All the rules and advice in the world cannot make a good cameraman; he must have natural ability and a great deal of practice. The first is beyond our control. Practice, however, is something which can be had even without a camera of any kind.

One can develop considerable skill in panning with a large still picture. The drawing reproduced inside the front cover of this volume is a good example. Cut a hole the size of a postage stamp in a piece of paper and make it the shape of a television screen. (Approx. 1" x 1⅓") Now move this frame around over the picture. Notice how easy it is to lose continuous interest during a pan-shot, how much better it is when you pan along something. Purposely make a very poor pan and then try to analyze what is wrong with it.

Purposes in Dollying

Dollying to change the field of view. The motivation for this movement usually arises from the audience's desire to see what is happening. If the action is reduced to a smaller area, the natural urge is to move closer and get a better view. A dolly-in can do this, or if there is not enough time, a cut to a closer shot will be better.

When the action takes a broader scope, a wider shot is needed, and the audience's desires are immediately answered when the camera pulls back to include it. The best camerawork is that which anticipates slightly the desires of the viewer and gives him the shot he wants before he is conscious of wanting it.

A dolly-back which forcefully takes one away from action which he is watching is sometimes useful at the conclusion of a program, provided the audience knows it has reached the end. If during the closing announcement, the camera is pulling back from the scene, a nice tapering conclusion is effected. This is often used on a program which began in the opposite manner, starting with a long-shot and dollying up close for the start of the action.

Dollying to follow action. An actor may have to cross the set, yet at the same time be involved in dialogue where it is necessary to show a fairly close shot. A cut to a wider "cover shot," although it would include the action, would still not show the audience what they wanted to see. The camera holding the actor in waist-shot at the beginning of the "cross" may dolly back as the actor moves (sometimes known as a *follow* or *truck* shot), keeping the same waist-shot throughout the cross. It is clearly better in such cases to use a camera in front of the actors rather than behind. However, an example may be given where the reverse is perfectly acceptable. Two characters are arguing heatedly "downstage," when one moves back to the window to escape the other. But the second character pursues the point and moves up to the window, too, and we dolly in to follow.

Dollying to adjust the composition. Whenever action takes place in a scene, the elements of the picture's composition change. The same framing will not continue to give a well balanced composition. Sometimes the camera can adjust slightly by panning or tilting, something that the cameraman always holds himself in readiness to do. The best cameramen, provided they have the right equipment, hold themselves in constant readiness for slight dolly movements also. Just as the framing may be off-center after movements of the subject, so the cameraman may find his framing too tight or too wide.

Adjustments of this sort should be made during the movement of the actors, not after, or attention will be called to the camera. The director may ask the cameraman to "ooze forward" just as he might ask him to "ease left" under similar circumstances where a slight pan is necessary.

Dollying for variety of shot. Occasionally, a cameraman will dolly forward or back during a lengthy shot, simply to add a little variety by changing the field of view. Sometimes this will be done on a shot of a vocalist, who begins a song in medium-shot, reaches the climax in close-up, and finishes in medium-shot again. This is a legitimate use of the dolly, but must be done very slowly and smoothly, if it is not to call attention to the camera.

Dollying rapidly for dramatic effect. In a dramatic program, the speed of the dolly movement can increase the impact if we surge in rapidly to a close-up of a crucial object, or to a tight close-up of an actor's face at a moment of intense emotion or revelation. This has much the same effect as a sudden surge of music in the background, and sometimes is synchronized with such a surge. The audience would have been impressed by the importance of the object seen in close-up, in any event, but having it rapidly swell in size on the screen provides additional excitement.

Vertical movement is often combined with dolly movement to produce the *zoom* shot effect, as we have already mentioned. This results in a diagonal movement through space: down-and-in or up-and-away. An illustration was given earlier of a high angle long-shot as used in a production of "The Medium." A later production of this same opera substituted a slow zoom-up-and-away for the high shot, with much the same dramatic effect. Again, the speed of the *zoom* may add further dramatic emphasis to an already exciting effect.

Purposes in Trucking

The camera may *truck* for any of the above purposes. A slight sidewise movement of the camera is sometimes necessary when one actor close to the camera is covering another who must be seen in the background. The camera will often *truck* to follow actors across the set, keeping abreast of them in their movements rather than actually preceding or following. Again a camera may *truck* or *arc* around a subject (preferably during some action of the subject) in order to bring a different background into the shot. Thus, if an entrance is to be made through a background door, the director will contrive to motivate a lateral camera movement which will bring the door into the shot at the correct time.

The most valuable effect of the trucking shot, however, lies in the increased feeling of depth which it imparts to the scene. Foreground objects move across the screen faster than objects in the background and reveal the distance between them in a very dramatic way. The gradual change of camera angle adds greatly to the visual interest of the shot. When properly motivated, the trucking shot provides a more interesting manner of moving across the scenery than the pan-shot, but is physically much more difficult to achieve.

Camera Effects

A number of effects are available in most television studios which can enrich a production if used with discretion. Some of these effects can be achieved with the equipment on hand, without the need of extra gadgets and requisitions to the special effects department. Other effects can be done optically with prisms, mirrors or masks in front of the camera. Some effects are achieved electronically—by means of the electrical circuits within the camera or by the addition of further electronic equipment.

The Superimposure

The most common effect is the superimposure, easy to accomplish with any standard switching equipment, and useful in many different kinds of production.

The superimposure has been used to excess in many programs, and frequently for no particular reason. Complaints from viewers that these effects confuse the picture and detract from the show are often well justified. When the pictures from two cameras are put on the screen at the same time, there should be a real purpose, a real value to the effect. The second camera should add something more than just a second image. In the most effective superimposure, the whole is really greater than the sum of the parts.

The Decorative Superimposure

Sometimes the superimposure is used for a purely decorative purpose. The superimposure of title cards on still or live backgrounds is an example in point. For this purpose, the lettering is usually done in white on a medium gray card. The video engineer easily brings the gray down to black level, and a cleaner picture results than if a black card is used. The background shot must be in a rather low key and without great contrast or spottiness. It would be impossible to superimpose letters on a background of contrasting foliage, for example, since they would very likely be illegible. A high key background (very light tones) would have to be faded down under the white letters in order for them to show at all.

Black letters may be superimposed on a scene also. It must be remembered, however, that in a superimposure, it is the white areas from each picture which dominate the dark areas of the other. Black letters on a title must necessarily be against a light ground. When such a card is superimposed over a scene, the light area of the card will fog the greater portion of the background scene. This fogging effect will not be noticeable, however, if the background scene is in a light tone. The dark letters will show up better if they are superimposed over dark areas of the background scene. There will be no light tone from the background scene to show through the dark letters and make them difficult to read.

Occasionally, the audience is given a shot of a singer or a conductor superimposed over a long-shot of the orchestra. Stars may be superimposed over a performer (Fig. 12). Sometimes a close-up of the fingering of an instrument will be superimposed over a long-shot of the musician, where the main purpose is not particularly to stress the musician's technique but simply to enhance the decorative value

Photo Courtesy Popular Science Monthly

Figure 12. Stars superimposed over performers. The star-effect is secured by using a "roller-towel" perforated with holes. As holes in the front sheet line up with those in back, light passes through and the stars twinkle.

of the picture. Caution should be exercised in using superimposures for this purpose. It is easy to be so concerned with the decorative effect that the clarity of the original image is overlooked. The director's responsibility is to give the viewers what they want to see and give it to them adequately. It is easy to let a decorative effect confuse the picture so the subject is hard to distinguish.

In the simple superimposure, no attempt is made to mask out portions of either shot. The elements of one scene show through those of the other. The only case where a composite effect can be achieved by simple superimposure is when the backgrounds of two shots are dark and contain nothing which could show through the foreground elements of the other. In a production of classical ballet on NBC-TV, a director superimposed two different shots of a pair of dancers and made them look like four dancers. This, in itself, is a very common

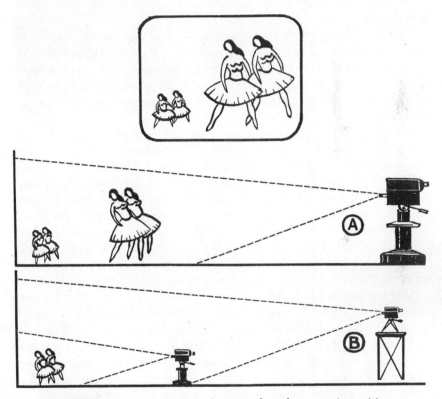

Figure 13. Two dancers become four by superimposition.

effect. However, one pair of dancers was normal size; another "pair" was midget size, repeating the same actions beside them. The illusion would have been spoiled, however, if a dancer from one shot had overlapped one from another shot; each would have shown through the other.

The effect of "ghosting" was prevented in this case because the backgrounds were dark and there was nothing in the background of either shot to show through the figures of the other. As in any composite shot, the problem of matching perspective is involved. If the second pair of dancers is to appear to be really in the same scene, the second shot must be taken from a different camera angle and a different distance. This must be the same relative angle and distance that the first camera would bear to a pair of diminutive dancers if they were actually there. In other words, since they are smaller, the camera angle is higher: instead of seeing them from their own eye-level, the camera looks down on them from a level considerably above their heads.

The composite superimposure has been used on dramatic shows to show two ends of a telephone conversation. Babette Henry did this on an ABC show, bringing up the intensity of each camera as the actor shown by that camera spoke. This reduced the ghosting effect on each subject in turn as the attention of the audience moved from one to the other.

Sometimes action and reaction can be shown together on the same screen by the superimposure method. In an *American Forum of the Air* program on WNBW in Washington, Vance Hallack once superimposed over a picture of a speaker a shot of his opponent, visibly reacting to the speaker's words, and planning his rebuttal. Hallack thus provided the viewer with close-ups of two subjects too far apart to cover in one shot. More important than that, however, he showed two sides of the story—the action and the reaction on the same screen.

CBS-TV, under Robert Bendick, did an even more sensational superimposure of this sort in connection with the circus at Madison Square Garden. A family of high-wire artists performed without a net, and only the season before had had a serious accident when one of them slipped and fell to the ground. The father was below, however, and broke the man's fall, so the accident was not fatal. During the later performance, the story was related to the audience who watched with bated breath as the family went through their act, with the father watching from below, superimposed on the same screen.

Superimposure with Special Meaning

Some of the most successful superimposures carry a special meaning not contained in either of the component shots. The *Philco Television Playhouse* used effects such as these on their commercials. The camera would dolly in to a close-up of a spinning record, the pick-up head would lower and the music begin. Then, superimposed on the turning record, the violinist would appear actually playing the music.

The special meaning was, of course, that the music sounded as good as though Mischa Mischakoff were actually there. (Fig. 14)

Figure 14. Violinist Mischa Mischakoff is superimposed over one of his records.

Photo Courtesy Philco Playhouse and Hutchins Advertising Company

The same effect was achieved another time by dollying into a close-up of the throat of a loud speaker and superimposing a shot of the musician or singer, as though he were emanating in real life from the cone of the speaker.

The best example the authors can recall of this type of superimposure in a dramatic show involved a girl who could not bear to hear a particular piece on the piano. A second character was engaged in driving her out of the house by constantly playing it. At one point in the show, when the tension became too great, the victim held her head in her hands and the director superimposed the hammers of the piano in such a way that they seemed to be pounding on her head.

A superimposition can often carry a symbolic meaning more readily than a straight shot.

On *Lamp Unto My Feet,* a CBS religious show, an ancient war was once depicted through a symbolic superimposure. One camera took a big close-up of an ornate brass brazier with an alcohol flame filling it and leaping across the screen. Across this was superimposed a silhouette of warriors in battle, swords meeting shields, spears raised and men falling. The effect conveyed the idea and the mood of the war much more graphically than realistic scenery and complex action might have done.

Sometimes the possibilities of fantasy in the superimposure technique lend themselves to comic purpose. Several shows have had great fun playing around with effects—this is especially true of Ted Mills' *Garroway at Large.* On one show, Dave was seen against a black background. He introduced a song, and then looked around for the singer. "Jack Haskell, where are you? Come on, here's the place where you sing." Jack Haskell superimposed dimly next to Dave. "Oh, a little stronger than that, Jack. Don't you feel very strong tonight?" Haskell came in a little brighter, then disappeared.

"Jack!"

Haskell came back.

"Will you stay if I go?" asked Dave. Jack nodded. "Okay. It's a cheap price to pay." Dave turned and faded out, leaving Jack to go into his song.

Another time on the same show, a very clever use was made of the fantasy superimposure. The script for the show carries only the following notation (since all dialogue on the program is ad libbed):

"Dave says most TV shows have big sets, big people, but we don't bother with that sort of thing. Here we have a fine star, Connie Russell, and a small person, Cliff Norton." Connie Russell then sang "Charley My Boy" to the diminutive Cliff Norton superimposed on the table-top in front of her. By the end of the song, Connie and Cliff were both full-size at the table and Dave was a little man on the table-top. The next page of the script carried the following notes:

"Dave is supered on table. Dismisses Connie and Cliff. Goes over to edge of table and calls (on echo) down to Betty. Says to go ahead and sing while he has cameramen get this size business straightened out." (Fig. 15)

Figure 15. Superimposition brings a very small Dave Garroway to the edge of a very large table-top.

Going over to the edge of the table was particularly well done. An exact mark was made on the floor of the black set in which Garroway stood, to mark the edge of the table. He started to walk away as though he had forgotten about being on a table-top, then stopped short just at the edge.

Matting

The *matte* shot, long in use in motion-picture special effects, is also done in television in several ways. A matte is a mask which blacks out part of the picture. An image from another camera may then be superimposed and will show clearly in this blacked out area because there is no background from the first camera to show through it. If opposite sides, for example, are masked off on two cameras, super-imposing the two will then result in either (1) the *split screen* effect—one picture on one side of the screen and another picture on the other, or (2) the *composite* shot—both images so blended in lighting, size, perspective, etc., as to give the illusion of a single shot taken with one camera.

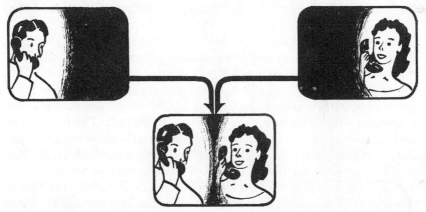

Figure 16. The off-set turret method of matting. The picture from Camera 1 is combined with the picture from Camera 2 by super-imposure.

The easiest method of achieving the *split screen* effect involves off-setting the lens turrets of two cameras in different directions. (Fig. 16) When a lens turret is turned slightly, the lens is no longer directly in front of the camera tube and a shadow area caused by the turret itself will cover part of the picture. One camera at a baseball game, for example, will frame the pitcher on the left of the screen with the turret offset so a dark area covers the right. Then the other camera frames up on the runner leading off first base on the right of his pic-ture with a shadow area on the left. A superimposure of the two will result in a *split screen* where each image is clear and distinct and separated by a soft curved line or thin dark area down the center (or diagonally, depending on the make of camera used). This effect is easiest to achieve if three cameras are in operation, since one camera can be used on the air while the other two adjust their turrets and are superimposed for the effect. However, if only two cameras are available, the effect can still be obtained if the second camera is made ready and superimposed on the first just at the time the first cameraman is turning his turret *on the air* and the dark area is creeping into his frame. This requires very skillful camerawork and must be practiced repeatedly if the cameraman has never done this before. He must pan the camera at the same time he turns the turret, to keep the image from moving off the screen entirely, as it would in an ordinary lens change.

Other methods of matting involve paper cups over the front of the lens, a pair of oatmeal boxes painted black inside with opposite areas cut out of the end of each, or a more complex matte box fastened to the front of the camera in the manner of standard motion-picture cameras.

The electronic split screen, requiring special circuits and electronic equipment, achieves the effect by *blanking* instead of optically matting. *Blanking* means turning off the scanning beam so it does not transmit an image as it sweeps across certain areas of the picture. If the second half of each scanning line is blanked out, for example, the right-hand half of the entire picture will show black. The first half of each scanning line may be blanked out in the other camera, and superimposure of the two will result in a *split screen* where the line of demarcation is sharp and clear. A further feature of the same electronic equipment which creates the *split screen* is that the position of this line of demarcation between two cameras can be altered. Thus, one camera may blank out the last three-quarters of each line, and the other only the first quarter, placing the line of demarcation nearer to the left-hand edge of the frame. This is controlled by a handle on the switching system which can be moved at any speed and produces the effect known as the *horizontal wipe*. As the handle is moved, the line of demarcation moves from right to left, or from left to right across the screen.

Still another method of *matting* involves blanking out a portion of the scene by providing a dark flat or drape across one side of the studio set. This was done for a trick effect in the *Garroway at Large* program where a large flat, painted a dark gray, was built with half a tree on either edge. One camera framed up on the right-hand side of the flat, showing the tree in the center of the shot, while the other camera framed up in the opposite manner on the left of the flat. The two halves of the tree joined in the superimposition and the effect

Figure 17A. An example of an optically produced split screen, combined with image inversion of one camera, as used in the CBS *Studio One* production of *Mary Poppins*.

Figure 17B. Example of an electronic split screen effect from the NBC production of *Lights Out*.

was a composite shot. This enabled members of the show to walk behind the tree and disappear, appearing again a few seconds later or changing into other people as they passed behind it. Finally, for a closing gag, the director had the entire studio orchestra walk out from behind the tree seemingly appearing from nowhere. (Fig. 18)

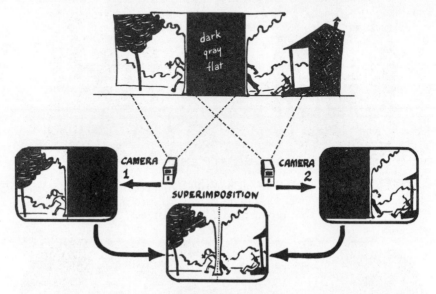

Figure 18. Matting technique accomplished by a large dark gray flat which takes up half of each camera's picture.

There are several types of prisms which can be affixed to the front of the camera lens to produce certain optical effects which are sometimes quite useful. The *image inverter* prism is perhaps the most commonly used. This may be a *dove prism* or a large *right-angle prism* placed on the lens in such a way that the camera looks directly through it in the longest dimension. It has the effect of reversing left and right in the same manner as a mirror. Then, if it is rotated, the left-right reversal will become a top-bottom reversal and the picture will turn upside down. The prism has been mounted in a free-turning mount controllable by means of a crank from the back of the camera so it can be rotated continuously if desired. Trick effects such as building a set upside down and then reversing both set and actors so the actors seem to be dancing on the ceiling, have utilized this *image inverter*. It has been used in *Space Cadet* to show an actor walking on the wall. In this case, the set was built on its side and then turned at a 90° angle by means of a partial rotation of the prism. An actor actually walking on the floor seemed to be on the wall. Perhaps the most useful effect this prism can achieve is the *canted shot*. (Fig. 19) The only disadvantage in its use, however, is the fact that left and right are reversed and the cameraman must reverse all his reflexes and pan left when he should pan right, etc. But even this problem can be eliminated by the simple expedient of reversing the scanning in the picture tube. *Scanning reversal* requires a little extra wiring in

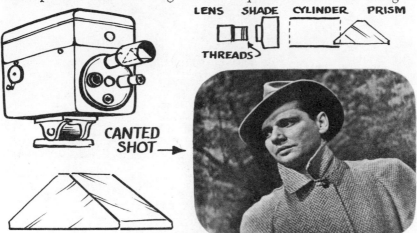

Photo Courtesy School of Radio Technique Studios and Bill Thompson

Figure 19. The image inverter prism and a canted shot achieved by partial rotation.

the camera, but this can be installed in short order, providing the cameraman with a switch with which he can invert the picture or reverse it left to right.

The reader will remember that the television picture is produced by scanning an optical image on the face of the camera tube by means of a tiny beam of electrons. Sweeping back and forth, it analyzes the picture into 525 horizontal lines. All cameras, monitors and home-receivers synthesize a picture in the same manner, beginning in the upper left-hand corner. If, however, a camera is altered so it starts scanning from the upper right, for example, the monitors and receivers are not going to know this, and will continue to start from the left, placing whatever information the camera picks up from the right side of its screen on the left side of theirs. The picture will then be reversed.

It was left for the *Garroway at Large* show to really have fun with the inverted screen. Characters jumped about from floor to ceiling; Dave appeared first right-side up, then upside down, in an attempt to

Figure 20. Example of a multiple image prism and its result.

keep up with them, and finally came back after titles for his usual closing gag, this time upside down and with his back to the camera. "Chicago," he said, "from you to came program this."

Another type of prism is used in front of the lens to produce a multiple image of the subject. This *multiple image* prism is a piece of glass, the back side of which is perfectly flat, but the front side is ground in several flat facets sloping slightly from the center to the outside. A two-facet prism will produce a double image, a three-facet prism a triple image, etc. A great variety of these prisms are available and have been used in the motion-picture field for years in the production of film trailers, etc., but only recently found their way into television. Some of these prisms produce a central image of the subject surrounded by several more images around the border of the picture. Rotation of the prism will then rotate these border images in a ring around the central picture. (They stay vertical, it should be noted, instead of turning upside down).

It has frequently been desirable to distort a picture in some manner, especially in a fantasy or dream sequence. This has been attempted with wavy glass in front of the camera, but recently a method has been devised where a great variety of distortions can be achieved electronically. This is made possible by the use of a piece of audio test equipment known as the audio oscillator. Electrical signals at regular sound frequencies are inserted into the circuits which control the scanning of the beam in the camera tube, causing it to move in an unnatural manner. The effect on the screen is a weaving or waving picture, looking sometimes like a water reflection. The waves can be made to move up the screen, slowly or rapidly, and they can be made large or small. The effect can be faded out, leaving a straight picture. One network (NBC) calls this device the *Flexitron*. It is often useful for transition effects where it may be used in place of the *defocus* effect.

Perhaps the most interesting of all camera effects is the *montage amplifier*. The term *montage* has so many meanings it is necessary to define it before proceeding further. As used in this context, a *montage* is a combination picture put together out of two or more shots taken by different cameras. It differs from the superimposure in that one camera's shot cannot be seen through the other. In the *montage*, all parts of the picture are solid. We have seen that a *montage* may actually be created by superimposing two cameras, provided the technique of matting is used. The *montage amplifier* is, in a sense, a method of electronic matting.

Two different effects can be achieved with this equipment. In the first, a definite geometrical area of one camera's shot (such as a circle, oval or heart shape) is inserted into the other camera's picture. Thus, to a shot of a man making a telephone call, might be added a small circular insert in one part of the frame showing a girl on the other end of the line.

The second type of montage effect, if used in the above example, would show the girl, not in an inserted picture area of her own, but in the same room with the man. To give a more practical illustration— a space cadet is shown standing in front of a dinosaur. The dinosaur

Figure 21. Space ca- dets at the bottom of the sea—or, at least, at the bottom of a small aquarium, by use of the ABC "Gizmo," de- veloped by G e o r g e Gould, Roy Fee and Rolf Drucker.

is actually a small lizard in front of one camera, while the actor stands before another camera in front of a black background. The *montage amplifier* then places him solidly into the picture of the lizard so that he actually seems to be within arm's reach of a giant reptile.

2. Pictorial Composition

The composition of the picture is not the concern of the cameraman alone. It is of great importance in the work of many others who contribute to the production. Being responsible for the appearance of the show, the director, of course, is more involved than anyone else. If the production is sufficiently complex to require a staging director as well as a television director, and perhaps a choreographer as well, these additional people will consider the composition of the final broadcast picture one of the principal aims of their creative work. Good staging of action or dance for television must be specially designed to make good shots. The scenic designer, too, will make sure that the set allows the director to frame interesting backgrounds for his shots.

Since many people who have nothing to do with the camera contribute to the composition of the pictures, it is evident that composition is as much a function of subject as it is of camera. Control over composition can be exercised in two ways: (1) through the handling of the camera: proper choice of field-of-view, camera angle, lens, and the other factors discussed in detail in the preceding chapter, and (2) through the arrangement of the various elements of the subject or scene. In most types of production, the television director is responsible for both the staging and the use of cameras, and he will exercise more control than anyone else over the composition of the picture.

There are many excellent books on composition, some written for the photographer, the majority for the graphic artist. But for this reason, they are of little practical value to the student of television. The graphic artist has every element of the picture under his control. He creates the shape and form of things. He considers the pattern of light and dark tones; he gives separate attention to the lines which separate areas and mark the boundaries of objects. Then he takes time to look critically at the background areas which are between and around the foreground subjects, and designs these elements of the composition as well as he can. This is real designing, but something that only the graphic artist can do. The television director (or cameraman) rarely is conscious of separate design elements like line and tonal pattern. In controlling the subject, the television director can only group people together, place them higher or lower in the picture, closer or farther from the lens, and control the kind of background they are seen against. In handling the camera, he is limited largely to the exercise of creative selection. He can pan his camera left or right, up or down, he can dolly in or pull back; he can choose this lens or that. He must select the portion of the scene which shows the subject to its best advantage.

He will do this, not according to rules, but according to "feel." This is where the pictorial sense comes in. There is no time to think things out; the cameraman (with or without the director's assistance), must automatically pick a good composition. If the composition is poor he must know it immediately and what to do to improve it. This feel for composition comes only from long experience with pictures. Sometimes a cameraman will not become proficient in this skill until he has spent many months on the job. Working with good directors will give him valuable training. The director will commonly alter a cameraman's framing, ask for a wider or a tighter shot, suggest a different lens or ask for slight panning adjustments for better balance. The cameraman will take the director's final word on questions of composition, and when he is working with a skilled director who has a finely developed sense of composition, he will learn rapidly.

Control of Composition With the Camera

Framing

Each aspect of camera handling makes a contribution to the improvement of pictorial composition, and these have been touched upon before. "Framing" of the shot, however, has not been discussed as such, and deserves separate mention because it is the operation through which the cameraman most frequently controls his composition.

The camera is always framing up a shot. When the adjustment which is necessary for the right composition is obvious, the director will simply ask the cameraman to "frame up." This would apply in the case of a simple title card or a close-up shot of a single person, where good composition consists only in centering the subject in the frame. The framing is considered "tight" when the subject is crowding the sides of the frame, and "loose" when there is considerable space around the subject. A loose composition is always safer than a tight one, since the camera is ready for broader action without having to dolly back, but the tight composition is usually the most pleasing.

Balancing

A large part of framing is concerned with what is called *balancing* the composition. This again is something which can only be done by feel. To give a simple example: A person looking at the camera must usually be centered to seem in proper balance. If there is an object in the background, however, or held in a man's hand out to the right, a better balance would center the man-and-object group, placing the man somewhat to the left of center.

Sometimes things outside the picture will affect the way it is balanced. For example: A profile shot of a person looking at something is usually framed with less space behind his head than in front to

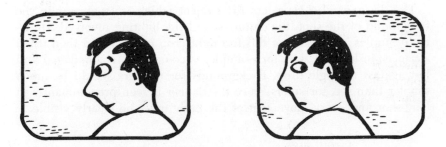

Figure 22. Two examples of good composition. Balance may be affected by unseen subjects outside the camera's field of view.

create proper balance. If, however, we are aware of something menacing him from behind, a better balance would show more space behind his head than in front. In each case, the unseen subjects beyond the frame of the picture have made the space on their side of the figure more important, and have affected the composition. (Fig. 22)

It is important to note that in composition, as well as in all the other phases of camera operation, there are many ways to skin the same cat. Two cameramen may frame up the same shot in two different ways, both equally pleasing. Then again, a better cameraman, without knowing why, will consistently frame up better pictures than his co-workers.

There is little that mechanical aids can do to assist in this creative process. Some cameramen mark their view-finders so they are sure to allow enough head-room (space above the actors' heads), and some like to have a center mark to refer to when panning with action. The cameraman generally "leads" a moving subject, keeping it always just behind the center mark in order to show the area into which it is moving.

Control Over Subject

Backgrounds

Good scene design can make pictorial composition easy. There are some sets in which you just cannot help but get good shots, at least from the standpoint of design. A good designer considers the shots that the director wants to use, and designs his set so that even when small portions of it appear, those portions will be pleasing in themselves and it will not be necessary to see the set as a whole.

The designer also considers the subject which is to appear in the foreground of the shot, the costumes and the lighting involved. Horrible examples of the lack of this foresight crop up now and then when a dancer in leopard skin, for example, is completely camouflaged and lost against a jungle drop. Backgrounds for dancers should be much simpler than sets for actors, since the dancer is seen predominantly in long-shot and every movement of the body must be clearly visible.

Groupings

Any analysis of beauty in design and pictorial composition discloses the fact that *simplicity* is the keynote. It can almost be said that the simpler a line (or a form or grouping), the stronger the composition will be. The grouping of actors in a shot serves to simplify the picture. By grouping people together instead of leaving them separated, we simplify the picture from a design made of many figures all the same size, to a simple mass composed of several figures grouped together. Almost any shape or mass formed by a group of actors is better than a disorganized number of separate people. Possibly, the grouping may consist only of moving a couple closer together so they make one form. (Fig. 23)

Figure 23. In the first picture, the figures are not grouped. In the others, grouping has improved the composition.

It there are three figures, they may be arranged in one group or in two. Possibly all that may be necessary is to move one of the actors closer to another, or if one is in the background, move him so that his figure will be overlapped by that of another in the foreground and together they will make one shape.

Michelangelo is supposed to have said that a statue should be so designed that it could be rolled down a hill and nothing would break off. He was after simplicity of mass. The simplest possible forms are, of course, the cube, sphere, pyramid, or, in two-dimensional terms, the square, circle and triangle. The t-shape, cross, and x-shape are also fairly simple forms. Of all these, the triangle is the most valuable for pictorial composition. Group people into a triangle, frame it properly, and a good composition will generally result.

The triangle has been the basis of good strong composition almost from the beginning of graphic art. It is particularly valuable in a rectangular picture, because the spaces left around the sides of the triangle are themselves triangular in shape, thus repeating the same form throughout the picture, but in different sizes, all subordinate to the main triangular form.

Another very fortunate aspect of this form is that it lends itself beautifully to placing the center of interest in a dominant and compelling position. The top point of the triangle is a very powerful spot in the design. There is no comparable point in a square or circle which can dominate the whole, unless one may choose to rotate the square into a diamond shape. The inverted triangle, on the other hand, has no dominant peak, and every point along the base or in the center of the form competes equally for attention. (Fig. 24)

Naturally, this device of composition, like anything else, must be given the right relative importance to other things. It would be running the thing into the ground, for example, to insist on forcing actors into triangular groupings at the sacrifice of natural action. Every

Figure 24. Which number dominates in each of these triangular groupings?

time a picture is composed, it is something new under the sun; there has never been anything quite like it before. That is why "rules" of composition cannot apply except in the very loosest way. We may borrow a page from the designer's book, from the painter's, from the photographer's, but mostly we must use our own good taste in determining just what devices are valuable to our particular purpose.

To make the triangular grouping simpler to obtain, sets with different heights, steps, etc., are very helpful. Seating people on the arms of chairs, on hassocks or stools that are lower than regular chairs, or having some people sit while others stand, will help toward this end.

Lighting can be a controllable element in pictorial composition in certain studios, where there is the equipment and the time and manpower to use it. This is particularly true in low-key scenes where each source of light illuminates new objects and adds new elements to the composition.

Dominance of one subject over others may be achieved with a concentration of light. This same compelling effect can also be achieved by lighting all portions of the set with a dim shadowless light, and striking the subject itself with a contrasting spot which gives it strong highlights and shadows.

By lighting a scene properly, it is possible to simplify the composition in many cases. Distracting elements in the background can be reduced in tone by cutting down the light on them so they will no longer compete with the subject for primary interest. The right amount of what is called "separation" between subject and background can often be achieved by lighting. Backlighting will do this by rimming the subject with a brilliant edge. Excessive backlighting, however, is an unnatural "movie" effect which does not help to convey television's peculiar feeling of actuality. A contrast in overall tone is often better for this purpose. The subject is either more brightly lighted than the background, or the background is lighter than the subject. This second possibility is of value in dance productions where the form and outline of the figure is most important. When details of expression on the face of an actor must be seen, however, this tonal relationship cannot be so easily used.

Figure 25. Which person is emphasized in this grouping?

Sometimes a gradation in light across a background will itself add an element to the composition. A blank area in the background, a wall or floor, perhaps, may be lighted in such a way that it has a subtle variation of tone within it, or even moves from a high to a very low intensity, and yet remains the same simple plane, unconfused by additional objects and points of interest which would distract from the foreground subject. Motion-picture cameramen light their backgrounds with small spots just for this purpose, so that the simple wall planes become rich in subtle variations of tone. This is not necessarily the unreal, stylistic device that backlighting has usually been in motion pictures. The unreal thing is to be seen when interiors are bathed in the merciless flat illumination of many television studios. In reality, interior illumination comes from a few sources and often these are low sources, so that the upper portions and far corners of walls are darker in tone.

We have shown how placing an actor at the apex of a triangle will give him a dominating position. The concentration of light on one actor will also pick him out from the others. Dominance may be achieved also by the use of converging lines of force. In Figure 25, for example, even though one actor stands at the top of a pyramid, his eyes and those of the girl direct attention to the man on the left. The converging lines of force, in this case, are invisible lines running from each of the actors to the spot at which they are looking, which then becomes the center of interest of the picture.

Books on composition cover many other techniques of achieving dominance. It is important, as in the illustration (Fig. 25), that two methods of achieving dominance are not applied to different subjects in the same shot or they may compete for the main interest and disorganization may result.

Unusual Composition

Occasionally, the temptation will arise to do something very unusual and sensational in the way of composition. Rarely, in the usual show, may this desire be indulged safely. Composition, like all other elements of production, must be the slave and not the master. It takes a strong motivation to call for a striking and unusual composition, and prevent its attracting attention to itself.

One of the best examples of the unusual in composition is the familiar *framed* shot. The camera looks into the room through the fireplace, or between the spindles of the balustrade. Sometimes one actor is framed by the arm or legs of another. (Fig. 26)

In the dramatic show, this special kind of composition demands a special motivation. It must be led into in some way. A shot in television, as in motion pictures, is not and cannot be independent. It is part of a series, dependent on the shot which came before and the one which comes after. A shot through the balustrade, for instance, cannot suddenly appear, in the middle of an ordinary sequence, without calling attention to the point from which the shot is taken and the camera taking it. The shot under the actor's arm is much easier to use in this respect, since it constitutes only a rearrangement of already existing elements. But to bring the stair-rail into sudden prominence calls attention to it and probably to the camera as well. If the shot were of the subjective type, of course, the situation would be entirely different. Showing someone peering through the railing before cutting to the framed shot would turn all camera-consciousness into consciousness of the eavesdropper instead.

Figure 26. "Framed shots," familiar examples of unusual compositions.

Sometimes a camera movement, which is itself motivated, may lead into the unusual composition. The shot might begin through the window, but with the camera too far in to show the window frame. An actor moving toward the window will then motivate a pull-back which will bring the window frame into view around the edges of the shot.

The opening shot in a sequence can often be quite unusual since it does not have to be particularly motivated, or led up to. Again, the shot up through the fireplace—the fire's eye-view, can sometimes be motivated when the actors are staring into the fire. We often see, and accept, the mirror's eye-view of the girl at her dressing table, or the oven's eye-view of the cook removing the turkey.

Another type of unusual composition is the *canted* or *cockeyed* shot (Fig. 19), where vertical and horizontal lines appear as diagonals on the screen. Diagonals are lines of action, of moving, kinetic objects, which impart a feeling of unrest. An unrealistic quality can also be suggested by this schizoid view of things. If the motivation calls, the canted camera may be used, but only when the motivation is very strong.

In the musical or variety show, these motivations are not as necessary. Anything which contributes, even superficially, to the visual interest of the production is desirable. Of course, the camera must not distract from the spirit of the performance; it would not be desirable, for instance, to use shots of a lovely singer, or of serious dancers, so that their actions seem to belie the law of gravity; but in the case of jazz musicians, trampolin acts, comedy dances, etc., the canted shot has been found to be most effective when properly used.

Poor Composition

In training people to recognize good composition when they see it, the consideration of poor composition is an excellent start. It is not hard to recognize poor composition, but it takes a great deal of knowledge and ability to know what makes it so and what must be done to correct it. Here is an exercise—see how you rate on sense of composition.

Make a small frame in a sheet of paper, as suggested before in Chapter 1, about 1″ high by 1¼″ wide. Now lay it on the picture inside the front cover of this book. John Groth's impression of the CBS Grand Central studios in New York, although perhaps a little short on accuracy, is certainly long on spirit, which is the important thing. This is an ideal picture for our purpose because it is full of detail and we can make from it many pictures of many things. The exercise is to set out deliberately to make a poor composition. Move the frame around until you find a framing that you know is not good in any way. Now explain what it is that makes the composition so poor. There are an unlimited number of framings on the page, but for some reason almost anything you try turns out to be rather good in its own way and it is very hard indeed to make a framing that is really poor. Why can't you find more poor compositions? Think about this while we examine some that the authors were able to find.

Turn now to the back endpaper where you will find the same picture with several framings outlined upon it.

Framing A is faulty because of the vertical line through the center of the picture. It divides the picture into two equal halves, neither of which is dominant. Worse than that, it calls attention to the frame of the picture. The line seems to come forward out of the plane of the picture and into the frame itself, becoming a sort of window mullion joining the top and bottom of the frame. It makes two pictures out of one. A vertical line anywhere in a picture is usually wrong, but it is worse when it cuts right down the center, making the frame look like a window. The same is true of a horizontal line cutting across the exact middle of the frame. This particular framing is made worse by the fact that there are almost identical forms in each of the halves, neither of which is subordinate to the other.

Framing B is poor for several reasons. In the first place, a point of interest is just visible on the lower edge of the frame, enough to attract the eye to that spot, yet not showing enough of the subject to satisfy the viewer's curiosity. Another fault is the line along the side of the frame which is not quite parallel to it. This also calls attention to the frame. It makes the frame look slightly askew. Even lines which are exactly parallel with the edges of the frame are to be avoided in television because distortions around the edge of the picture, either in transmission or in the home receiver, often make these lines distorted and askew.

Framings C and D are not good because they do not frame a picture of anything in particular, unless it may be an area of floor. As a picture of the floor, however, neither is much good because of the interesting elements around the edge of the frame, each of which is partly shown and calls for further investigation. Framing E is another half-and-half proposition, half-torso, half-floor, with the action moving rapidly out of the frame. Framing F, like many similar framings that can be made in the top area of the picture, shows nothing recognizable, although it is difficult to keep the lines from making at least some sort of a pleasing abstract pattern.

If we start canting the camera so that the framelines are no longer vertical, we can make lots of poor compositions. This is because most forms and lines in this picture, or in any scene you may wish to photograph, are either vertical or horizontal. That is why we usually frame pictures in a rectangular area which is held vertical while viewing,

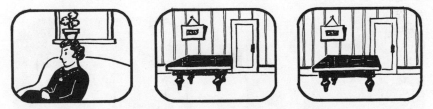

Figure 27. Odd juxtapositions. A slight change in lateral camera angle has improved the second picture.

instead of some irregular shape or a rectangle at an angle. The major forms are in keeping with the frame. When these forms run at an angle to the frame, they fight with it. Not only that, but when the picture is eventually viewed in an upright position, the forms which were originally solid and stable become very unstable, and are imbued with a feeling of motion which may be out of keeping.

A characteristic of faulty composition which cannot be demonstrated in this same picture, but which crops up very often in television camerawork, is odd juxtaposition. Unfortunate effects result from these juxtapositions; near objects seem to connect with far objects when the camera is wrongly placed, and the classic example of the man with the halo around his head illustrates what may sometimes be seen. The juxtaposition of chair and table in Fig. 27 makes it seem as though the door and table are fastened together. Just a small change in camera placement (c) is all that is needed.

Why is it that so few poor compositions can be made? The answer is that a subject had not been assigned. Each time you moved the frame, you were making a picture of another subject. If a specific subject were asked for (the couple on the piano, for example) only a few positions of the frame could create satisfactory composition. It is mostly a matter of balance. The conventional framing on a subject such as this is indicated in Fig. 28.

Figure 28. Three framings on a portion of the studio scene reproduced on the endpapers of the inside covers of this volume.

a

b　　　　　　　　　　　　　　　c

A little room is left above the head, and the legs are cut off wherever the lower edge of the frame may fall. In practice, a subject such as this would be shot with a longer lens, or closer camera, to make the faces as large as possible on the screen. Note that the artist has arranged this grouping in a roughly triangular shape, placing the girl's head a little higher than the man's. If both were the same height, the grouping would be less pleasing. Various off-center framings of this group are possible, using the basic frame with which we began, but these all bring additional elements, objects or floor areas into the picture. If these new elements had meaning, the off-center compositions would be acceptable. If, for example, the girl were singing to the accompaniment of the piano, a shot such as (b) would be usable, showing singer, accompanist and audience in the same shot. Extraneous background objects, stage-hands and odd cameramen, tend to confuse the issue and should be removed. The grouping still forms a triangle. The framing is a little tight; you can "dolly the camera back" a little by closing one eye and bringing the frame closer to you. If constant traffic behind the couple interferes with their tête-à-tête, a framing such as (c) would be desirable in order to include the traffic in the background.

Another example can be taken from the stagehand on the catwalk. (Fig. 29) A conventional well-balanced framing of this subject might be secured with Framing (a), if it were not for the fact that the man

a   b

Figure 29. Two framings on a detail from the endpapers of the inside covers. One of these gives a better feeling of height.

is looking down, apparently leaning from a high place. Framing (b) shows the empty space beneath him and puts across the idea of height. The fact that he is looking down almost requires us to give the picture more space beneath than above him. Whatever he is doing is below him, and consequently, no one is going to be interested in the space above.

Much can be learned about camerawork by moving the small frame around over this picture. The effects of panning the camera can be experimented with, as well as the effect of zooming in or out on a scene. Note that moving the frame in or out (or better, holding the frame stationary while moving the page closer or farther from the eye) is not the effect of dollying a camera closer to the subject, but the effect that is secured by a zoom lens which brings the viewer closer to the subject by changing focal length. Note also, while you are making these experiments with one eye, that the picture assumes a striking three-dimensional quality. This is the old Chinese trick of looking at a picture through a hollow fist. Anyone may enjoy stereoscopic television who is willing to squint at a set through his fist.

This has been a very brief chapter covering an important and wide field. It is the authors' hope that the study of this material will stimulate further thinking on creative composition, especially by those who operate the cameras. Only the experience of working with *pictures*, however, can really develop the "feel for good composition" which the television worker must have. Some teachers of television, lacking electronic equipment, have made maximum use of pictures of all kinds in teaching the subject. The student is required to sketch out his shots (ability to draw is not necessary for this); he is asked to crop pictures and improve their framing; he is taught the making of pictures with simple still cameras. During rehearsal he is encouraged to watch the action through a portable viewfinder so that he may be conscious at all times of the frame surrounding the picture area. Television is, after all, a photographic medium, and creative mastery of the camera's picture is essential to successful producing and directing.

3. Shots in Sequence

In recent years, some television directors and producers have begun to question the old theory that a television program, like a film, is a sequence of shots. They are beginning to feel instead that a television show is a continuous flow of events, which the camera picks up and brings to the viewer in the most effective way. In film, each shot is separately planned, lighted, and given a camera setup, rehearsed, and filmed several times over until perfected. In television, on the other hand, all the shots must be planned at once, the entire area pre-lighted, and invariably, some artistic decisions are made while the program is in progress. However carefully we may pre-plan our shots, we are still compelled by the spontaneous nature of the medium to take things as they come. As a result, not all the cuts in any given television program can be assured the perfection they have in film, where the editor can spend hours determining the exact point at which to make each cut. Accordingly, some television directors prefer to avoid cutting as much as possible, considering it in the nature of a necessary evil, rather than as an advantage.

Whichever of these approaches may be more accurate, the fact remains that the process of going from shot to shot, and the selection of the shots which adjoin one another is a very important part of creative television. The most important concept, in the opinion of the authors, is that the sequence of shots must provide a flow of continuity. There must be a connection between shots as they carry us along in a smooth progression from view to view, always showing us what we want most to see, always bringing us further information. Anything which disturbs that flow interferes with our enjoyment of what we are watching, unless the disturbance is a deliberate punctuation which informs us that one train of thought has ended and another is about to begin.

Changing from Camera to Camera

There are three basic ways in which we may change from the shot on Camera 1 to the shot on Camera 2. These are the *cut*, the *dissolve*, and the *fade*.

The *cut* is an almost instantaneous switch from one camera's picture to that of the next. It is used when the director wishes to achieve a maximum of continuity and a minimum of interruption. Viewers are so conditioned to cutting in films that the eye-blink of the cut goes almost unnoticed. The viewer is simply aware that something else is on the screen; he is not aware of how it got there.

The *fade,* or more properly, the combination of fading out one shot and fading in the next, is used when the director wishes to achieve a minimum of continuity and a maximum of interruption. It is the equivalent, in television, of the lowering of the theater curtain.

The *dissolve,* sometimes called *lap dissolve,* is a blending of one shot into the next. It provides a minor break in continuity, a moderate interruption. In dramatic programs, it usually indicates a discontinuity of time or space, and can hardly ever be used for any other purpose. In non-dramatic programs, on the other hand, the *dissolve* has a variety of uses.

As in almost every phase of television, there is no hard and fixed rule about the choice of *cut* or *dissolve*. It comes down once again to a matter of taste and style, as modified by convention and custom. The experienced director will not hesitate to depart from tradition to achieve an effect he feels is justified by the demands of the particular situation.

Cutting Techniques

Cutting is obviously more than a matter of saying, "Take 1," "Take 2," whenever the director feels the audience has seen enough of the previous shot and should be given another view. If the cut is to achieve its primary function of showing the viewer what he wants, then cutting must be done smoothly and carefully, from the right shot, and at the right time. Readjustment on the part of the viewer should not be necessary. If the viewer must mutter to himself, "Oh, I see . . . the guy on the left is the one with the gun . . . the one who was on the right before," the cutting has not been good. Similarly, if the cut is obvious, if it jars the viewer so that he becomes aware of the cut, the director has not been cutting smoothly.

To cut or not to cut is the first question. As we have pointed out in the previous chapter, television directing is a matter of making the right decision. In *cutting*, the first decision is whether to cut at all—not only at any given moment, but throughout the entire show. There was once a successful dramatic series called *Stories for One Camera.* Some fine dramatic programs have been done entirely on one camera, with a tremendous amount of imagination and ingenuity involved in dollying and panning, as well as in having the performers "make the shots" by their movements about the set, nearer and farther from camera. Even in a show blessed with four cameras, an imaginative director may find a sequence of several pages of script in which he will choose to hold on one camera, knowing that no purpose would be served by cutting to another.

On the other hand, by holding on one camera, the director must sacrifice the advantages of *cutting:* the ability to set up the following shot with a camera that is off the air and can be adjusted or repositioned more accurately, the variety of shots made possible by *cutting*, the increased tempo which may be secured by *cutting* to new shots of new interest, and the added ability to concentrate attention quickly on the subject of his choice.

Why to Cut. Fundamentally, the most urgent reason for *cutting* is that it usually is the quickest method to show the viewer what he wants to see, when the preceding shot cannot include it, or cannot show it closely enough to make it recognizable. For example, in a discussion program, the audience usually wants to see the person who is speaking, and it is the responsibility of the director to cut to a shot which includes that person as soon as he begins to speak. Then, if he continues to speak for any length, the viewer will probably want to see him more closely. It is the director's job then to show him in close-up, so that his reaction will be clearly understood.

The jarring effect of a cut may be put to good use, especially in a dramatic show, in order to *punctuate* or *emphasize* a dramatic moment. Thus, if a character enters the scene with important news, we may be sure the viewer gets the news in one of two ways. The character may enter at some distance from camera and walk down into a medium shot to get his message across, or we may cut to him, once his entrance has been established, and lend additional importance to what he is saying, by the abruptness of the shift from long-shot to close-up.

Another instance in which the cut—the shortest distance between two shots—must be used, is the capturing of a quick reaction. The inspector tells a suspect that he has pinned the crime on one person.

Whether the suspect registers relief or guilt, the audience is entitled to a quick close-up shot of his expression. Sometimes speed is not so crucial, as in the case of two young people whose intimate conversation is being overheard by an older person. The latter's reaction need not come at any pre-determined second, this time; but a cut is still indicated. The only other alternative would be camera movement, which would be difficult to motivate, and which might take us away from the young people for too long a time.

Even in a sequence in which the director has set out to stay on one camera as much as possible, he finds himself forced to cut by circumstances. A highly dramatic scene between two people has ended with the girl leaving the room. To give her a dramatic exit, the camera has panned with her to show the slamming door. In order to show the man standing disconsolately on the other side of the room, the director has a choice of camera movement or cutting. Choosing the former, he may have the camera pan back across the room, risking an unmotivated movement across an empty set. His other alternative might be a second camera ready on a shot of the actor left behind, to which the director might cut as action is completed in the preceding shot.

When to Cut. When to cut depends on the nature of the two shots which are to be joined. If these are *both of the same subject* and the second shot shows nothing new, we are in one category. When the second shot is *something entirely new or different,* we are in another. Let us list a few cuts in each:

1. *Same subject:*

    close-up of one person, to medium shot of same

    tight shot of several persons, to wider shot of same

    medium-shot to long-shot (so long as no new subjects of importance are introduced)

    any shot of a group, to a shot of part of the group

2. *Different subject:*

    close-up of one of two people, to close-up of the other

    any shot of a group of people, to a shot of another group

The cutting will be done at different times, and based on different motivations, when we change from one to another of these categories. There are some cutting situations which are intermediate between these two categories; that is, the second shot contains the same subject *plus* additional subjects. A cut from a close-up of one person to a two-shot containing the first person is a case in point. Cutting from a two- to a three-shot is another example. In these cases we can usually practice the cutting techniques which apply to either of the above categories.

When shall we cut in each case? When cutting between two shots of the same subject, it is usually best to choose the moment of some definite action. Sitting, rising, turning, gesturing, etc. are typical motivations for *cutting on action*. The cut should come in the midst of the action, so that movement begun in one shot is completed in the next. This then forms a bridge between the two shots and minimizes whatever abruptness there may exist.

When cutting between shots of different subjects, it is meaningless to cut in mid-action, because the movement will never be completed in the second shot. In the different subject category, it is advisable to wait until action, if any, has been completed, as in the example of the closing door behind the young lady who left her companion. The primary motivation for cutting between close-ups of different people in the same scene is *dialogue*. As one actor finishes a line and the next is spoken by an actor who is not in the same shot, we cut to the second actor, just as he begins to speak. *Cuts on dialogue* may be marked on a script, and even the script-bound student-director, who does not watch his monitors, has a chance of cutting accurately on lines. But describing the action in your script will not give you the precise second in that action at which to cut. Only by watching the monitor and choosing the right instant can this be done.

But there are other timing cues which help the director get precise and neat cutting, especially in the second category of shots of different subjects.

The *reaction shot* has been mentioned as one of the purposes for cutting. One character tells the second some startling news. Although the first is still speaking, the viewer must watch the second character's reaction to the news, if the plot is to be advanced. Since the cut must be made as the new emotion dawns on the second actor's face, this would seem to be a *cut on action*, or rather, a *cut on reaction*. In actual practice, it is usually convenient to agree in rehearsal that the reaction will dawn at a given word in the first actor's dialogue, and the cut may be made on that word. If the reaction comes a second or two late, we simply are on hand to see the dawn break.

Cutting on the direction of attention is often desirable, especially when an actor sets up an attention—by pointing or looking at some object which is out of the frame of the current shot. The actor sees something which is off-camera at that instant; the viewer immediately wants to know what he has seen. That wish is satisfied by cutting to a shot of the object in question.

Cutting at the end of a phrase of music is a procedure that makes for neatness and dispatch in the handling of song or dance numbers. In a ballet, it may sometimes be preferable to cut on action, even when that action is not at the end of a phrase, since a visual flow of images and the continuity of action is always the most important factor.

But in a song number, particularly a popular song whose musical structure is mathematically rigid, it is both convenient and effective to cut at the end of an eight-measure segment, or just before the release, or as the vocalist pauses for an instrumental break. Cutting in the middle of a phrase brings about a discrepancy between visual and auditory phrasing, causing a ragged effect.

Cutting on a sound cue also combines convenience and effectiveness. In the case of the example of the young lady who walked out on her dejected lover, the slam of the door (both in sight and in sound) is a natural moment at which to cut back to the man she left. Any similar sound—a shot, a breaking window, a shout or a sob, would motivate a cut, especially if the cut showed either the source of the sound or its effect upon some member of the cast.

In any event, a little experimentation during rehearsal soon reveals the exact second at which a cut will be most effective, and both director and technical director will have a surer feel for cuing the cut precisely.

How to Cut Effectively

Smooth cutting depends not only on the timing of the cut, but even more on the nature of the two shots between which the cutting is done. Wherever possible, too great a discrepancy between the shots is to be avoided or compensated for in some manner. If shots cannot match, in any one of the ways listed below, then cutting on action is the safest recourse. Cutting on action joins a shot whose nature is changing right up to the instant of the cut, to a new shot whose nature is also changing as the action is completed. The continuous action welds the two shots together. It is interesting to note that when other factors, such as relative camera angle, etc., are inappropriate, or not conducive to a smooth cut, the director may stage an action which will make a smooth cut possible.

In what respects should two shots be related to insure smooth cutting between them? In any of the following:

Relative angles. In a two-camera show, the student-director is tempted to place his cameras at opposite edges of the set, shooting inward, in order to get variety of camera angles. Yet cameras placed so widely apart may create a seeming change in screen direction. Screen direction is the direction in which characters or subjects seem to be moving across the receiver screen. There are only two screen directions: left and right. The classic example of misguided camera placement is the use of a camera in the infield of a race-track, in one of the earliest pick-ups of horse-racing. With no opportunity to rehearse the shots before the race, the director watched the horses come into the stretch on Camera 1, at the top of the stands. Then he cut to a closer shot on his infield camera, only to see the horses apparently face about and head back the other way. As seen on one camera, they were going from the left edge of the frame to the right. On the other camera, they ran from right to left.

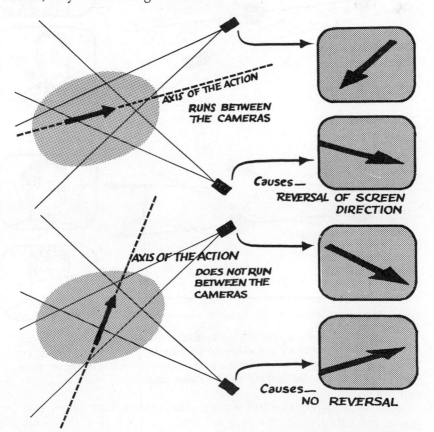

Figure 30. When the axis of the action runs between the cameras, cutting from one to the other will reverse the direction of the action.

Whenever the axis of the action runs between two cameras, the direction of the action is reversed on the screen. The screen direction problem crops up also in dramatic shows, when two people are conversing. Instead of an axis of action, we have here a "conversational line" joining the two people. As long as both cameras are on the same side of this conversational line, no screen direction problems will arise. If, however, one of the cameras is placed on the opposite side of this axis, a cut to this camera will reverse the apparent direction in which the subject is looking.

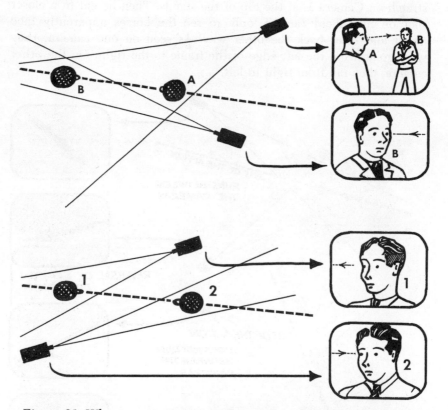

Figure 31. When cameras are on opposite sides of the conversational axis, screen directions are reversed in cutting. In the first example, Actor B is mistaken for Actor A; in the second, both people seem to be looking in the same direction.

Another unhappy effect of widely unrelated camera angles may involve the background. We may cut from one shot of a single subject to another shot of the same person, but the background as seen from the new angle may be so different as to make us feel, for a moment, that the actor has jumped over to another set. Such an effect becomes a very rough cut indeed.

Again, overwide separation of cameras may give so different an angle on the same subject that as the cut is made, it may seem that a new actor has been added to the scene. One of the actors seen on Camera 1 looks like a couple of other fellows when seen from the rear on Camera 2.

Relative composition. While it is said that shots must have a reasonable relationship in relative composition, it is not advisable to cut from a medium-shot of a singer seen from the left to a medium-shot of the same singer seen from the right. Cutting to a shot identical except in angle is valueless, with the notable exception of the reverse angle shot described on page 31. These shots, of course, are identical in composition but completely opposite in emphasis.

What should be avoided is the cut in which a subject seems to jump from side to side of the frame. In Fig. 32 it is clearly seen what hap-

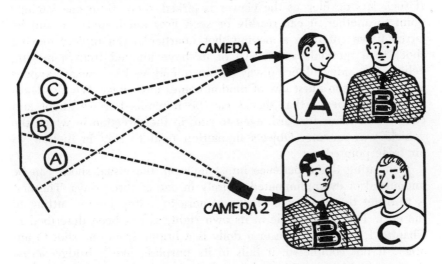

Figure 32. Cutting between these two shots results in Character B jumping from one side of the frame to the other.

pens when characters A, B, and C are seated side by side and photographed with two two-shots. First, we see B on the right of the frame in the shot with A. Then, as we cut, we see B on the left of the frame alongside C. Clearly, with each cut B has become much too agile for comfort.

Even when there is a change of subject in two successive shots, it is possible to maintain visual continuity by similarity of composition.

If the center of interest in the two successive shots is in approximately the same position in the frame, the cut is less distracting, even when the subject changes, than if the eye must jump to a different part of the screen.

The reader may well ask about the most familiar example of cuts between totally different shots which one is likely to see on today's TV screens, the cut from long-shot to extreme close-up. It is almost impossible to match two such shots in any way, and the jar occasioned by the cut is marked. Yet such a cut is thoroughly justified when a definite shock value is desired by the director. The extreme effect of such a cut can be dramatically valid because the very shock of the rough cut underscores the drama of the revelation provided by the close-up.

Relative movement. If the most pleasing effect of good cutting is the smooth continuity of progression from shot to shot, then the avoidance of any sudden jar must be one of the director's objectives. If such jars develop as the viewer is jerked about from one vantage point to another, it can readily be seen how much more he will be jarred if we cut from a moving shot (particularly a *rapidly* moving shot) to a motionless shot. All of us have jumped from a moving vehicle to a sidewalk or railway platform, and we know what happens as Isaac Newton's first law of motion comes into effect. We also learn through experience that shocks can be minimized if we alight and continue to move forward, even to run, in the direction in which the vehicle was moving. Objects in motion tend to stay in motion, as Sir Isaac pointed out.

Translating this experience into television, the visual shock can be minimized or even eliminated entirely in one of three ways. The first is to bring the movement of one camera to a stop before cutting to the next. This is advisable in its own right, as has been described in Chapter 1, because a pan or a dolly is a bridge from one shot to another; if not completed, it fails in its purpose, like a bridge across a river which never quite reaches the opposite shore. The important point in connection with cutting, however, is the fact that when a camera movement is completed before cutting, one stationary camera is cut to another. In other words, we have waited for the train to come to a stop before jumping off.

The second way, as any hobo who has flipped a moving train can tell you, is to match your speed to that of the train. If two cameras are following the same action (a quarterback carrying the ball, or an actor crossing the set), they will both be panning in the same direction, and a cut between them is generally smooth. If the two shots involve different subjects, this becomes a tricky bit of camerawork, calling for a good deal of rehearsal or a camera crew experienced in this type of shooting. But it is a rewarding device. If Camera 1, for example, is panning from left to right, then, well before the instant at which the cut is planned, Camera 2 starts to pan in the same direction, on a shot with almost the same framing, panning at the same rate of speed. A cut made at this moment will be smooth. This method was used, for example, in the "roll call" of a student discussion program called *There Ought to be a Law*. As the members of a "high school legislature" reached the vote on an issue which had been discussed throughout the program, the camera took tight close-ups of the individual students. Camera 1 started panning down the front line of voters to the mid-point of the row, catching each face as its owner voted. At the mid-point, Camera 2 (already in motion and on an identical close-up shot) was picked up and continued to the end of that row. Meanwhile, Camera 1 was lining up on the first student at the left-hand end of the second row, and the process was repeated. The cuts were smooth and the continuity was clear.

A third way in which a cut from a moving camera shot to a stationary one can be made less obvious, involves the actors. If the actors continue, in the second shot, to move in the same screen direction in which they *and* the camera were moving in the first shot, the cut will be made on action, and the eye is less likely to be aware of the stationary frame in the second shot.

Obviously, if the director must provide such action just for the sake of "saving" his cut from being ragged, he must be careful that the staging does not seem contrived. But when the motion is appropriate, it can well be made a part of the pictorial continuity as well as a point of dramatic action.

Going from Shot to Shot by Other Means Than Cutting

The *cut,* then, is an instantaneous switch to a different shot. But there are other ways of going from one shot to another, chief of which are the *dissolve* and its many variations, and the *fade*. Our concern here is not so much with the psychological contribution of each type of transition, but with its function in pictorial continuity.

The Dissolve

The dissolve, often known as the *lap dissolve*, or simply the *lap*, is the process whereby the picture on one camera blends gradually, and at a controllable speed, into the picture on a second camera. The flexibility of the *dissolve* and its intriguing effect pose a dangerous temptation to the new director. He is likely to be so entranced with the effect that he uses the *dissolve* at every opportunity, appropriate or not, and almost forgets the clean, incisive effectiveness of a neat cut. Harvey Marlowe, Program Manager of WOR-TV, makes the statement that "Every new director goes 'dissolve-happy' for a time. He has to get that phase out of his system before he can get back to using the *dissolve* only when it is more appropriate than a *cut*."

When, then, is the use of the *dissolve* justified? There can be no hard and fast rule, no question of right and wrong. As in so many aspects of camera handling, *dissolving* or *cutting* is a matter of individual preference and style.

The reader must bear in mind the difference between the use of the *dissolve* in dramatic programs and in non-dramatic programs. In television drama, the *dissolve* is reserved by almost all directors to indicate a discontinuity in time or space. The viewer is steeped in that convention from his film-going, and any other use of the *dissolve* in a drama disorients him. Since the *dissolve* is a more gradual switch to a different shot, the change to a different angle or composition will not be as noticeable as in a *cut*. Nevertheless, for a brief second, both shots are on the screen at the same time, and relative matching is still helpful in achieving smoothness.

In the non-dramatic program, the *dissolve* cannot be used as an indication of change in time, since all time is in the present. The non-dramatic program may involve change in place, however, and the *dissolve* may be used, not so much to indicate the change as to bridge it.

Similar to this is the use of a *dissolve* to create a false bridge between two elements of a program that actually need no bridging but which are set up more effectively when separated and connected, simultaneously, by a *dissolve*. For example, in a ballet we may watch two principal dancers complete a movement, after which they are joined by six other dancers. When the music and the pattern of the dance changes, the viewer's feeling about the dance should change simultaneously. By *dissolving* to the long-shot which shows the six new dancers entering, we may emphasize the fact that the dance is entering on a new phase, and we even make the sequence just beginning seem like another number. A cut would not have given the viewer the brief breathing space in which he adjusts himself from his enjoyment of the *pas de deux* to his enjoyment of mass movement.

In a "format" show, in which a narrator or MC introduces the enactment of a vignette or skit which will explain his point, we may "frame" the dramatic segment by *dissolving* into it and *dissolving* out of it at the end as we rejoin the MC.

The *dissolve* usually gives us a slower and smoother switch to another shot. The speed of the cut is beyond our control, but a *dissolve* may be paced to fit the mood. It may be timed to coincide with the last measure of an instrumental introduction to a song, for example, terminating in a shot of a vocalist about to sing.

Variations. Variations on the *dissolve* are possible through the use of camera effects or electronic effects, which have already been described. One such effect is the *defocus*. This involves ending a sequence by cranking the camera out of focus until a vague blur fills the screen. Previously, the shot on the next camera has been *defocussed* to the same vague blur. The director then may *cut* or *dissolve* from blur to blur; in either case, the viewer will not be too aware of the change until the shot on the second camera is brought into focus.

The *Flexitron* provides still another variation of the *dissolve* (described in the preceding chapter). A shot can slowly begin to wave and wiggle, building up to a point where the picture is no longer recognizable. Then a *cut* or *dissolve* can be made to another waving shot which immediately quiets down into a straight picture. Or, if desired, the second shot may have no *weave* at all, simply *dissolving* out of the first shot as soon as that picture has wiggled into unrecognizability. The latter technique is frequently the best, since it saves time in making the transition. The *defocus* transition is also improved by defocusing only the first camera and dissolving into a clear shot.

The Fade: In the television drama, a minor discontinuity in time or space is usually accomplished by a *dissolve*. This is comparable to a new scene in the theater, for which the stagelights are lowered and then raised again on another setting. A major pause in the flow of the drama, comparable to the end of an act in the theater is indicated in television by fading to black and then fading in the next shot. The *fade* gives a conclusive feeling, and is very properly used at the end of a drama to "ring down the final curtain" to prepare for the commercial. Many programs use a standard title card or program symbol to separate the program from the commercial, although some agency producers protest this device as "flagging the commercial" and possibly driving the viewer from the set. Whether used alone or combined with a title card, the *fade* is a clean and definite separation of two unrelated elements. It results in a break in continuity.

For this reason, the relative appearance of the two shots which are separated by the *fade* is not as important as it is in the *cut* or the *dissolve*. The *fade* provides time to lose the visual image of the first shot, and no matter how different the second may be, no continuity is attempted, and the viewer is not jarred by the change.

The pace of the *fade* may, of course, be regulated by the switching system, and some directors prefer to fade fairly rapidly within the body of a drama and to fade rather slowly as a final curtain. Equally important in determining tempo is the length of time during which nothing but black is on the screen. Some directors feel that the maximum time during which the screen should stay black is three seconds. Any longer period may not only break the mood of the program but may even cause an attack of the fidgets among the viewers.

Nevertheless, "When in doubt, fade it out." Why? Because a black screen is preferable to one upon which the viewer may see things going awry, or an actor who has finished his scene, doggedly holding his pose and peering frantically for a signal that the camera is off so he may step out of character. (To say nothing of the horrible possibility of the actor's stepping out of character and stepping off the set in full view of the home audience!) Therefore, even if the next shot is not quite ready, it is best to fade to black, hold in black, and fade up again as soon as possible.

We have seen so far how the individual shots are beads to be strung on the string of the director's inventiveness. Unlike most necklaces, these are composed of beads which are not alike, nor are they spaced with perfect evenness. It is the selection of the individual beads, their placement next to adjacent beads which are pleasantly, not discordantly, dissimilar, and the delicate adjustment of their connection and separation by *cuts, dissolves* and *fades,* which makes the complete string either a work of art or a gewgaw.

4. TV Terms and Script Marking Symbols

So that the reader may have before him for ready reference all the standard symbols and cues that are used on the director's script, such a collection is given below. This is by no means complete; indeed, every director will devise some cues and symbols of his own, but the standard markings which appear on every script are here included.

TERM	SYMBOL or ABBREVIATION	MEANING
Terms connected with field of view:		
Single shot One-shot	*1- shot*	A shot including only one person
Two-shot	*2- shot*	A shot including two persons
also Three-shot Four-shot; etc.	*3-shot*	
Group shot	*GR - shot*	A wide shot of an entire group
Long shot	*LS*	A wide-angle shot showing the maximum area of the scene. This usually means the actor is shown full length.
Close-up	*CU*	A shot of a single person or object which fills the screen. A full head or a head and shoulders, occasionally a shot as low as the waist, is called a close-up.

TERM	SYMBOL or ABBREVIATION	MEANING
Medium shot	MS	Almost anything in between the above two definitions. Usually a shot where actors are shown in waist shot or longer, but not full length.
Knee shot Thigh shot Bust shot Shoulder shot Head shot Waist shot	KS TS BS SS WS	Terms in which the field of view is defined in term. of the lower frame line of the picture. If this cuts the actor at the knee, for ex- ample, the shot is known as a knee shot.
Tight shot	Tight CU etc	A shot composed so the sub- ject crowds the edge of the frame.
Loose shot	Loose 2-shot etc	A shot so composed that there is space around the subject.
Combination shots (LS-CU) Special composition		Unusual shots of this na- ture can be described in words, but are much easier described in with a sketch (see script "Line of Duty")

Terms connected with camera angle:

High shot	High	A shot taken from consid- erably higher than eye level.
Low shot	Low	A shot taken from consid- erably lower than eye level.
Top shot	Top	A shot where the camera is

TERM	SYMBOL or ABBREVIATION	MEANING
		looking vertically down, or almost so.
Over-the-shoulder shot	O.S.	A two-shot, usually, showing the person further from the camera in full face, but only the shoulder or side of the head of the near person. The camera literally looks over the near person's shoulder. (Note that the abbreviation O.S. when applied to sound means "off-screen.)

Terms connected with camera movement:

TERM	SYMBOL or ABBREVIATION	MEANING
Pan (left or right)	Pan L	Camera rotates to left or right, sweeping across the scene.
Tilt (or pan) up or down	Tilt up	Camera rotates to look up or to look down.
Dolly in	DI	Camera rolls forward toward the subject.
Dolly back Pull back	DB (DB)	Camera rolls backward, away from the subject or scene.
Truck (left or right)	Tr R	Camera rolls crosswise (or diagonally), not toward or away from subject.

TERM	SYMBOL or ABBREVIATION	MEANING
Zoom in	*Zoom in*	Camera simultaneously dollies in and lowers from a high to a low angle.
Zoom out	*Zoom out*	Camera simultaneously raises and pulls back. (Zoom effect may also be obtained with zoom lenses, in which case the cues are the same.)
"Let" actor in		Camera holds steady so actor enters frame.
"Let" him out		Camera holds steady as actor leaves the picture -- does not attempt to follow him.
Let him into close-up		Camera does not dolly back as actor comes toward camera.
Take actor across set up stairs, etc.		Camera follows actor, panning or tilting as necessary, dollying or trucking (sometimes) without further cue.
Cross with him		Similar instruction leaving details of operation up to the cameraman.
Standby for rise Watch the rise		Warning to cameraman of action to come. Also warns boom man to be ready to lift boom.

TERM	SYMBOL or ABBREVIATION	MEANING

Terms connected with switching:

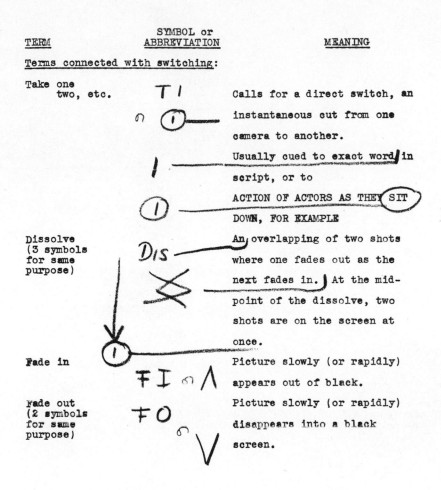

Take one
    two, etc.
                    Calls for a direct switch, an
instantaneous cut from one
camera to another.
Usually cued to exact word in
script, or to
ACTION OF ACTORS AS THEY SIT
DOWN, FOR EXAMPLE

Dissolve
(3 symbols
for same
purpose)
                    An overlapping of two shots
where one fades out as the
next fades in. At the mid-
point of the dissolve, two
shots are on the screen at
once.

Fade in
                    Picture slowly (or rapidly)
appears out of black.

Fade out
(2 symbols
for same
purpose)
                    Picture slowly (or rapidly)
disappears into a black
screen.

Part II

THE SIMPLER FORMATS

5. An Interview Format

INTERVIEW WITH DR. X
INTRODUCTORY NOTES AND PRODUCTION SUGGESTIONS

The interview type of program is one of the most popular in television. Whether it is as popular with the public as it is with the producers has not been established, but there can be no question that the interview will be a staple item on the schedule of the small station for a long time to come. It does provide one essence of television—reality. And a skillful interviewer, if he has a guest with an interesting personality, can provide a very pleasant quarter-hour.

From the viewpoint of production, the interview is a very good opening exercise for student-directors. Using two cameras, the director has his choice of four basic shots: a two-shot and a close-up of the interviewer, let us say, on Camera 1, and a two-shot and a close-up of the guest on Camera 2. The close-ups may vary from medium close-ups to tight close-ups; the two-shot may occasionally (perhaps at beginning and end) be pulled back for a long-shot which shows most of the set and facilitates smooth handling of the guest's arrival or departure, if the guest is not to be seated beside the interviewer throughout.

Some interview formats have two or three guests in succession, each one joining the interviewer in turn. Or the host may move about the set, joining one guest after another. But once these transitions have been accomplished, the visual problem becomes the same again: two people conversing. For our purpose here, we have assumed a spot in a larger program involving only one guest. If the material can hold interest, it might easily run seven or eight minutes.

Some indication of visual materials—photographs, objects or whatever is available—is provided in the script, although the inclusion of such items will, of course, depend on the local situation. The guest, the mythical Dr. X, is assumed to be any member of the faculty who has recently been abroad, on a field trip, or to an important professional conference. Most people in such a position will be gracious enough to help out in a student exercise, either through natural kindness or in the interests of facing a television camera and getting that experience over with. In early trial-runs, it may be more convenient to use a stand-in for the visitor, just to set the shots, and to postpone bringing the guest down to the studio until the time scheduled for dress rehearsal.

Many college FM stations make a practice in the summer session, for example, of putting on a radio interview series featuring visiting faculty members. This format, the "Who's in Town" type of program, has general interest and public relations value. Its TV equivalent is seriously recommended for a beginning television station as simple programming which will combine the need for minimum preparation with maximum effectiveness. But don't let "minimum preparation" lead you to avoid out-of-studio pre-planning, or to shirk spending time and effort on collecting visual materials, mounting photographs, selecting appropriate objects, and other supplementary items. Finally, remember that any interview program depends on two factors for its success: the personality of the interviewer, and the story which the guest has to tell. Not even superb lighting and camerawork can make a good interview out of a haphazard conversation between two uninteresting people. Ed Wegener put it very well: "People in stupors don't get high Hoopers!"

Suggestions to the Producer and Director

One effective way of covering this type of format is to deploy cameras as shown in Fig. 33. If small objects are to be exhibited by the guest, they may be placed on the coffee table or held by the MC while the guest describes them. Use of a 135-mm. lens on Camera 1 can probably take care of all but the smallest objects, and an 8½-inch lens on Camera 2 can cover that contingency.

The "script" as provided gives only a bare outline on which the MC will elaborate, of course. Additional questions, particularly those which will stimulate the guest to relate a personal anecdote or describe a dangerous moment, will enrich the program. As planned here, the interview would run about ten minutes, depending always on the brevity or length of the guest's responses. Controlling the flow of the guest's replies is one of the first techniques to be mastered by an interviewer. By adding two or three questions, the MC can easily extend the program to fifteen minutes, always subject to the guest's ability to sustain interest for that length of time. One safe way of controlling time is to provide two expendable questions, tentatively scheduled to come just before the last or next-to-last queries. If the guest under-

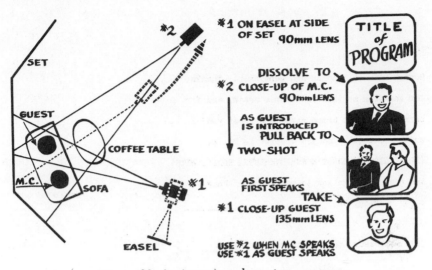

Figure 33. An interview show—two cameras.

stands that these two expendable items provide a "cushion" and will
be eliminated if his other remarks run longer on the air than in rehearsal, he will not be upset at their being dropped. He may even be
brisker in his earlier replies if he really wants to make all his points.

INTERVIEW WITH DR. X*

MUSIC: SERIES THEME, UP AND UNDER	TITLE CARD: Title of Series (With Us Today, Who's in Town, etc.)
ANNOUNCER:	
Yes, be <u>With Us Today</u>, as Station _____	
brings you another visit with an interesting	
guest who has been places and seen things,	
places and things about which you'll enjoy	
knowing more.	
Today's guest is Dr._____ of the	
Department of _____, and here to in-	TITLE CARD: Name of Guest
troduce him to you is your regular host on	
<u>With Us Today</u>, _____(Name of MC).	
MUSIC:	DISSOLVE TO MC
OUT	

* No rights required

MC:

Good afternoon, ladies and gentlemen. Thanks
for inviting me into your homes again, and for
permitting me to bring with me a guest you'll
enjoy meeting.   Today's visitor is Dr. X.
(BRIEF LIST OF GUEST'S ACHIEVEMENTS, ENDING WITH)
And now, I'd like you to meet a man I know you'll
enjoy hearing, Dr. _____.

DR. X:

It's a pleasure to be with you, Mr._____.

MC:

Dr._____, one of the reasons why we
are particularly eager to bring you to our tele-
vision audience today is your recent (TRIP ABROAD,
FIELD TRIP, COMPLETION OF A RESEARCH PROJECT,
GOVERNMENT SERVICE OR ATTENDANCE AT AN IMPORTANT
PROFESSIONAL MEETING). Won't you tell us about it?

DR. X:

DESCRIBES CIRCUMSTANCES UNDER WHICH HE WAS SELECTED
TO TAKE PART IN RECENT EVENT, PURPOSE OF HIS TRIP,
WHERE IT WAS HELD.

MC:

Who were some of the prominent people you met
there, Dr._____, whose names might be
familiar to our audience?

DR. X:

NAMES AND IDENTIFIES THEM.

MC:

What were some of the impressions you received in
the course of this (TRIP, RESEARCH, SERVICE, ETC.)?

DR. X:

(IF POSSIBLE, SHOWS PHOTOGRAPHS, FILM OR OTHER
VISUAL REMINDERS OF SCENES HE VISITED WITH
DESCRIPTIONS.)

MC:

It's an experience we all envy you, Dr._____.
I'm sure many of our viewers would like to have
been with you. But which part of the time you
spent there seemed most significant?   What is
your most memorable experience?

DR. X:

ANSWERS AND, IF APPROPRIATE, SHOWS ILLUSTRATIVE
MATERIAL. IN SCIENCE FIELD, ACTUAL OBJECTS
FOUND OR INVENTED MAY BE SHOWN AT THIS POINT.

MC:

And now that you're back, what is your next move?

DR. X:

DESCRIBES ADDITIONAL RESEARCH, BOOK HE IS GOING
TO WRITE, OR OTHER FUTURE PLANS.

MC:

Dr. _____, what is the importance of this
event to the average man or woman who is watching
us now?

DR. X:

RELATES SUBJECT OF INTERVIEW TO LIVES OF VIEWERS

MC:

And for this insight into the effect of _____
on the lives of all of us, we are deeply grateful,

Dr._____. Thank you for coming today and
for sharing with us your recent experience in
_____. Come again soon, won't you?
(TO CAMERA)   And that, ladies and gentlemen,
concludes our visit with you today. But won't you
invite us into your homes again at this same time
next week? I know you'll enjoy meeting _____,
the noted _____. Until then this is
_____ bidding you good afternoon.   DISSOLVE TO CLOSING TITE
                    MUSIC:
THEME SNEAKS IN UNDER ANNOUNCER
                    ANNOUNCER:
Station _____ has brought you _____
(program title), the informal and entertaining
visit with an interesting guest whose story we
hope you enjoyed hearing. Today's guest was
_____. Join us again next week
at this time for another television visit (tele-
visit, if you dare) with _____ (Name
of MC). This has been a _____
production.

                    MUSIC:
UP FULL AND HOLD TO TIME

6. A Demonstration Format

INTRODUCTORY NOTES AND PRODUCTION SUGGESTIONS

In a wide range of program types, running from commercials through cooking and fashion shows to the finest educational programs, the demonstration format has proved its worth. It is truly televisible; it proves what we are trying to express. While it has certain obvious hazards, such as the need for the demonstration to work the very first time (or, at least, the second), its advantages are well worth the risks.

As an example of a demonstration subject which would be readily available to any organization with studio equipment, we have chosen television itself, a demonstration in the simplest possible terms of how a program comes "from us to you." The only piece of equipment which is not part of any studio is the physics apparatus, which shows how a beam of electrons is deflected by magnets. That may be secured from the physics department of most colleges and even some high schools. In a pinch, the unit may be omitted entirely, although it is greatly helpful in clarifying the key operation of television—scanning. The exact format of such a demonstration depends largely on the facilities and layout of the particular studio in which it is produced, so that only a *suggested* format can be given here, with the knowledge that it will have to be rewritten to fit the local requirements. For example, much of the demonstration in the script that follows involves the control room. In some studios, it may be possible to dolly a camera up to the control room window and obtain adequate shots of the interior. This same camera can then be dollied back and used as a second camera on the floor. In other studios, shots of the audio console and camera monitors can only be obtained by placing a camera permanently in the rear of the control room. In a two-camera studio this would leave only one camera for the rest of the demonstration on the floor. Ideally, of course, a third camera will make this full demonstration possible. A look into the control room and a chance to see the director, TD and engineers at work is a revelation to most viewers, and it is suggested that if only two cameras are available, one of these be used in the control room in spite of the problems which will be raised in doing the floor portions of the demonstrations with only one camera.

"From Us to You" may be presented by one MC, with studio assistants who handle equipment but do not participate verbally, or by an MC and two associates, each of whom takes over one part of the demonstration and explains what his particular apparatus does. In any event, an MC should ad lib around the framework which is suggested, rather than try to memorize a script.

FROM US TO YOU*

MUSIC:

SERIES THEME, UP AND UNDER

TITLE CARD: Title of Series
(See for Yourself, We Take you
Now, In the Spotlight, etc.)

ANNOUNCER:

Once again, Station _____ and the University of _____ invite you to SEE FOR YOURSELF.   Today, SEE FOR YOURSELF how a television program comes From Us to You.

TITLE CARD: From Us to You

MUSIC:

DOWN AND OUT

ANNOUNCER:

(NO PAUSE) And here to welcome you into our studio is your regular host on SEE FOR YOURSELF, _____.

DISSOLVE TO MC
(SUGGESTION: EXTREME LONG-SHOT
SHOWING AS MUCH OF STUDIO AS
POSSIBLE, INCLUDING MIKE BOOM OVER
MC'S HEAD, THEN DOLLY IN ON MC.)

MC:

GREETS VIEWERS AND SHOWS THEM STUDIO, POINTING OUT LIGHTS, CAMERAS,SETS, ETC., VERY BRIEFLY. SAYS LET'S START WITH THE SOUND PART OF THE PROGRAM AND SEE HOW THAT IS PRODUCED. SOUND IS SOMETHING WE ARE FAMILIAR WITH — WE HAVE

* No permission required

BEEN BROADCASTING SOUND TO YOU OVER THE RADIO

FOR MANY YEARS.   IN RADIO INSTEAD OF MY GOING

OVER TO A MICROPHONE, HOWEVER, THE MICROPHONE

COMES OVER TO ME.   HE SHOWS MICROPHONE BOOM,

HAS THE OPERATOR HANDLE THE CONTROLS AND DEM-

ONSTRATES WHAT EACH ONE DOES.

(Note: This calls for inter-cutting between
two shots, one a close-up on the control in
the hands of the boom-operator; the other a
shot of the MC and the microphone showing the
result of each action.)

MC EXPLAINS THAT SOUND VIBRATIONS HITTING

MICROPHONE GENERATE SMALL ELECTRICAL VI-

BRATIONS -- SHOWS CABLE ALONG WHICH THEY

PASS TO CONTROL ROOM. INTRODUCES CONTROL

ROOM.

AFTER A QUICK LOOK AROUND -

We'll tell you about those other interesting

looking pieces of equipment in just a moment,

but first let's look at the audio console. The

audio engineer is controlling the volume of my

voice. As you can see (BEGIN TO FADE MC'S MIKE)

he can fade me down to a whisper (PAUSE, THEN

FADE UP) he can bring me out of a whisper to

as near a shout as our equipment can handle.

By turning that dial he keeps my voice at the

best level for listening comfort.

HE POINTS OUT THE TURNTABLES IN SIMILAR MANNER

AND DEMONSTRATES THE SNEAKING IN OF THEME MUSIC

UNDER THE SPEECH.

EXPLAINS HOW THE AUDIO CONSOLE IS THE "GRAND
CENTRAL STATION" OF THE AUDIO SYSTEM. EXPLAINS
AMPLIFIERS AND THE MIXING OF SOUNDS, AND HOW   (CHART) on studio camera)
ALL GO THROUGH THE MASTER GAIN TO THE TRANS-
MITTER.

LEADS NOW TO A DISCUSSION OF THE PICTURE PART
OF THE PROGRAM. SHOWS BRIEFLY THE CAMERA CON-
TROL UNITS, THE MASTER MONITOR AND THE SWITCHING
SYSTEM, RELATING THESE TO THE CAMERA.   NOW   CHART SHOWING RELATION OF
                                                       THESE ELEMENTS
HE TRANSFERS HIS ATTENTION TO THE CAMERA AND
SHOWS ITS VARIOUS PARTS.   HE DESCRIBES THE
TUBE WITHIN THE CAMERA WITH THE AID OF A SIMPLE
CHART. HE ACTUALLY TAKES THE VIEWFINDER OFF THE   CHART OF CAMERA
CAMERA AND PUTS IT BACK AGAIN.   HE DRAWS PARALLEL
WITH SOUND PORTION OF BROADCAST -- HERE WE HAVE A
PICTURE MADE OF LIGHT AND DARK PORTIONS CONVERTED
INTO ELECTRICAL IMPULSES AND TRANSMITTED. SAYS
THE ONLY THING WHICH CAN BE BROADCAST IS ONE LONG
CONTINUOUS ELECTRICAL CURRENT. THE PROBLEM IN
MAKING TELEVISION WORK IS TO CONVERT A TWO-DIMEN-
SIONAL PICTURE INTO A ONE-DIMENSIONAL, CHANGING
CURRENT. COMPARES THIS TO A SINGLE LINE VS. AN
AREA. EXPLAINS SCANNING WITH CATHODE-RAY TUBE AND
PERMANENT MAGNET. SHOWS HOW BEAM OF ELECTRONS IS
DEFLECTED BY THE MAGNET. SHOWS IMAGE ORTHICON
TUBE, AND KINESCOPE TUBE AND DRAWS PARALLEL. NOW,
HE SAYS, LET'S SEE HOW THE CAMERA AND THE CAMERAMAN
PUT THE RIGHT PICTURE ON THE END OF THIS TUBE.

(NOTE: If only one studio camera is available, and
the camera in the control room cannot get a suitable
shot of it, then a setup of mirrors must be used so

it can see itself. Put up two mirros in the fashion
of a clothing store so the camera can look into one
and see a side view of itself reflected in the other.
This may require an adjustment in studio lighting.
The mirrors will have to be fairly large).

MC SHOWS THE LENS TURRET AT THE FRONT OF THE CAMERA

AND THE HANDLE AT THE BACK WHICH CHANGES LENSES.

POINTS OUT WIDE-ANGLE AND NARROW-ANGLE LENSES AND

ASKS CAMERAMAN TO CHANGE FROM ONE TO THE NEXT.

SHOWS LENS CHANGE ON THE AIR, AND EACH LENS COMING

INTO FOCUS. POINTS OUT FOCUS CONTROL ON CAMERA

AND DEMONSTRATES NEED FOR CONSTANT FOCUSSING.

WALKS TOWARD CAMERA AFTER ASKING CAMERMAN

NOT TO FOCUS. WALKS AWAY FROM CAMERA AND

SHOWS DEPTH IN WHICH HE IS KEPT SHARP. THEN

DOES SAME AGAIN AFTER ASKING CAMERAMAN TO

FOLLOW FOCUS.

NOW, HE SAYS, LET'S GO INTO THE CONTROL ROOM

AGAIN AND SEE WHAT HAPPENS TO THE VARIOUS

PICTURES FROM THE DIFFERENT CAMERAS WHICH

ARE BEING USED ON THIS SHOW. HE MENTIONS

FIRST THE CAMERA MONITORS AND INTRODUCES THE

VIDEO ENGINEER.

(NOTE: MC must have studio monitor to watch
control room shots, unless he can move quickly
into the control room or turn over the discussion to someone else who is inside).

VIDEO ENGINEER DEMONSTRATES SEVERAL OF THE

CONTROLS HE USES: BEAM, ORTH FOCUS, BLANKING,

ETC. CAMERA PICKS THIS UP OFF OTHER CAMERA'S

MONITOR.

NOW WE GO TO THE TECHNICAL DIRECTOR AND THE

SWITCHING SYSTEM. SINCE ONLY ONE CAMERA CAN

BE ON THE AIR AT ONE TIME, SOMEONE HAS TO

SWITCH BETWEEN CAMERAS. A ROW OF BUTTONS
CONTROLS SWITCHES AND CUTTING IS DONE BY
PUNCHING THE BUTTONS. FOR EXAMPLE (assuming
a close-up of the buttons is possible), BUTTON
TWO IS DOWN NOW SO YOU ARE SEEING THE PICTURE OF
THE CONTROL ROOM WHICH IS BEING PICKED UP ON
CAMERA TWO. WHEN THE DIRECTOR SAYS "TAKE ONE"
THE T.D. PUNCHES THE TWO BUTTON - LIKE
THIS - AND NOW YOU ARE LOOKING AT THE STUDIO
ON CAMERA ONE. TO GET BACK INTO THE CONTROL
ROOM WE HAVE TO TAKE TWO AGAIN.
MC THEN DEMONSTRATES THE FADE-OUT AND FADE-IN
EFFECT, FIRST ON THE SAME CAMERA, THEN BETWEEN
CAMERAS. THEN A FADE-OUT AND A FADE-IN COM-
BINED, WHICH IS A DISSOLVE. SHOW IT SLOW AND
FAST. NOW MC INTRODUCES THE DIRECTOR AND
SHOWS THE INTERCOM HEADSET THAT HE WEARS.
INTERCUT SHOT OF CAMERAMAN TO SHOW THE OTHER
END OF THE CONVERSATION. HAVE THEM TALK BACK
AND FORTH A FEW TIMES. HAVE THE DIRECTOR
GIVE THE CAMERAMAN A FEW SIMPLE DIRECTIONS FOR
CAMERA MOVEMENT. (DOLLY IN OR REPOSITION LEFT,
ETC.)
MC THEN THANKS EVERYONE IN THE CONTROL ROOM,
SUMS UP THE STORY ON A CHART OF THE EQUIPMENT -
SAME CHART USED AT BEGINNING OF VIDEO DISCUSSION.
(THIS SUMMARY WILL CONSTITUTE A GOOD FILL SINCE
THE MC CAN PRESUMABLY EXPAND IT AS MUCH AS HE
NEEDS - ACCORDING TO THE TIME SIGNALS HE IS
GIVEN.)

HE STARTS THE WIND-UP WITH: - WELL, I HAVE JUST
TAKEN A LOOK AT ANOTHER VERY IMPORTANT PIECE OF
EQUIPMENT - THE STUDIO CLOCK (SHOT OF CLOCK IF
POSSIBLE). I HAVE TO WIND UP THIS PROGRAM AT
EXACTLY _____ AND THAT GIVES ME _____
TO GO. NEXT TIME YOU WATCH A TV PROGRAM, THINK
OF THE THINGS THAT ARE GOING ON. IF WE SLIP
OCCASIONALLY, AS WE ALL DO, I HOPE YOU WILL
UNDERSTAND. SO UNTIL WE MEET AGAIN ON THE NEXT
BROADCAST OF _____ THIS IS _____
_____ BIDDING YOU GOOD AFTERNOON
(EVENING, NIGHT, OR WHAT HAVE YOU).

      MUSIC:

SNEAK IN THEME, HOLD UNDER

      ANNOUNCER:

Station _____ has just conducted an informal tour of our television studio, in which we
have shown you something of what it takes to
bring one of our programs From Us to You.
Be with us again next week at this same time
when you can SEE FOR YOURSELF how _____
_____.
Your host on today's broadcast has been
_____, and this is _____
speaking for the University of _____.

      MUSIC:

UP FULL AND HOLD TO TIME

7. A Panel Discussion Program Using a Film as Its Springboard

IT'S WORTH KNOWING

INTRODUCTORY NOTES

This film-and-panel-discussion format was developed by Dr. Franklin T. Mathewson of the Department of Audio-Visual Instruction of the National Education Association, whose idea it was originally, and Robert Herridge of WCBS-TV, who served as writer and producer for the station. The film used on the sample program which appears on the following pages was the McGraw-Hill production, *This Charming Couple.*

The format of *It's Worth Knowing* is reproduced here as an example of a discussion program which uses a film as its springboard. It will be noted that only the continuity read by an off-camera announcer is fully scripted. The moderator, Edward Stasheff, ad libbed his remarks around an outline provided by the writer-producer. The panelists ad libbed completely, following the questions thrown out by the moderator. This format has been used by other CBS affiliated stations by permission of the flagship station WCBS-TV, New York, and the Metropolitan branch of the Department of Audio-Visual Instruction of the NEA. Suggested topics and the films to introduce them may be secured by writing to DAVI Producer, *It's Worth Knowing,* WCBS-TV, 485 Madison Avenue, New York 22, N. Y. College and school stations may present the sample script on closed circuit without further permission, but should secure clearance if the broadcast is to go out on the air.

NOTES ON THE DRAMATIC FORM OF DISCUSSION PROGRAMS

By ROBERT HERRIDGE

It is not new, the idea that a serious discussion—the exploration of a subject or problem by two or more persons—creates essentially a dramatic situation. One of the most important elements of the drama, by Aristotle's definition, is the "intellectual element," the exchange of ideas by persons reacting to a given situation. Bernard Shaw has demonstrated again and again that an exchange of ideas is a dramatic event of great excitement. The deliberate and systematic utilization of a proper form—the dramatic form—for the situation created by a discussion group is, so far as television is concerned, a relatively new experiment.* The program *It's Worth Knowing* is an experiment of this kind.

The intent of *It's Worth Knowing* is to provide the audience not with the mere spectacle of a quarrel of opinions, but with the stimulating and satisfying experience of a discussion group developing and drawing out a body of ideas concerning a given subject—the satisfying experience of a dramatic exchange of ideas by persons of long experience in the field and for whom the ideas are a matter of belief.

The important words here are "development"—the concern of the producer in relation to his material; and "satisfaction"—the concern of the producer in relation to his audience. With any discussion group, if the subject or problem is important, clash of opinion, conflict of ideas and viewpoints are normal. The producer's problem is to handle this conflict so that the end result is meaningful—so that there is not only smoke but fire and light. The problem is to give the conflict shape and form so that it must, because of various controlling factors, work through definite stages of development and come to something meaningful for the audience. Thus the audience is left with the satisfying sense of having watched something grow, a body of ideas develop—a discussion with a beginning, a middle, and an end. It has seen an exposition stage developed into a conflict stage and then seen the conflict resolved and rounded out by a final summation. And the form best equipped to handle this conflict of ideas is, as briefly noted above, the dramatic form.

The form underlying the surface script form of *It's Worth Knowing* is dramatic: there is a beginning, a middle, and an end; there is exposition, conflict, and resolve. There is also the prologue and epilogue delivered by the moderator, who is, in addition, a kind of stage manager directing and controlling the action on stage. It is his job to see to it that the discussion develops and that a properly rising dramatic line is maintained according to the way it has been worked out in rehearsal.

This does not mean setting any hard and fast dialogue rules, or

---

* The general meaning of the term "dramatic form" as used above is not to be confused with its more specific meaning, i.e., the form of the play.

scripting the program in advance. It means only setting up certain key questions and key statements that move and develop the discussion. If the moderator, who is a key figure here, has a sense of the dramatic, the work is that much easier. What is most important is that the end-result appear simple and spontaneous. And that, of course, takes work. It takes work and a properly functional form for the discussion program—the dramatic form.

IT'S WORTH KNOWING[*]

March 22, 1952

ARE YOU READY FOR MARRIAGE?

BLACK ON THE LINE

FADE UP MS, BOOKCASE

SUPER TITLE FROM TELOP:
"IT'S WORTH KNOWING"

CUE STUDENTS IN: START ARC
LEFT AND DOLLY IN SLOWLY
WITH THEM TO DISCUSSION AREA

TAKE OUT TITLE

TAKE THEME UNDER AND CUE ANNOUNCER

ANNCR:

This is Studio 53 in Liederkranz Hall -
where every Saturday afternoon at this
time - in association with the Metropolitan branch of the Department of Audio-
Visual Instruction of the National Education Association - WCBS-TV presents the
educational series - IT'S WORTH KNOWING.

Here in Studio 53 - set aside by WCBS-TV
for the purposes of this series - you see
objects representing various fields of our
culture. And each week, with the help of
an educational film and discussion group,
we present a subject or problem selected from
one of these many fields - a subject or problem

[*] See opening of this chapter for permission required

about which IT'S WORTH KNOWING.   Your moderator,
Edward Stasheff, is television supervisor for the
Board of Education of New York City.
And now in the discussion area, Mr. Stasheff and
his guests are ready to begin. Mr. Stasheff...

STASHEFF:

Welcomes viewers to 9th in series on Understanding
Yourself and Others.
Today's program the second in special series of
three on problems of marriage.
Importance of problem stressed by fact that one
out of every four marriages in America ends in
divorce.
Many theories as to cause advanced; almost as many
solutions. Perhaps our discussion group can offer
suggestions.
Dr. Margaret Benz, as Professor of Sociology at
New York University, and an expert on family living, let me ask you this: If there is any one
factor that causes so many marriages to end in
divorce, what would that be?

DR. BENZ:

ANSWER

STASHEFF:

And Dr. Abraham Stone, as physician and psychol-
ogist, as author of books on marriage counselling,
and thus a man with both theory and professional
practice in the field of marital relations, what
would you name as the chief factor?

                         DR. STONE:

ANSWER

                         STASHEFF:

And, finally, Mrs. Frances Shepherd, as one
with practical experience in the field of
marriage counselling, what do you consider the
major reason for marriage failure?

                         MRS. SHEPHERD:

ANSWER

                         STASHEFF:

Now let us see what factors led to the failure
of Ken and Winnie's marriage, in the film
story, That Charming Couple.   Winnie and Ken
were so in love; they seemed to have so much
to hold them together.   Was divorce inevitable,
or could it have been avoided?   See what you
think as our film story unfolds.   And it be-
gins where so many marriages end - in the   ROLL FILM
divorce court.

WE COME OUT OF FILM ON LONG-SHOT OF DISCUSSION   DISSOLVE TO FILM
GROUP. WE DOLLY IN AND ANNOUNCER IN BOOTH
IDENTIFIES EACH MEMBER OF THE DISCUSSION GROUP
AS THEY CONVERSE.

                         STASHEFF: CUE STASHEFF:

COMMENTS ON FILM AND LEADS INTO DISCUSSION.
KEY QUESTIONS:

    1.   Could their divorce have been pre-
vented?

    2.   What caused their marriage to fail?

3. How do we define a "successful marriage"?

4. How often is money, or the lack of it, a factor in causing marriages to fail?

5. What is the "romantic illusion"?

6. What do girls expect of their future husbands?

7. Why is it impossible for most men to live up to these ideals?

8. What can society do to prevent divorce caused by this factor?

ON TIME CUE:

STASHEFF ASKS DR. STONE TO SUM UP PROBLEM AND SUGGESTED SOLUTIONS

DR. STONE:

ONE-MINUTE SUMMARY

STASHEFF:

(INTERRUPTING SPEAKER WHO FOLLOWS STONE) Regrets that time does not permit further exploration of problem; reminds audience that they may well go on with discussion where studio group left off. Asks viewers to send their conclusions to station, along with comments on program and suggestions for future subjects. Points out how fine educational film can provoke stimulating discussion. Thanks guests. Announces that next week we'll continue with exploration of problems of marriage, particularly the problem of competition between husband and wife, as we view and discuss the film story, Who's Boss?

And so, until we meet again next week at this same

time on WCBS-TV, Channel 2, this is Edward Stasheff,

bidding you good afternoon.

MEMBERS OF GROUP RISE AND CHAT INFORMALLY. KILL
STUDIO MIKES. START SLOW PULL OUT AND SUPER CREDITS
FROM TELOP IN SYNC WITH ANNOUNCER

                         ANNCR:

Groups interested in the McGraw-Hill film shown on

today's program may obtain information by writing to:

IT'S WORTH KNOWING, WCBS-TV, Department 1, 485 Madison   SUPER ADDRESS

Avenue, New York 22, New York.

From Studio 53 in Liederkranz Hall - WCBS-TV has

presented - IT'S WORTH KNOWING -

In cooperation with the Metropolitan branch of the

Department of Audio-Visual Instruction of the National

Education Association.

IT'S WORTH KNOWING is produced with D.A.V.I. by   SUPER CREDITS OVER

Franklin T. Mathewson -   SHOT OF BOOKCASE

For WCBS-TV by Robert Herridge -   AT REAR OF STUDIO

Directed by Jon Fogel -

Parts of this program were mechanically reproduced.

Next week we shall present and discuss another

phase of the problem of Understanding Yourself and

Others - another problem about which .....

IT'S WORTH KNOWING.

8. An Educational Panel Show

DEBUNKING CAMPAIGN BUNK

An educational script on national politics and elections

INTRODUCTORY NOTES AND PRODUCTION SUGGESTIONS

(First broadcast on *The Living Blackboard,* the New York City Board of Education Series for home-bound high school students, presented over the facilities of Station WPIX, New York City. Produced by Edward Stasheff and directed by Freddie Bartholomew)

The Living Blackboard was begun in October, 1951, as an extension of the Broadcast Service of FM Station WNYE, the Board of Education station, which for several years had broadcast twenty-five programs a week for high school students whose physical condition made it impossible for them to attend school in the usual fashion. Although designed for this specialized audience, *The Living Blackboard* soon attracted thousands of adult viewers who were interested in educational programs.

In the late spring of 1952, shortly before the Republican and Democratic nominating conventions, Martha Caccamo and Albert Sayer, radio teachers on the High School of the Air staff at WNYE, prepared five programs for a special sub-series entitled "Presidents, Politics and Public Opinion." The individual program titles ran as follows:

"Election Fun and Fury"
(highlights of past elections)

"Choosing 'The People's Choice'"
(primaries, conventions, and elections)

"Debunking Campaign Bunk"
(the script reproduced on the following pages)

"You Can't Tell the Candidates without a Program"
(the candidates and the issues)

"The People and The People's Choice"
(elections and the democratic way)

119

"Debunking Campaign Bunk" was chosen for inclusion in this volume because its subject matter makes it appropriate for broadcast in the fall of any year, since it can easily be slanted toward local or state elections by slight modification of the opening discussion. It was also selected because of its use of highly effective visual methods and sound educational techniques. As the reviewer for *Variety* wrote, the program ". . . was informative for adult viewers, as well as for the high school set, and its approach to the subject was fresh and engaging." It used several methods to get its point across: cartoons which jested at baby-kissing candidates, matched with photographs of actual candidates using the very techniques satirized by the cartoons; a puppet candidate "with a platform full of inconsistencies and contradictions, promising all things to all men," as *Variety* commented; a soapbox department, with student orators performing before a rear-screen projection of Columbus Circle. *Variety* concluded by recommending, "This telecast of *Living Blackboard* would bear repeating in time and adapting for viewers of voting age. Perhaps it should even be expanded to a pre-election evening series."

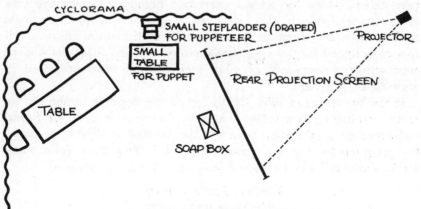

Figure 34.

As presented here, names of actual participants have been omitted, so that any group which produces the program may substitute the names of its own participants in the blanks provided in the script. For Columbus Circle, any appropriate street corner may be substituted, either by rear projection if such equipment is available, or against a blank drop with a single lamp-post, bearing the names of suitable streets in the local community. The puppet presents no problem in this day of community marionette companies, and the superimposition of the names of the propaganda devices requires simple white lettering on dark cards. The soapbox scene may use for its spectators and orators high school or college students or older people. The only real "acting" is done by the puppet. Old magazines are a good source of political photographs and cartoons, if no newspaper picture "morgue" is available.

DEBUNKING CAMPAIGN BUNK[*]

by

Martha Caccamo and Albert Sayer

HIT THEME	OPENING TITLES
ANNOUNCER:	DISSOLVE TO ANNOUNCER

Once again the voice of the candidate is heard in the land.   Once again the weary voter is assailed by claims and counter-claims, by promises and compromises. Whom are we going to believe?   Today (tonight), we're going to do a bit of Debunking the Campaign Bunk you've been hearing and will continue to hear between now and Election Day.   But before we join our host, _____, let's see what three of our students here at _____ think of the election issues. Left to right, we have _____,

SHOT OF STUDENTS TALKING ANIMATEDLY (DEAD MIKE)

_____, and _____. Let's join them, shall we?

STUDENTS' MIKE IS OPENED AND THEY DO BRIEF EXCHANGE OF CURRENT ISSUE. ORIGINAL PROGRAM USED AD LIB ON WHETHER THE ONE BOY IN THE GROUP WOULD BE WILLING TO VOTE FOR A WOMAN PRESIDENT. HE WAS WILLING, PERSONALLY, BUT WASN'T SURE WHETHER THE AVERAGE MAN WOULD AGREE WITH HIM.

GIRL:

Well, let's find out. Let's ask the man in the street ... I mean the man in the studio, our announcer, Mr. ____.

Oh, Mr. _____ !

[*] No permission required. Courtesy of the authors, Martha Caccamo and Albert Sayer

ANNOUNCER:

What is it, _____?   Anything wrong?

GIRL:

No, Mr. _____. We just wanted to ask you

a question. How would you feel about voting

for a woman President? (OR COUNCILMAN,

MAYOR, OR GOVERNOR)

ANNOUNCER:

I don't know...I've never thought about it.

But I don't have any objection....there isn't

any law against it, is there?

GIRL:

I'm not sure...let's ask_____. He's an

expert on that sort of thing. (CALLS)

Mr. _____ !

MC: (ENTERING)

What is it,_____ ?

GIRL:

Is there any law against a woman's being

President of the United States?

MC:

(LONG ANSWER: NO LAW AGAINST IT, JUST CUSTOM,
ETC. LEADING UP TO WHY CAN'T ANNOUNCER RUN...
NO CUSTOM OR TRADITION AGAINST HIS BEING A
CANDIDATE.)

ANNOUNCER:

You know, it might be fun at that. But I don't

know if I'd be rugged enough to stand the pace

of campaigning. It's a hard life any way you

look at it - racing from one place to another,

making speeches to all kinds of groups in all

parts of the country.

MC:

And don't forget all the years you would have
had to give to the party and its activities before they would even consider you worthy of
nomination.

ANNOUNCER:

Even that doesn't scare me as much as some of the
silly things that a candidate is expected to do
during the course of his campaign. I'd feel
awfully foolish.

CARTOON OF CANDIDATE IN
SURGICAL MASK, KISSING BABY

BOY:

Do you mean this sort of thing, Mr._____?
Here's a candidate standing for clean government
and wearing a surgical mask while he kisses a
baby in the crowd of people listening to his speech.

ANNOUNCER:

That's right. Not that I don't like babies, but
to do that sort of thing just to get votes isn't my
speed. And don't think that that cartoon is far
wrong. Why, look at this picture, taken of Senator   PIC: SENATOR TAFT
Taft during the current campaign. And just see what
Al Smith had to do. Even Calvin Coolidge had   PIC: SMITH BEING HANDED
himself decked out in an Indian head-dress to   INDIAN HEAD-DRESS
gather a few votes.

MC:

What other tactics do candidates use?

(STUDENTS LIST SEVERAL OTHER HACKNEYED DEVICES)

ANNOUNCER: PIC: PRETTY GIRLS

Of course, there's the other side of the pic-

ture. The party headquarters would be sure to   PIC: DISTRIBUTING BUTTONS

have a lot of pretty girls on hand to help in

the publicity campaign - and I like pretty

girls, no matter where you find them.   Those

volunteers work very hard distributing emblems,

buttons, banners, etc. to everyone they can grab.

MC:

But don't forget, Mr._____, you wouldn't

have much chance to meet those pretty volunteers.

You'd be making all those whistle-stop speeches

which every candidate has to survive if he wants

to catch the votes.   You might even have to do   PIC: CANDIDATE ON STEEL GIRDER

this sort of thing. Such nimbleness and such

self-restraint!   Imagine lunch hour after lunch

hour with no food for yourself, just speechmaking.

ANNOUNCER:

It does sound gruesome.

MC:

Thank you, Mr. _____, we can understand why

you're not too enthusiastic about running for

the office of President yourself.

(ANNOUNCER LEAVES. MC CONTINUES)

All this baby-kissing, this wearing of Indian head-

dress, this posing so that the candidate appears to

be a regular fellow, has come to be traditional in

our national campaign. But these shenanigans are

merely incidental to the serious purpose of an
election campaign. In the course of his campaign, the candidate may declare himself on
certain issues, he may make certain promises,
and may even be pinned down to specific answers
to certain embarrassing questions.

BOY:

Of course, a skillful candidate is very clever
about not letting himself be pinned down to definite answers and commitments. It's up to us,
his voters, to see through his tricks and to de-
tect his inconsistencies. Let me introduce to
you the very model of a modern model candidate -   PUPPET BOWING AND SMILING
John J. Barkis - because Barkis is willing to
serve as a model of all that is bad.

MC:

We want it distinctly understood that any resem-
blance between Mr. Barkis and any real candidate,
living or dead, is not only a coincidence but
downright impossible. And now, ladies and gentlemen, a few remarks from Mr. Barkis.

PUPPET:

Dear Friends: For many months I've been looking
forward to this visit, which brings me back to
this little village where I was born and brought
up. How good it is to stand here among you - my
neighbors - and to say hello again to the boys and
girls I went to school with. Last night I slept
again in the humble cottage, little more than a

log cabin, where my folks spent forty-
seven years together, working side by
side with you people to build this great
country. Yes, it was a hard life in those
days. But though I have been away from
you these many years, my heart has always
been with you.

INTERRUPTION FROM FIRST GIRL:

Mr. Barkis, this "log-cabin" stuff you're
handing us now, hasn't that worn rather
thin since Lincoln's day? Let's get down to
brass tacks. What are you going to do about
the high cost of living?

                    PUPPET:

Oh yes, the high cost of living. Hmm. Yes,
you're having a hard time keeping up with the
cost of living; food prices are high, and rents
are still climbing. As soon as I'm elected,
I'm going to take steps to lower farm prices,
so that food costs can come down.

INTERRUPTION BY BOY:

But what will the farmers say about that? Do
you think they'll like having farm prices go
down?

                    PUPPET:

The farmer? Oh yes, the farmer. The farmer is
the backbone of our nation and of our national
economy. I believe that the welfare of the

farmer is of the utmost importance to, and is
the responsibility of, the rest of the nation.
Farm subsidies should be raised. Loans and
other credit facilities should be made for the
farmer. If I'm elected, I promise to see that
he gets a "Square deal."

INTERRUPTION BY SECOND GIRL:

But, Mr. Barkis, that sounds as if the government is going to do a lot of butting into the
farmers' affairs. Do you believe that the government should interfere with our economic system?

PUPPET:

No interference. The greatness of this nation
has always been based on freedom of enterprise.
If I'm elected, there will be no government
interference with industry. There will be no
seizures of industry by the government; there
will be no government ownership or operation
by the means of production or distribution. If
you want a government that believes in free enterprise, elect me for your next President.

INTERRUPTION BY BOY:

Oh, wonderful! My father will certainly vote
for you, Mr. Barkis. Only the other day he
said it was about time our government saved us
from being destroyed by the labor unions.

PUPPET:

Labor. Since the days of the thirteen col-
onies, labor has created this nation's wealth.
By the sweat of their brows the workers have
built this glorious country brick by brick.
And, my friends and fellow-Americans, my party
has always been the party of patriotism. Don't
be carried away by the glib phrases of candidates
who by their policies and actions have given aid
and comfort to disloyal individuals and subversive
organizations. In voting for me, you will be
choosing a man who has never for a moment wavered
in his devotion and loyalty to American institutions.
A man who is always for what the voters want. A
man who is willing —

INTERRUPTION BY MC:

Thank you, Mr. Barkis. I'm sure that your audience
is fully aware of just what it is that you stand for.
I believe that we can summarize it briefly by saying
that you promise all things to all men and that you
are holding out a paradise for each and every one of
us.

PUPPET BOWS OUT

            MC: (TURNING TO STUDENT GROUP)

And let's bear in mind that Mr. Barkis resorted to
many of the tricks that have fooled some of the
people some of the time since voting first took
place in the history of mankind. The Institute

of Propaganda Analysis once enumerated the seven

standard propagandizing devices. In a moment we

are going to adjourn to Columbus Circle where

some speakers are holding corner meetings. As

the speakers talk, I am going to ask you students

here in the studio, and you also at home, to guess

which device each speaker is using. First let us

review the seven best known devices.

(NOTE: IF THE TITLES WHICH ARE TO BE SUPERIMPOSED
ON THE BOTTOM OF THE SCREEN, OVER THE PICTURE OF
THE MC, ARE MADE ON A DRUM, THEY CAN BE QUICKLY
CHANGED AFTER EACH PARAGRAPH WITHOUT LOSING THE
SUPERIMPOSITION. AN OPENING JUST LARGE ENOUGH TO
SHOW THE LETTERING SHOULD BE MADE IN A MASK IN
FRONT OF THE DRUM SO THE LETTERS WILL NOT ROLL ALL
THE WAY UP THE SCREEN AS THEY ARE BEING CHANGED.
THIS MASK SHOULD BE REMOVED BEFORE THE DRUM IS
USED AGAIN DURING THE GUESSING, SO THAT ALL SEVEN
DEVICES CAN BE ROLLED BY TO HELP THE HOME AUDIENCE
GUESS, AND AS MANY CAN SHOW AT ONCE AS POSSIBLE).

1.   Namecalling.   A device to influence judgment

without an examination of the evidence on which

it should be based. The propagandist appeals to

hate and fear by pinning "bad names" on individual

groups, nations, races and policies which he wishes

the public to condemn and reject.

SUPERTITLE:
"NAMECALLING" AT
BOTTOM OF SCREEN

2.   Glittering Generalities.   A device by which

the propagandist identifies his program with vir-

tue by use of "virtue words," such as truth, free-

dom, honor, social justice, progress, democracy.

SUPERTITLE:
"GLITTERING GENERALITIES"

3.   Transfer.   A device by which the propa-   SUPER:
gandist carries over the authority, sanction and   "TRANSFER"
prestige of something we respect and revere to
something he would have us accept.   Symbols
(the cross for the Church, the Flag for the Nation) carry the emotional feeling of an established
institution to the subject for which the propagandist seeks to enlist our support.

4.   Testimonial.   A device by which we are in-   SUPER:
duced to believe something is good because famous   "TESTIMONIAL"
people support it (or are alleged to), or that
something is bad because famous people are against
it.

5.   Plain Folks. A device in which the leaders   SUPER:
attempt to win our confidence by having us believe   "PLAIN FOLKS"
that they are people like ourselwes - just plain
folks among the neighbors.

6.   Card Stacking.   A device in which the prop-   SUPER:
agandist stacks the cards against the truth by   "CARD STACKING"
giving partial facts, resorting to underemphasis
and overemphasis, to distortion and false testi-
mony. Basically, it is a device of confusion and
diversion, the technique of "the big lie."

7.   Band Wagon. A device to make us follow the   SUPER:
crowd, to do what the propagandist wants us to do   "BAND WAGON"
because "everyone is doing it," or so he says.
Basically, it is an appeal to the human instinct
to back a winner, whether it is a candidate or an
idea.

And now let's visit Columbus Circle.

(DISSOLVE TO REAR PROJECTION SET WITH SLIDE OF
COLUMBUS CIRCLE: GROUP IS GATHERED AROUND
SPEAKERS STANDING ON SOAP-BOX)

FIRST SPEAKER:

Every American is entitled to share in the bene-   SUPER:
                                                                 "GLITTERING GENERALITIES
fits of democratic government. We must make sure

that every threat to the American way of life is

met. We must guarantee to each and every individ-

ual the right to life, liberty, and the pursuit of

happiness. Special privileges to vested interest

must be avoided if we are to continue calling this   AT END OF SPEECH SUPER
                                                                 DRUM TITLES WHILE GROUP
nation of ours a land of equal opportunity for all,   IN STUDIO GUESSES.
                                                                 MC WILL CLINCH POINT.
a land where honest toil brings its own reward and

every person is free to better himself.

SECOND SPEAKER:

Ladies and Gentlemen: On you rests the responsi-

bility of electing the next President of the United

States. I place before you Mr. Barkis, whose integ-

rity and loyalty are beyond question. His record of

public service is known to all of you. Now let's

examine the record of those who run against him.

Alexander Throttlebottom's record, and wealth, was

made, not in the public service, but on Wall Street.

A plutocrat of plutocrats, he knows nothing of the

life of the common man. A conservative capitalist,   SUPER: DRUM TITLES
                                                                 WHILE STUDIO AUDIENCE
he seeks to overthrow all the social and economic   GUESSES

progress that has been made in the past decade.

His platform is more worthy of a Fascist dictator

than that of a leader of a democratic nation.

THIRD SPEAKER:

I stand here today to help you make a wise choice

for President. I will not rely on glittering gen-

eralities, nor will I lower myself to calling my

opponents names. Instead I will read to you what

people of good repute have said about my candidate,

John J. Wintergreen:

> "John J. Wintergreen is so kind to dumb
> animals!" Signed Lavinia Q. Flutterbush,
> Director, Home for Aged and Homeless Cats.

And again, from Hortense Z. Powderpuff, mother of

Mr. Wintergreen's wife. She says:

> "Any man can be kind to his mother on
> Mother's Day, but John Wintergreen is
> kind even to his mother-in-law and for
> three months of the year."

And the Thrifty Citizen's Association has this to

say about my candidate: SUPER: DRUM TITLES

> "We know John Wintergreen to be for lower
> taxes and higher budgets."

FOURTH SPEAKER:

Ladies and Gentlemen: As I look down into your

eyes, I can see reflected in them that intelligence

which will enable you to vote wisely and well.

As you know, the veterans are voting for my candi-

date; the farmers are voting for my candidate; the

workers and even the small businessmen are voting

for my candidate. My neighbors and your neighbors

are voting for my candidate. My candidate has run

for Major, for Governor, for Senator, and has never

lost.   Be a winner yourself by voting for my candi-   SUPER: DRUM

date.

MC ENDS COMMENT ON FOURTH SPEAKER WITH:

That's right. That's the bandwagon appeal. We

all like to be in the swim; so we dislike the

thought of not doing what the crowd is doing.

We like to feel that we're on the side of the

winner.

(IF TIME WILL ALLOW, THE INDIVIDUAL DIRECTOR
MAY ADD MORE SPEAKERS EXEMPLIFYING THE OTHER
THREE DEVICES.)

                    STUDENT:

(IN GROUP AROUND SOAP-BOX)

But, Mr. _____, whom are we to believe then

if there are so many ways of fooling the public,

of confusing the voter?

                    MC:

Let's ask our discussion group what methods of

checking up on the candidates they would sug-

gest.

(CUT TO DISCUSSION AREA. STUDENTS AD LIB SUG-
GESTED TECHNIQUES OF EVALUATING CAMPAIGN MATER-
IAL. MC JOINS THEM TO LEAD DISCUSSION.)

POINTS:

DISCUSSED BY GIRL I:

Let's beware of the candidate whose sign reads   PIC CARTOON:
                                                        "PLATFORM FOR RENT"
"Platform for Rent," whose appeal is filled with

glittering generalities, whose approach is that

of the humble background, or who uses the flag-

waving technique.

DISCUSSED BY BOY I:

Let's beware of the candidate who does not stand   PIC: PHOTO OF LANDON-
                                                    LINCOLN BANNER
on his own record, but who seeks to shield himself

behind the fame and traditions of a past hero.

DISCUSSED BY GIRL II:

Let's be wary of the candidate who promises to have   PIC: CARTOON OF
                                                       UTOPIAN SETUP
a sure cure for all of society's ills and who prom-

ises a land of milk and honey for every one of us.

CUSHION QUESTION TO STUDENTS:

Do you think that the candidates of 195_ will try

to use these same devices?

(STUDENTS AD LIB ANSWERS)

CUSHION QUESTION:

Do you think television will have a helpful effect

on campaign techniques?

(STUDENTS AD LIB ANSWERS, UNTIL TIME CUE)

                    MC: (WRAP-UP)

1. Suggestions for sending in for pamphlets

about propaganda and intelligent voting.

2. Opportunity to test critical judgment in

current or future broadcasts by candidates.

3. Repetition of advice to audience to be alert.

4. Turns program back to announcer.

                    ANNOUNCER:

This brings to a close our program on "Debunking

Campaign Bunk," the _____ in a series on Pres-

idents, Politics and Public Opinion. Today's   CLOSING CREDITS

script was written by Martha Caccamo and Albert

Sayer, and was directed by _____.

Members of the cast included _____
as our Moderator, and students from the
Television Workshop of _____
University.
Join us again next week for the next program
in this series, _____
_____ speaking; this has been a
presentation of the _____ University
Television Workshop.

                    MUSIC THEME.

9. A Debate Format in a Courtroom Setting

PUBLIC VERDICT

Introductory Notes and Production Suggestions

Since the earliest days of television, producers have found dramatic value in the use of a courtroom setting for discussion and debate. The trial atmosphere heightens the sense of conflict and makes the discussion of important issues both personal and intense. As far back as 1945, CBS in New York had a long-running series called *Opinions on Trial* in which not a person, but an idea, was put on trial each week, prosecuted and defended. The setting was the mythical "Court of Public Opinion," through whose doors the camera (and hence the viewer) entered to observe the proceedings. The verdict was left to the audience.

More recently, Irving Sulds produced over the DuMont Network a series called *Court of Current Issues,* in which prominent members of the bar participated as presiding judge, prosecutor and defense attorney. While the latter program used a jury on the set, with members of the studio audience seated in the jury box, the real decision was made by the viewers who were invited to send in their individual decisions. In both cases, the viewer had a definite sense of participation, since his opinion was not only invited but clearly considered important.

While a courtroom trial of a public issue does not have the reality of such a proceeding as the hearings of the Senate Crime Investigating Committee, it does create a far greater impact than the televising of a conventional platform debate. Readers of this volume who are familiar with current trends in forensics are familiar with such variations on the older pattern as the Minnesota and Michigan debates, in which members of each team question their opponents, in addition to the formal presentations. The cross-examination technique is believed by many to provide a better opportunity for coming to grips with differences of fact and opinion than the older style of rebuttal.

136

The script outline which follows provides an opportunity for students of debate to join with students of television production in a joint effort. While close cooperation throughout is of great value, it is quite possible for the two classes to meet together once to discuss the preparation of the program, and then not again until a day or so before the actual broadcast. Only the director need sit in with the debaters as they prepare their material, once the limitations of time and physical position are clearly understood by all. In the interim period, the debaters may prepare content while the television students work on the production, secure in the knowledge that the "talent" will arrive ready for the first dry-run. Use of "dummy topics" is recommended for all rehearsals so that the opponents will not expend their ammunition in trial-runs.

While the program as outlined on the following pages is planned to run for half an hour, a forty-five minute time-slot would permit more thorough development of the ideas. The extra fifteen minutes could be distributed proportionately throughout the format. A student or adult "jury" may be used to represent the home audience or dispensed with entirely.

The shots planned by Director Al Story for a University of Michigan production are provided here as a guide for student-directors, with the comment that they were used as a basic camera pattern for two cameras, from which the director frequently departed on the air. Other directors may do it in other ways. Even the format, as devised by Professor N. Edd Miller and Edward Stasheff of the University of Michigan, should be varied to fit the local situation. However, as it stands, it will serve as a working point of departure.

The "attorneys" are the equivalent of debating team captains, with rather more responsibility. They must be ready to raise objections which the "judge" may sustain or overrule. Wherever possible, they will be ready with not only verbal but visual evidence: chart maps, enlarged photostats, etc. The "Defense Attorney" upholds the affirmative, the "Prosecutor" represents the negative.

The "Judge" has a most important role to play. He requires a background in law (or at least in courtroom procedure), in debate, and in time-keeping, since it is he who must get the program off the air on time by shutting off each segment. It should not be difficult to find him from among the attorneys of a community. Ideally, he may even be a local judge who was himself a debater or debate coach, with recent radio experience. (Lucky the producer who finds such a paragon!)

PUBLIC VERDICT[*]

ANNOUNCER:

(OFF CAMERA) It's your turn to serve in the
Court of Public Verdict!

MUSIC:

THEME UP, DOWN AND UNDER

ANNOUNCER:

Each week at this time the Speech Department of
the University of _____ presents the Court
of Public Verdict in which students of argumenta-
tion and debate and students of television combine
their efforts to put current issues and opinions
on trial before the jury that matters most - The
Jury of Public Opinion!

MUSIC:

UP AND OUT

COURT CLERK:

Hear ye, hear ye, hear ye. This first session
of the Court of Public Verdict will now come to
order! Scheduled for hearing today is the proposition, Resolved, _____

_____.

Presiding at this trial is his Honor, Judge
_____. Everybody, rise.

TITLE CARD: Court of
Public Verdict

TITLE CARD: Presented by
the Speech Department of
the University of _____

TITLE CARD: Wording of the
Resolution

---

[*] No permission required

JUDGE ENTERS AND TAKES HIS PLACE ON THE BENCH.
EVERYONE SITS AND JUDGE BEGINS HIS EXPLANATION
OF PROCEDURE TO BE FOLLOWED, AD LIBBING AROUND
THESE POINTS:

1. This is not a real trial, so certain unorth-
odox procedures will be followed, such as having
each attorney cross-examine the other. Witnesses
will not be sworn.

2. Unlike actual trials, attorneys and witnesses
will be held to strict time limitations.

3. Each attorney will be permitted to present
two witnesses, but must yield them to his opponent
for cross-examination.

4. Finally, each attorney will cross-examine
his opponent, then sum up.

(CONCLUDING)   And now, the Attorney for the Defense of the Resolution has one minute in which
to present his case.

DEFENSE ATTORNEY:

PRESENTS HIS CASE (1 minute), THEN CALLS HIS
FIRST WITNESS
DIRECT EXAMINATION OF FIRST DEFENSE WITNESS
(2½ minutes)
CROSS-EXAMINATION OF FIRST DEFENSE WITNESS
(1½ minutes)

JUDGE:

The Attorney for the Prosecution now has one
minute in which to present his case to the jury.

PROSECUTING ATTORNEY:

PRESENTS HIS CASE (1 minute), THEN CALLS HIS FIRST
WITNESS.

DIRECT EXAMINATION OF FIRST WITNESS FOR THE PROS-
ECUTION ($2\frac{1}{2}$ minutes)

CROSS-EXAMINATION OF FIRST WITNESS FOR THE PROS-
ECUTION ($1\frac{1}{2}$ minutes)

JUDGE:

The Attorney for the Defense will now call his second witness.

DIRECT EXAMINATION OF SECOND DEFENSE WITNESS

($2\frac{1}{2}$ minutes)

CROSS-EXAMINATION OF SECOND DEFENSE WITNESS

($1\frac{1}{2}$ minutes)

JUDGE:

The second witness for the Prosecution.

DIRECT EXAMINATION OF SECOND WITNESS FOR THE PROS-
ECUTION ($2\frac{1}{2}$ minutes)

CROSS-EXAMINATION OF SECOND WITNESS FOR THE PROS-
ECUTION ($1\frac{1}{2}$ minutes)

JUDGE:

All evidence to be introduced through witnesses
having now been presented to the jury, the
Attorney for the Prosecution may now cross-examine
the Defense Attorney.

CROSS-EXAMINATION OF DEFENSE ATTORNEY (2 minutes)

JUDGE:

The Defense Attorney may now cross-examine the
Prosecuting Attorney.

CROSS-EXAMINATION OF PROSECUTING ATTORNEY

(2 minutes)

JUDGE:

The Defense Attorney will now sum up the case

for the Defense.

SUMMATION OF THE CASE FOR THE DEFENSE (1 minute)

JUDGE:

CHARGES THE AUDIENCE AS A JURY TO RENDER A VERDICT

ON THE MERITS OF THE CASE AS THEY SEE IT ($\frac{1}{2}$ minute).

JUDGE THEN ADJOURNS COURT UNTIL SAME TIME NEXT WEEK.

ALL STAND AS HE LEAVES BENCH. HOLD ON MILLING

CROWD BEFORE BENCH UNTIL TIME TO DISSOLVE TO FIRST

OF CLOSING TITLES. FADE AUDIO IN COURTROOM SET

AND BRING IN ANNOUNCER'S VOICE OVER CROWD SHOT.

ANNOUNCER:

(OFF SCREEN) You have tried the case, ladies and

gentlemen. Now, what is your verdict? Send your

decision to the Court of Public Verdict in care

of this station, _____.

The majority decision of our home audience jury

will be announced on next week's broadcast, when

the opinion on which we ask a public verdict will

be _____.

Today's program was prepared and produced by the

debate and television classes of _____

and _____. The program was directed

by _____, and this is _____

_____ speaking for the University

of _____.

MUSIC:

UP AND HOLD TO TIME

10. Three Dramatic Vignettes

CASTING CALL

Introductory Notes and Production Suggestions

"Casting Call" was designed as a course exercise, in this case, for a class which is predominantly or entirely masculine. Nevertheless, it makes an excellent ten-minute element for insertion in a longer program of varied elements, and stands on its own merits as a dramatic script. It will interest students to know that the author, Robert Foshko, wrote it while he was an undergraduate in the radio and television classes at the University of Michigan.

Certain production problems have been deliberately included, and their solution will provide young directors with valuable experience. Although it is not absolutely necessary to have a dressing-room mirror, for example, the use of mirror shots is an exciting part of good camerawork. When George Palmer enters Walter Bain's dressing room, a mirror shot shows us Bain in close-up, facing the camera, and Palmer entering through the door. We see Bain's face; Palmer, presumably, does not. Thus, Bain's expression reveals to the audience how he feels about the interruption and how he feels about Palmer.

Another problem arises from the changing of the names on the dressing-room door. When Palmer shows Bain his own name-plate, saved from more successful and bygone days, we must see it clearly. If Palmer holds it steadily as he shows it to Bain or rests one end on the make-up table, a camera can get a tight close-up on an 8-inch lens without moving in too closely. Then, at the end, when Palmer leaves Bain, the latter notices the old sign on the door. He looks at it, presumably, and the viewer must see what he is looking at. Bain can walk to the door and thus lead the camera to the name-plate; we can pan to the door, indicating the direction of his gaze, and then dolly in to a tight shot into which Bain's hand will come as he removes the sign; or if this takes too long, we can simply cut to the name-plate on another camera. The director may try all three methods and see which works better for his set and his camera positions.

The opening scene, before the callboy enters, provides an opportunity for creating a little back-stage atmosphere. We can begin as the script has with Bain seated at his dressing-table, finishing the removal of his make-up, or we can begin with a shot of the outside of his door, with other actors moving past in the corridor. The callboy knocks and we cut to the inside of the room, join Bain, and with him hear a second knock. Creating the familiar orderly confusion of a dressing-room provides an interesting problem in set dressing, the addition of those little props which establish a locale and lend authentic atmosphere.

"Casting Call" abounds in opportunities for reaction shots. Whereas standard directing technique puts the camera on the character who is speaking, in this script it is frequently more important to see the expression on the face of the listener as he hears an important line and reacts to it.

No two directors will stage and shoot this script in the same manner, and therein lies the value of experimental production for the director who is learning to find his way with cameras.

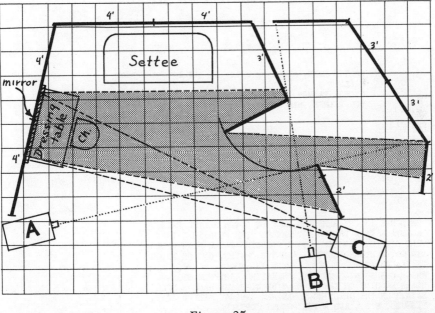

Figure 35.

The floor plan in the accompanying illustration is a suggested set for this production. Three camera positions are plotted representing the extreme side angles from which cameras might be used. The camera at position A can see a certain area through the open door, the downstage limit of which is indicated by the dotted line, and the backing must therefore extend at least this far. Position B indicates the other extreme and determines how far the backing must extend upstage. Camera position C is the furthest upstage that a camera is likely to be placed. The shaded area indicates that portion of the set which will be reflected in the mirror. The wall of the set holding the mirror must be so angled that the mirror does not reflect an area beyond the set. It is obvious that if the wall is opened out any further (forming a greater angle with the back wall), a camera in this position will see itself in the mirror. Mirrors must be placed only on the side walls of sets such as this so an opposite wall can be reflected. There have been many unfortunate instances of mirrors or even glass-covered pictures placed on the back walls of sets which reflected cameras, lights, stagehands and other extraneous activities having nothing at all to do with the dramatic situation at hand.

C A S T I N G   C A L L

A Dramatic Sketch for a Male Cast

by Robert Foshko

C A S T

WALTER BAIN, a rising actor in his late thirties
CALLBOY
GEORGE PALMER, a former star, now in his fifties
TOM PALMER, his son

CASTING CALL[*]

by

Robert Foshko

THE SCENE IS THE DRESSING-ROOM OF ACTOR WALTER BAIN,
BACKSTAGE IN A BROADWAY THEATER. THE FURNITURE IS
VERY SIMPLE, FUNCTIONAL: A DRESSING-TABLE WITH WALL
MIRROR, A WICKER SETTEE, AND TWO CHAIRS, ONE OF WHICH
IS PLACED AT THE TABLE. THERE IS A DOOR, RIGHT,
WHICH OPENS INTO THE SET, REVEALING A SIMPLE SIGN-
BOARD HANGING ON THE OTHER SIDE WITH THE NAME WALTER
BAIN. ON THE DRESSING-TABLE ARE SEVERAL MAKEUP JARS,
TISSUES, ETC., AND A TELEPHONE. OPTIONAL PROP IS A
CLOTHES-RACK OF SOME SORT LEFT OF TABLE WITH BAIN'S
COSTUME ON IT - AN ARMY OFFICER'S UNIFORM.

[*]No permission required

WE FIND BAIN SITTING AT THE DRESSING TABLE, OBVIOUSLY
REMOVING THE LAST OF HIS MAKEUP, COMBING HIS HAIR.
HE IS HANDSOME, LATE THIRTIES, MOVES AND TALKS WITH
GREAT POISE AND ASSURANCE.

AFTER A MOMENT THERE IS A KNOCK AT THE DOOR.

                    BAIN:

Yes?

                    CALLBOY: (OFF)

Telegram for you, Mr. Bain.

                    BAIN:

Come in. (RISES, CROSSES TO DOOR. BOY IN SHIRT-

SLEEVES ENTERS AND HANDS HIM TELEGRAM.)   Thanks,

Willie.

                    CALLBOY:

Mr. Bain, do you want to see Bertha before she

leaves for dinner?

                    BAIN: (STARING ABSENTLY
                          AT TELEGRAM)

Hm? Oh, no. It's just a loose button on my cos-

tume. She can take care of it later, before the

show tonight.

                    CALLBOY:

I'll remind her when she comes in.

                    BAIN:

Good.

CALLBOY EXITS. BAIN OPENS TELEGRAM, READS IT,
SMILES SLIGHTLY AT ONE POINT, THEN SIGHS AND
SHAKES HIS HEAD SLOWLY. HE WALKS TO TABLE,
LIFTS TELEPHONE RECEIVER AND DIALS A NUMBER.

Hello. Mr. Thompson, please, Walter Bain calling.

(PAUSE, HE SITS AT TABLE) Hello, Charlie? Yes.
Fine. Look I just got a telegram from the coast...
from Gilligan. Yes. Didn't you send him a wire
explaining the situation? (INDICATES TELEGRAM)
Well, he seems to think I'm holding out for more
money. Here...I'll read it to you. (LIFTS TELE-
GRAM) 'Majestic guarantees thirty-eight weeks
our price. Don't be stubborn, sweetheart. Script
tremendous. Budget tops. Studio aiming for
Oscars all around. Please reconsider. Gilligan.
Now look, Charlie...(SLIGHTLY ANNOYED) We've been
all through that. (LAUGHS) Believe me, I'd love
to, you know it. (SERIOUS) Charlie, you're a good
agent. Best in the business. But try to understand.
(PATIENTLY) I've got a good supporting role in this
play. A natural for me. The show is a hit, and the
cast is tops to work with. But forgetting that for
a minute - look, I've got a run-of-the-show contract,
and...what? Sure, Carrington would let me go if I
could get a replacement. What? Sure, there's an
understudy. Why? Oh, he's all right for two-three
nights if I catch a cold but for the rest of
the run...no hope. What? But that's just
it! I scoured every booking office in town,
and there's nobody I'd trust with the part.
It's highly stylized stuff. Well, yes, Myron
Anderson could do it but he's tied up in a

new musical.   That's it.   I can't run out and

leave them with a clunker!   If I could dig up

a dependable guy who could handle the role,

I'd leave in a minute.   But...well, that's the

breaks.   Movie or no movie, I'm sticking with

the show.   Yes.   (SHRUGS HIS SHOULDERS)   So

look, get in touch with Gilligan, will you?

Tell him it's out of the question.   (THERE IS

A KNOCK AT THE DOOR.   BAIN COVERS MOUTHPIECE)

Come in.   (BACK INTO PHONE)   Okay, Charlie?

(SMILES)   Don't fret, we'll hit it next time.

Goodbye.

BAIN HANGS UP AND TURNS TO FACE GEORGE PALMER WHO
HAS ENTERED THE ROOM AND WAITS HUMBLY NEAR THE
DOOR.   PALMER IS MIDDLE-AGED AND PRETTY WELL
CRUSHED BY HARD TIMES.   BUT HE ONCE WAS A STAR,
AND THE POLISH IS STILL EVIDENT.

PALMER:

Sorry to disturb you, Mr. Bain.

BAIN

(FRIENDLY)   Not at all, George.   (HE INDICATES

FOR PALMER TO SIT, BEGINS CAPPING HIS MAKEUP JARS)

(SIGHS)   Wednesday is a long day.

PALMER:

(SMILES SLIGHTLY)   Oh, I sort of like matinees

myself.   They seem to be...well, right with

you...hanging on every line.   A matinee crowd

is pulling for you every minute.   (NOSTALGIC)

You want to work your heart out for them.   (HE

IS LOST IN THOUGHT)

BAIN:

(RESPECTFULLY) You ought to know, George - you're

one of the best.

PALMER:

(SLIGHTLY BITTER)   You mean was...

BAIN SHRUGS AND FINISHES CLEARING HIS TABLE. THERE
IS AN AWKWARD PAUSE WHILE PALMER GATHERS HIMSELF TO
HIS INTENTIONS.

PALMER:

Mr. Bain...there's something I want to talk to you

about.

BAIN:

Sure, George, what's on your mind?

PALMER:

I'm just a bit player now, I know - but, well,

I've been watching you, Mr. Bain, as long as you've

been with the show. You...you're all right. You're

not swell-headed or cocky like some. I...I think

you're the kind of man I can talk to.

BAIN:

(BRUSHES THIS ASIDE)   What is it, George?

PALMER:

(INTENT)   I've got a favor to ask.

BAIN CONSIDERS THIS A SECOND, THEN REACHES FOR
HIS WALLET TO SAVE PALMER EMBARRASSMENT.

BAIN:

Sure, I understand, how much do you...?

PALMER:

(SHAKES HIS HEAD QUICKLY) No, it...it isn't

money. (GATHERS HIMSELF) Mr. Bain, I know

this will sound foolish to you but...please try

to understand. (BAIN NODS) I have a son.

(PAUSE) Haven't seen him in a long time...he's

been away at school out West. A fine boy...

a good boy. I'm very proud of him. (LOWERS

HIS HEAD) And I want him to be proud of me.

So...so I never told him...I couldn't.

                    BAIN:

Couldn't tell him what?

                    PALMER:

That I'm on the skids.

                    BAIN:

Don't talk like that! You're not a bum! You've

got a part in a show and you're doing a good job.

                    PALMER:

(SHAKES HIS HEAD) You don't understand. He

thinks I'm still way up there...a big man. He

thinks I've got...the supporting lead in the

show, a private dressing-room...instead of shar-

ing a room on the fourth floor with three other

men like a green walk-on.

                    BAIN:

You wrote him....

                    PALMER:

(TERRIBLY ASHAMED) Yes...I lied.

                    BAIN:

(QUIETLY) What is it you want, George?

PALMER:

He came East this afternoon, called me a little
while ago. He has a three-hour stopover in New
York on his way to an Army camp, basic training.
He wants to see me. (FLAT) He's on his way here
now.

BAIN:

(QUIETLY)   You want to use my dressing-room?

PALMER IS ALMOST OVERCOME BY SHAME, CAN ONLY NOD,
HIS EYES AVERTED.

BAIN:

(RISES AND TOUCHES PALMER'S SHOULDER) I can dress
tonight in Carrington's room.

PALMER:

I need it for only a few minutes.

BAIN:

Sure...

PALMER:

(LOOKS UP AT HIM)   Thanks, Mr. Bain.

BAIN:

(SUDDEN THOUGHT)   Wait...my name-plate on the door.

PALMER TAKES A SMALL NAME-BOARD OUT FROM UNDER HIS
JACKET. IT IS RATHER OLD, BUT SERVICABLE. THE
NAME IS CLEAR: GEORGE PALMER.

PALMER:

I...saved this. From the old days.   Would
you mind?

BAIN SMILES, TAKES THE NAME-PLATE FROM HIM,
CROSSES TO DOOR, OPENS IT, REPLACES HIS NAME
OUTSIDE WITH PALMER'S, CLOSES DOOR, CROSSES
TO DRESSER AND PUTS HIS OWN PLATE OUT OF
SIGHT.

                    BAIN:

I'll be out of here in just a minute.

HE REMOVES HIS JACKET FROM BACK OF HIS DRESSING-
CHAIR, SLIPS IT ON, STRAIGHTENS HIS TIE IN MIRROR,
SMOOTHS HIS HAIR. THEN HE WINKS AT PALMER TO GIVE
HIM COURAGE AND TURNS TO LEAVE.

THERE IS A KNOCK AT THE DOOR. BOTH MEN LOOK AT
EACH OTHER. BAIN NODS FOR PALMER TO ANSWER. THE
OLD MAN IS ALMOST PARALYZED, BUT BREAKS OUT OF IT.

                    PALMER:

Who...who is it?

                    TOM:

(OFF) It's me, Dad, can I come in?

PALMER IS GALVANIZED INTO ACTION, RUNS TO DRESSING-
CHAIR, SITS, QUICKLY RUMPLES HIS HAIR, LOOSENS HIS
COLLAR AS IF FINISHING HIS MAKEUP REMOVAL

                    PALMER:

(QUICKLY) Yes, yes, Tom, come in!

TOM ENTERS, YOUNG, CLEAN-CUT. PALMER SPRINGS OUT
OF HIS CHAIR TO GREET HIM. THEY EMBRACE

                    PALMER:

(PUSHES HIM TO ARM'S LENGTH) Tom, let me look at

you, son! Ha ha! Why, you're as tall and tan as

a Hollywood cowboy! (CLAPS HIM ON THE SHOULDER)

I hardly recognize you. You're a man.

                    TOM:

You look real fine yourself, Dad - just the

way I remember you.

                    PALMER:

Me? Ha! Tom, I never felt better in my life,

never better, son. (REALIZES SUDDENLY THAT

BAIN IS STILL IN THE ROOM) Oh, I'm terribly

sorry. Tom, I want you to meet Mr. Bain here -
a very fine gentleman.

THEY SHAKE HANDS.

              TOM:

How do you do, sir?

              BAIN:

A pleasure, Tom.

              PALMER:

(HURRIEDLY) Mr. Bain just dropped in talk over a
little business. (FEEBLE CHUCKLE) You know how
it is. Don't let you rest a minute.

              BAIN:

Well, I've got to be running along. Oh, thanks
for your time. Mr. Palmer.

              TOM:

Oh please don't go. (TO PALMER) Dad, I've got
to dash over to the hotel to change. I...I'm
afraid we'll just have time enough for dinner before my train leaves.

              PALMER:

Sure, son. I..I'll be finished up here in just
a few minutes. I'll meet you at the hotel, okay?

              TOM:

Fine. (TURNS, THEN HAS A THOUGHT) Oh, Dad,
how about those pictures you promised me?

              PALMER:

Of course. (RISES) I'll get them right now
from...uh, from the cast dressing-room. I

was...visiting before and forgot them. Won't

take but a minute.

PALMER CROSSES TO DOOR AND EXITS. TOM SMILES
AT HIM AS HE LEAVES, BUT AS SOON AS HE IS GONE
THE BOY SITS ON THE SETTEE. HIS FACE BECOMES
SUDDENLY VERY SAD. BAIN LEANS AGAINST THE
DRESSING-TABLE, WATCHING HIM NARROWLY.

   TOM:

How is he, Mr. Bain...really?

   BAIN:

(GUARDEDLY) What do you mean, Tom?

   TOM:

Has he been...drinking?

   BAIN:

Drinking! Why, your Pop is right as rain, kid.

   TOM:

You needn't pretend...now, anyway. I know who

you are, Mr. Bain...I read the papers. (FLAT)

And I know about Dad.

   BAIN:

This is level, Tom. He's all right. He hasn't

touched a drop in months. It's a long road back..

but he's a trouper. He'll make it one day. But

it's tough on him now.

   TOM:

(COVERS HIS EYES) I wish I could help him...

but I don't know how. (LOOKS UP SUDDENLY,

HEARTBROKEN) Why must he try to fool me,

why must he lie, why can't he trust me!

BAIN:

(SOFTLY)   He loves you, Tom, and he's afraid
he'll hurt you. Try to understand him...he's
been through a lot. You're his whole world now.

TOM:

(LOOKING OFF SADLY)   I'm sorry, Mr. Bain. I
didn't mean to say anything...please, please
don't let on that....

BAIN:

I know, son.

DOOR OPENS AND PALMER COMES IN BRISKLY WITH A
PHOTO ENVELOPE. TOM IMMEDIATELY PUTS ON A
SMILE FOR HIM.

PALMER:

There you are, m'boy, safe and sound. You just
take them along so you'll be sure and have them,
eh? (HANDS TOM ENVELOPE)   Now get yourself a
shower and a few minutes' rest and we'll have the
best dinner this old town can set up! Ha ha!
You name it - French, Italian, Chinese, steaks -
what do you like?

TOM:

We'll see, Dad. I warn you - I'll be on straight
Army chow for the next three months and I want a
meal to remember tonight! (BOTH LAUGH)   See you
soon. (TO BAIN)   Goodbye, Mr. Bain.

(THEY SHAKE HANDS AND THEIR EYES LOCK FOR AN INSTANT.)

BAIN:

Goodbye, son. Good luck.

TOM EXITS. PALMER STANDS LOOKING AFTER HIM
A MOMENT, THEN THE SMILE FADES FROM HIS FACE,
AND HE BITES HIS LIP. HE SINKS DOWN ON THE
CHAIR, EXHAUSTED.

                    PALMER:

(WHISPER) He's...a fine boy, isn't he...

                    BAIN:

He's from good stuff.

                    PALMER:

(A MIRTHLESS LAUGH)   From me?   Good stuff.

(BITTER)   I don't deserve to have a son like

that.

                    BAIN:

(CRUELLY) Maybe you're right! Maybe you don't

deserve him at all! (PALMER SHUTS HIS EYES)

I'll tell you something, Palmer. My father was

a failure - you understand?   A down-and-outer.

He flopped in every business he ever tried. He

lived poor all his life...and he died poor. But

he was the greatest man I ever knew. I wouldn't

have loved and respected him more if he'd been a

king! He tried...and he was honest - not lucky -

but honest, with himself and with us. He was a

man...

                    PALMER:

(STARING AT THE FLOOR)   And what will my son say

about me...

                    BAIN:

That you were a coward.

                    PALMER:

A coward...

                    BAIN:

Palmer - I think you will have to tell him.

(SOFTLY) He won't remember the lights or the

dressing-room, or the phony glitter. Only that

his father had a backbone - or didn't!

PALMER RISES SLOWLY, HIS MIND RACKED WITH IN-
DECISION. BAIN LOOKS INTO HIS FACE.

        BAIN:

He loves you, George.

        PALMER:

(QUIETLY TO HIMSELF)   How can I tell him?

PALMER TURNS AND WALKS SLOWLY OUT OF THE ROOM,
LEAVING THE DOOR OPEN. BAIN STANDS LOOKING
AFTER HIM A LONG MOMENT, NOTICES THE NAME-PLATE
ON THE DOOR, TAKES IT DOWN AND WALKS TO HIS
DRESSING-TABLE, LOOKING AT THE SIGN, THINKING.
THEN HE PUTS IT DOWN, LIFTS THE TELEGRAM FROM
THE TABLE. HIS EYES NARROW. HE PICKS UP THE
TELEPHONE RECEIVER AND DIALS A NUMBER.

        BAIN:

Mr. Thompson, please. (PAUSE) Hello, Charlie,

this is Walter. Look, have you sent Gilligan

that wire yet? No?   Good. I want you to hold

off on that until tomorrow morning. You know, a

funny thing happened just now in my dressing-room.

I saw one of our bit players give a great perform-

ance. He's got the stuff - no question about it.

He could step into my role easily...Yes, I'm sure

of it. But there's one thing, Charlie. I don't

know if he's solid inside or all rotten. But

I'll see him tonight...after a certain dinner party.

And I'll know. If he does what I think

he's going to do, we're on our way to

California!

FADE OUT

"WON'T YOU TELL ME, DOCTOR . . ."

INTRODUCTORY NOTES AND PRODUCTION SUGGESTIONS

The sketch, vignette or skit (call it what you will) which follows was designed to serve two necessary functions. It provides a bit of dramatic material for a cast of four women, thus solving one of the casting problems which confronts a woman's college or a co-ed course in which the acting talent is chiefly feminine. It also provides a ten-minute dramatic unit which can be made part of a longer variety show or which can be produced as a unit in itself.

A ten-minute script offers obvious advantages to a class in TV production. A short script can be rehearsed in one or two class-periods, and then given a dress rehearsal and a closed-circuit production within another class hour. It can be memorized readily and can be blocked for camera by a student-director in an evening. Once it is running smoothly it is possible to rotate directors (and other personnel) on each run-thru, making three changes in an hour, provided each new director does not deviate too much from what the others have done before.

"Won't You Tell Me, Doctor . . ." has been deliberately designed to pose several interesting production problems. Much of its action takes place with two characters seated at a desk. Assuming two cameras, the director must plan a variety of two-shots and one-shots which will avoid monotony. There is ample opportunity and justification for reverse angles, discussed on page 31. Two brief scenes are played outside the consultation room, in the waiting room or anteroom which leads to the psychiatrist's inner sanctum. As shown in the floor plan, the two scenes may be fully provided or the anteroom may be suggested by the two-sided common wall around the connecting door. In either case, the camerawork suggested by the action offers a variety of choices. The camera may shoot through the door as Mrs. Albright enters at the beginning and as she follows Dr. Benton at the end. Or the camera may follow them, trucking across the "cross-section" of the dividing wall. Or one camera may walk them to the door, while the other picks them up on the inside and then follows them to the desk.

The close-up of the snapshot in the script may be done either with Camera No. 2 over Dr. Reid's shoulder as she holds the picture in her hand, or a duplicate photo may be held in the floor manager's hand close to the more convenient camera. If the former method is chosen, an 8-inch lens will make it unnecessary for the camera to move in extremely close.

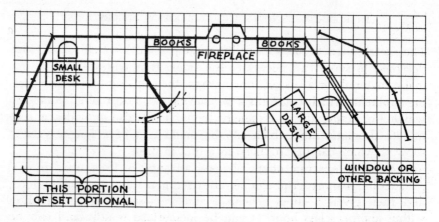

Figure 36.

An opportunity is given in this script to show a time-lapse effect, indicating that a conversation has been going on for a long time. As indicated, this is done by fading to black, since some props must be changed during the time lapse. The risk involved here is that the screen will remain black too long and thus destroy the necessary continuity. It will probably be found that the effect will be better if the camera makes some change during the fade-out so the new shot is not identical with the one which faded out. The reader will note that two transitions have been combined here: the fade-out-fade-in plus the change in condition of the ashtray. The fade alone, or a dissolve, would be sufficient. The student-director should be encouraged to find his own way to make this minor transition in time.

The entrance of Dr. Benton near the end of the script poses a camera and staging problem. Dr. Reid is talking, and must be placed in such a fashion that she will not see the door as it opens. Some directors will arrange to have the door show in the background of a wide two-shot. Others may simply cut a medium shot of Dr. Benton into the conversation at the moment she enters.

There are several ways of handling the cameras on each action, just as there are several ways of staging the actions themselves. The most successful director will be the one who devises natural and believable action which also lends itself to complete and satisfactory coverage with the camera.

WON'T YOU TELL ME, DOCTOR?[*]

A Dramatic Skit for Four Women

CAST

Mrs. Albright
Dr. Reid
Dr. Benton
Nurse

THE SCENE IS A DOCTOR'S OFFICE, LATE IN A FALL
AFTERNOON.   AS THE CONSULTATION ROOM OF A
WOMAN PSYCHIATRIST, IT COMBINES PROFESSIONAL
DIGNITY WITH A DEGREE OF WARMTH AND CHARM.
THE CONVENTIONAL CONSULTATION DESK WITH ITS
SWIVEL CHAIR FOR THE DOCTOR AND A COMFORTABLE
CHAIR FOR THE PATIENT IS OFFSET BY PICTURES
AND DRAPES THAT SHOW TASTE AND IMAGINATION.
A BOOKCASE SHOWS SLIM VOLUMES AS WELL AS PRO-
FESSIONAL ONES, WHILE A VASE OR TWO OF FLOWERS
UNDO ANY IMPRESSION OF SEVERITY.

IF FACILITIES PERMIT, THE OUTER OFFICE OF A
NURSE-SECRETARY IS ALSO SHOWN AS INDICATED.
IF ONLY ONE SET CAN BE PROVIDED, THE OPENING
SHOTS CAN BE FRAMED AGAINST THE OUTER-SIDE
OF THE DOOR WHICH LEADS INTO THE CONSULTATION
ROOM.

WE FADE FROM OPENING TITLES INTO A SHOT OF A
NEAT PROFESSIONAL SIGN READING Edith Benton,
M.D.   A HAND COMES INTO THE SHOT AND AS WE
DOLLY BACK WE SEE THAT THE SIGN WAS ON A
DOOR, THAT THE HAND HAS MOVED ACROSS THE
SIGN TO THE DOORKNOB, AND THAT IT HAS HESI-
TATED THERE, RELUCTANT TO TURN THE KNOB. BY
NOW WE SEE THE HAND'S OWNER, MRS. LEONA
ALBRIGHT, A WOMAN IN HER THIRTIES.   SHE IS
WELL DRESSED, JUST SHORT OF THE POINT OF
OSTENTATION, BUT LINES OF DISCONTENT ARE
ETCHED ABOUT HER MOUTH. AT THE MOMENT SHE
IS MORE THAN USUALLY WROUGHT UP. SHE GLANCES
ABOUT HER, SHOWS PETULANT ANNOYANCE, AND
CALLS IMPATIENTLY.

MRS. ALBRIGHT:

Hello! Isn't there anyone here?

[*] No permission required

                    DR. REID:

(OFF CAMERA, OFF MIKE AND FROM BEHIND
DOOR TO INNER OFFICE)

Yes? Who is it?

                    MRS. ALBRIGHT:

Oh, Dr. Benton . . there's no one out

here. May I come in?

DOOR OPENS AND A PLEASANT, QUIET-MANNERED
YOUNG WOMAN IN A SEVERELY TAILORED SUIT
STANDS IN DOORWAY

                    DR. REID:

Were you looking for Dr. Benton? I'm

afraid the nurse has stepped out on an

important errand.

                    MRS. ALBRIGHT:

(SWEEPING RIGHT IN AND PLUMPING HERSELF
DOWN IN THE ARMCHAIR FACING THE DESK)

Oh, Doctor, it's such a relief to find you

here. I know I'm simply hours too early for

my appointment, but I got to worrying about

it, and I just couldn't wait another minute.

(THE OTHER YOUNG WOMAN HAS PAUSED AT THE DOOR
FOR AN INSTANT DURING ALL THIS BUT HAS COME
AROUND TO THE DESK DURING THE SPEECH. SHE
STANDS BEHIND THE DESK IN INDECISION.)

                    DR. REID:

I think you're making a mistake. I'm not ...

                    MRS. ALBRIGHT:

Not able to see me now? But you simply must.

The other patients can wait, I'm sure. Be-

sides, there's no one out there at the moment,

and this is my first visit to a psychiatrist's

office, and if I have to wait any longer the

suspense will be very bad for me, I'm sure.

                DR. REID:

(SITS DOWN WITH SUDDEN DECISION)

Just what seems to be troubling you, Mrs...?

                MRS. ALBRIGHT:

Albright...Mrs. Leone Albright. Won't you

tell me, Doctor?....

                DR. REID:

I take it there's something on your mind?

                MRS. ALBRIGHT:

Something on my mind? Oh, Doctor, you can't

imagine what it's been like. I've been married

for six years now, and I must admit that the

first two were perfectly happy years, but then...

                DR. REID:

Have you any children?

                MRS. ALBRIGHT:

(DOESN'T LIKE BEING INTERRUPTED)   No. I've

thought it best not to have any. My husband

wants them, but somehow...Doctor, you believe

that a couple can be perfectly happy without

children, don't you?

                DR. REID:

I've known a few couples who seemed to manage

it, but...

MRS. ALBRIGHT:

Oh, I'm so glad you agree with me. I wish my
husband could hear you say that. Ed is always
complaining and I'm always having to show him
where he's wrong. Why, only the other evening
I read to him that story in the paper about the
man who was backing his car out of the garage
and his two-year-old child was playing on the
lawn and...

DR. REID:

(WITH EFFORT)   Yes...I know about that accident.

MRS. ALBRIGHT:

You read it, too?   Then you know how I felt when
I saw it. Such a well-educated couple, too.
Just think, they were both Ph.D.'s!   Well, as
I pointed out to Ed, when you have children you're
just inviting unhappiness.   Something is always
happening to them.

DR. REID:

And you and your husband are unhappy because you
can't agree about children?

MRS. ALBRIGHT:

Oh, it's not only that, although that is the main
thing. It's the sort of man that he's turned
into. Here...(RUMMAGES IN HANDBAG)   Here's a
snapshot...you see the sort of person he's turned
into?

(HANDS THE SNAPSHOT TO DR. REID. WE SEE THE SNAP-
SHOT IN SOMEONE'S HAND, PRESUMABLY DR. REID'S.
ED SEEMS A VERY PLEASANT LIKABLE MIDDLE-AGED MAN.
MRS. ALBRIGHT'S VOICE GOES ON.)

You see how insensitive and dull he's become?

Now during our courtship - we had a long one

and he was utterly charming then - Ed was so

considerate of my feelings. He was always

thinking of me, and of ways to let me know how

much I meant to him. But in the last few years,

he's become a changed man!

               DR. REID:

In what way has he changed? (RETURNS SNAPSHOT)

(MRS. ALBRIGHT HAS BEEN SMOKING IN A NERVOUS
FASHION THROUGH THIS.   AS DR. REID RETURNS THE
SNAPSHOT, MRS. ALBRIGHT PUTS OUT HER CIGARETTE
IN AN ASHTRAY ON THE DESK. WE DOLLY IN ON
SNAPSHOT AND ASHTRAY.)

               MRS. ALBRIGHT:

Why, he hardly seems to know when I'm in the

room. He's lost all respect for my opinions.

He pays no attention to what I have to say ...

(WE HAVE FADED OUT DURING THIS SPEECH.   AS WE
FADE IN AGAIN THE ASHTRAY IS STILL IN VIEW BUT
WITH THREE OR FOUR HALF-SMOKED CIGARETTE BUTTS
IN IT. THE SNAPSHOT IS GONE. MRS. ALBRIGHT'S
VOICE FADES IN WITH THE PICTURE AND AS WE DOLLY
BACK SHE IS STILL TALKING BUT DR. REID IS
STEALING A GLANCE AT HER WRIST-WATCH.)

...but most of all, it's his whining and com-

plaining. He just can't understand that with my

delicate health...

               DR. REID:

You've mentioned your health before, Mrs. Albright.

Just what is the matter?

MRS. ALBRIGHT:

Oh, nothing I can put my finger on. I've
been to several doctors, and they can't seem
to find a thing wrong with me. But I just
can't seem to get to sleep. I tumble and toss
and lie there listening to Ed's awful snoring,
and first thing I know it's morning.   When he
goes down to breakfast, I doze off at last...

DR. REID:

I take it you don't have breakfast with your
husband, Mrs. Albright?

MRS. ALBRIGHT:

I should hope not!   I never look my best in
the morning, and I do think I owe it to my husband to let him see me only when I'm fit to be
seen.

DR. REID:

(RISES AND PACES AWAY FROM DESK, THEN TURNS
BACK)
Mrs. Albright, what makes you think that a
doctor can help you?

MRS. ALBRIGHT:

(THUNDERSTRUCK) But you're a psychiatrist!
Ever so many of my friends have been psycho-
analyzed, and they tell me that life has been
so much happier for them once they could get
rid of their repressions and inhibitions and
things. And one of them even had her husband

go to the analyst with her, and then he
continued after she had finished, and now
they're both so much happier.

          DR. REID:

Mrs. Albright, a psychiatrist spends ten to
fifteen years in very intense and difficult
professional training.   Then he...or she...
feels that this training should be used to
help those who are really sick at heart, who
are emotionally disturbed or mentally distraught.
Do you think you qualify?

          MRS. ALBRIGHT:

(FLOUNCING UP) Well, I never!   I certainly
don't think I'm ready for an institution if
that's what you wish to imply!   But I'm a
very sensitive woman - all my friends tell me
so - and I thought that you, being a woman,
as well as a doctor, would understand. I'm
sure there are others . . .

(BOTH WOMEN ARE TOO WRAPPED UP IN THEIR ARGUMENT
TO NOTICE THAT THE DOOR TO THE OUTER ROOM HAS
OPENED AND THAT A MATURE, GRAY-HAIRED WOMAN HAS
ENTERED QUIETLY.)

          DR. REID:

But I'm not that kind of doctor, Mrs. Albright.
I would have told you so if you had let me.
And I couldn't help thinking that your suffering
is largely imaginary, and that Dr. Benton....

DR. BENTON:

(WHO HAS BEEN WATCHING THIS LAST EXCHANGE)

I beg your pardon...were you waiting to see

me? (TURNS TO DR. REID) I'm sorry it's

been so long, Dr. Reid. It took a bit of

time...

MRS. ALBRIGHT:

(INTERRUPTING)   Are you Dr. Benton?

Then who is....(RECOVERS) I'm Mrs. Albright,

Doctor, Mrs. Leone Albright, and I had an

appointment for five o'clock.

DR. BENTON:

It's just ten minutes to five now, Mrs. Al-

bright, and I'll be with you in a moment.

If you'll just step into the waiting room...

(SHE GENTLY BUT FIRMLY EDGES MRS. ALBRIGHT
THROUGH THE DOOR AND CLOSES IT BEHIND HER.
WE NOW SEE MRS. ALBRIGHT ON THE WAITING ROOM
SIDE OF THE DOOR. A NURSE COMES UP TO HER.
COMPREHENSION IS SLOWLY DAWNING ON MRS.
ALBRIGHT'S STARTLED COUNTENANCE.)

NURSE:

Won't you have a seat, Mrs. Albright? I'm

sorry I wasn't here when you arrived, but I

had to step out for just a moment and I

suppose you walked right in.

MRS. ALBRIGHT:

(THOUGHTFULLY)   Tell me...if that was Dr.

Benton who came in just now, who was that

woman I've been speaking to? Don't tell me

(DISTASTEFULLY) that she's a...a patient!

NURSE:

(SYMPATHETICALLY)   No, though it's a wonder
that she isn't.   She's the wife of one of
Doctor's patients...and a brilliant young
woman...a Ph.D. in Sociology. She's Dr.
Marilyn Reid.

MRS. ALBRIGHT:

The one whose husband was in the papers last
week? The man who backed his car out of the
garage and ran over his own child?

NURSE:

That's right. He collapsed yesterday and
Dr. Benton is treating him. He's over at the
Neuro-Psychiatric Center now, and Doctor has
just come from there.

MRS. ALBRIGHT:

And to think that I told her all my troubles.
Oh, dear...

(DOOR OPENS. DR. BENTON AND DR. REID COME
THROUGH. MRS. ALBRIGHT BARELY MOVES AWAY
ENOUGH TO LET THEM GO BY, AND LISTENS
AVIDLY AS DR. BENTON SAYS:)

DR. BENTON:

So that's the story, Marilyn. He seems to be
adjusting to the Center pretty well, and the
hydrotherapy helped this afternoon. Tomorrow
or the next day we may try shock treatment.
But I'll let you know.

DR. REID:

Thank you, Doctor. I know you're doing

all you can. (TURNS)   Goodbye, Mrs.

Albright. I hope you find the help you

need. (EXIT)

DR. BENTON:

(SLIGHT SMILE AT EXCHANGE, THEN GETS DOWN
TO WORK)

Now, Mrs. Albright, if you'll come in...

(THEY MOVE THROUGH THE DOOR AND WE SEE
THEM CROSS TO THE DESK AND TAKE THEIR AP-
PROPRIATE PLACES. MRS. ALBRIGHT LEANS
FORWARD EAGERLY ACROSS THE DESK.)

MRS. ALBRIGHT:

Won't you tell me, Doctor, if there is

anything you can do for me?

(FADE TO BLACK BEHIND IRONIC MUSIC
CLOSING SCENE)

"SHE WALKS IN BEAUTY"

Introductory Notes and Production Suggestions

Few vignettes which the authors have read or seen surpass James Truex's "She Walks in Beauty" in warmth and charm. For students of television acting or production it provides challenging problems; for the viewer it provides a sentimental but satisfying experience. The script calls for two men and two women; for two mature actors and two young ones. It has two "character" parts and two which might be called "straight" but which possess definite individuality. Finally, its theme has universal appeal, for it treats not only of young love but of love in the later years. Mr. Truex has treated his characters with kindliness and warmth, and even the unhappy Miss Ingersoll arouses our sympathy.

Whether the director chooses to present "She Walks in Beauty" in the *Cameo Theatre* style, about which its originator, Albert McCleery, has much to say on page 280, or whether he prefers to give it a realistic setting, he will find much delight and the proper amount of difficulty in producing it. Clearly, the window through which Mr. Bernard watches Miss Riley each day as she crosses the lawn to her classroom must be strategically placed in the set. The location of Mr. Bernard's desk is another problem. A principal's desk usually dominates his office, as the usual principal dominates his visitors. But Mr. Bernard is not the usual principal; will his desk also be different?

But different or not, that desk will serve as the center of much of the action, so it must be carefully located with reference to the shots that can be taken of the man behind it and the visitor who sits beside it or stands before it. The director will need good shots of Mr. Bernard and Miss Ingersoll in the opening pages, of Mr. Bernard and young Hawkins a little later on. But they do not stand in the same relationship to Mr. Bernard, and one outward indication of this difference is where they sit or stand while speaking to the principal. Miss Ingersoll obviously feels that she has a proprietary right to sit or stand where she pleases, and will automatically march to the seat reserved for distinguished visitors—either across the desk or at one side of it. Hawkins is literally on the carpet, or thinks he is; he will sit only when ordered to, and then possibly will find it difficult to face Mr. Bernard until rapport has been established.

The director should remember that good shots of the two individuals involved in such scenes are not enough; he must judiciously intermix two-shots to keep the relationship between the principal and the teacher or the principal and the student clear in the mind of the viewer. Moreover, when Miss Riley enters the scene, the director will be faced with the problem of three-shots. Will he keep Miss Riley on one camera and her two admirers on the other, once the basic orientation attendant upon her entrance has been accomplished? That's one way of doing it. But "She Walks in Beauty" abounds in opportunity for reaction shots: Mr. Bernard's feelings when Hawkins betrays his secret to Miss Riley; Miss Riley's feelings when she learns how she has misjudged the principal; Hawkins' violent reaction to the news that Miss Riley is already betrothed to the chemistry teacher.

The director must so arrange his actors and his cameras that he can get good shots of their facial reactions, from as near a head-on position as possible. Yet they cannot hold fixed positions for three or four pages, nor can the director permit their movements to become artificial and forced. There are many ways of solving these problems, and the authors are going to make only two suggestions:

1) Keep the desk as small as possible without its looking silly. Try a large desk and you'll soon see why.

2) Experiment with various placements of furniture, cameras and actors in *dry-run,* using rehearsal furniture of approximately the same size as the pieces you'll use in the studios. But work your experiments out with a viewfinder in dry-run until you're satisfied you have the best solution. It will be too late to go shopping for shots when you finally go on camera!

THE   KATE   SMITH   DAYTIME   HOUR

Friday, May 9, 1952

presents

SIR CEDRIC HARDWICKE

in

"SHE   WALKS   IN   BEAUTY"

by

JAMES TRUEX

Devised by ALBERT McCLEERY for

MR. TED COLLINS

C A S T

MR. BERNARD . . . . SIR CEDRIC HARDWICKE
MISS INGERSOLL. . . . . LUCILLE CALVERT
YOUNG HAWKINS . . . . DAVID ANDERSON
MARY ALICE RILEY. . . . . SUSANNE SHAW

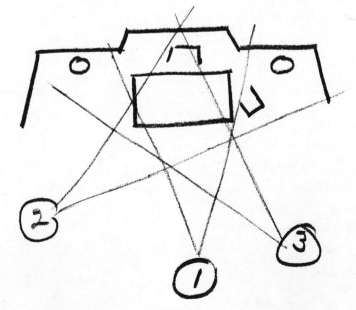

*Permission to reproduce this script in any form
may be obtained by writing to the author's agent,
Mrs. Blanche Gaines, 40 East 49th Street, New
York, New York.

②= on Miss Smith's introduction

DISSOLVE TO . . . . .PRINCIPAL'S OFFICE *①*

(Sound: Background Spring Noises

(MR. BERNARD ~~WRITING AT DESK~~ *At Window!* HE

LOOKS UP, STARES DREAMILY OUT WINDOW,

THEN WRITES.

~~SOUND: OF KNOCKING ON DOOR~~. MR.

(Comes To Desk)

BERNARD ∧HASTILY SLIDES PAPER INTO

DESK DRAWER.)

               MR. BERNARD

Come in.

(Sound: Door Open + close)

(MISS INGERSOLL STRIDES INTO ROOM)

               MISS INGERSOLL

Mr. Bernard ....

               MR. BERNARD

Yes, Miss Ingersoll?

               MISS INGERSOLL

There's something going on in this

school that I feel it my duty to

call to your attention.

               MR. BERNARD

Go right ahead, Miss Ingersoll.

What is it this time?

               MISS INGERSOLL

Read this!

                    (MORE)

-2-

MISS INGERSOLL (Cont'd)

(SHE TOSSES PIECE OF PAPER ON DESK.
HE READS IT, THEN LOOKS UP)

Well, what do you think of it?

MR. BERNARD

I think it's a love poem, Miss
Ingersoll. Did you write it?

MISS INGERSOLL

Please, Mr. Bernard. This is a
serious matter. This piece of
obscenity was written by one of
my students right in the middle of
my geometry class.

MR. BERNARD

Oh, now, I wouldn't call it obscene,
Miss Ingersoll. Passionate, perhaps,
but not obscene. We must not forget
that it's spring. Didn't you ever
write this sort of thing when you
were young?

MISS INGERSOLL

That's neither here nor there, Mr.
Bernard. The important thing to
notice is the dedication "To M.A.R."
They are the initials of the new
English instructor, Miss Mary Alice
Riley.

MR. BERNARD

Then obviously the poem is intended
for her. What are we doing with it?

-3-

MISS INGERSOLL

Mr. Bernard, as the new principal,
I should think you would try to be
more aware of what's going on in
this school. That young lady has
caused dissension and trouble ever
since she took up residence here.
She's a disturbing influence on the
young ... this poem proves it. She
doesn't dress like a teacher, act
like a teacher ...

MR. BERNARD (CUTTING IN)

Or look like a teacher. You've
pointed that out before, Miss
Ingersoll. Go on.

MISS INGERSOLL

I know you seem to regard it lightly,
but when students begin writing lewd
verses in honor of Miss Riley in my
geometry class, I feel that something
drastic should be done.

MR. BERNARD

What do you want me to do, Miss
Ingersoll? The young lady in question has a contract to teach high
school English until June of this
year. She is pretty, she dresses
well, and at least one young member
of the junior class seems to have
fallen in love with her. But don't

-4 -

MR. BERNARD (Cont'd)

you see that none of these things
can possibly be construed as a
breach of contract?

MISS INGERSOLL

I can see that my twenty years of
service here in this school means
nothing to you, Mr. Bernard. When
the late Mr. Green was principal,
he seemed to welcome my advice.

MR. BERNARD

I welcome it, too, Miss Ingersoll,
but in this instance, I'm at a loss
to know what steps I should take to
satisfy both yourself and my conscience.

MISS INGERSOLL

(INJURED DIGNITY)

Would it be too much for me to ask
you to speak to the author of this
-- poem and see that he is properly
discip¯ined? He's waiting outside.

MR. BERNARD

Then show the culprit in.

MISS INGERSOLL

Thank you.

(SHE GOES TO OPEN DOOR)
(Sound: Door open)
Hawkins, come in here.

(HAWKINS ENTERS RELUCTANTLY)

Mr. Bernard will take care of you.

-5-

HAWKINS

Yes, ma'am.

(MISS INGERSOLL EXITS. HAWKINS STANDS,

HEAD DOWN)

(Sound: Door Close

MR. BERNARD

Come here, Hawkins.

(HAWKINS SHUFFLES TOWARD DESK. MR.

BERNARD HOLDS OUT POEM)

Did you write this?

HAWKINS

Yes, sir.

MR. BERNARD

In Miss Ingersoll's geometry class?

HAWKINS

Yes, sir. I'm sorry.

MR. BERNARD

That you wrote the poem?

HAWKINS

No, sir. That I wrote it in Miss

Ingersoll's geometry class.

MR. BERNARD (Rises)

I see. Hawkins, while writing

poetry is not altogether reprehen-

sible as a pastime, I should advise

you in the future not to indulge in

it during school hours. In that way

you can make more certain that the

poem reaches the person for whom

it is intended and no one else.

-6-

HAWKINS (SOMEWHAT PUZZLED)

Yes, sir.

MR. BERNARD (WALKS TO WINDOW)

As for the poem itself, I think it
has considerable merit. But that
line: (READING)
"She walks in beauty like the night"
Didn't Lord Byron write that one?

HAWKINS

Yes, sir, but it seemed to fit in
so well.

MR. BERNARD

I know it's tempting, but we poets
must be careful not to borrow too
much from the past. We must create
our own images.

HAWKINS

Yes, sir. Did you say, "we" poets,
sir?

MR. BERNARD

Why, yes. I've tried my hand at
poetry myself from time to time.

HAWKINS

No kidding, sir!

MR. BERNARD

No kidding. As a matter of fact,
I was working on one today.
(REACHES IN DRAWER)
I'd be grateful if you'd glance at
it and give me your opinion on it.

-7-

MR. BERNARD (Cont'd)
(HANDS PAPER TO HAWKINS)
Unfortunately, I was interrupted
before I was able to finish the
last line.

HAWKINS (HURRIEDLY READING)
Gee, Mr. Bernard, you're a real
poet. This is terrific. It's
a sonnet, isn't it?

MR. BERNARD
It hopes to be. If I can ever
find anything to rhyme with "gazelle".

HAWKINS (STARING AT PAPER)
But Mr. Bernard! The dedication!
"Lines written to M.A.R.!"

MR. BERNARD
Mary Alice Riley.

HAWKINS
You, too, huh?

MR. BERNARD
Me, too, Hawkins.

HAWKINS
Gosh, Mr. Bernard, isn't she a pip!

MR. BERNARD
She's all of that, Hawkins, and more.
It is my privilege to watch her every
morning as she travels across the
lawn to her classroom. That journey
is a sonnet in itself.

-3-

HAWKINS

I'm taking her course in the Romantic
Period..Eighteen hundred to eighteen
hundred thirty-two.

MR. BERNARD

You're a lucky fellow.

HAWKINS

Say, this makes us rivals, doesn't
it?

MR. BERNARD

In a way, Hawkins, though youth is
on your side. 3

HAWKINS

I've got too much youth, Mr. Bernard.
When you're fifteen years old, nobody
takes you seriously. *C U Mr B* 2

MR. BERNARD

When you're fifty, you can't take
yourself seriously. I don't know
which is worse! 3

HAWKINS

Gosh, Mr. Bernard, I had a hunch
you were pretty human for a school
principal, but I never dreamed you
were this human! 1

MR. BERNARD

Some people regard it as a failing,
Hawkins. You'd better get back to
class. (HOLDS OUT HAND) I think

(MORE)

-9-

          MR. BERNARD (Cont'd)

we should keep this poetry business

a secret between ourselves, don't

you?

          HAWKINS

(~~TAKING HIS HAND~~)

Yes, sir. And may the best man win!

          MR. BERNARD

Oh, uh. No more writing in Miss

Ingersoll's geometry class. Under-

stand?

          HAWKINS

Absolutely!

          MR. BERNARD

In a way, Miss Ingersoll suffers

from your complaint and mine ...

a lack of reciprocal affection.

She is caught on the horns of an

isosceles triangle. We must be

kind to her.

          HAWKINS

Yes, sir.

(SOUND: Door Knock + Open & close

(AS HAWKINS TURNS TO GO, DOOR OPENS.

MARY ALICE RILEY ENTERS SHOT)

          MISS RILEY (ANGRILY)

I see I've arrived just in time.

Don't go, Hawkins. What I have

to say concerns you.

-10-

MR. BERNARD

Won't you sit down, Miss Riley?

MISS RILEY

No thank you. A moment ago in the
faculty room, Miss Ingersoll announced that she had reported this
young man for writing a poem dedi-
cated to me. Is that so?

MR. BERNARD

It is.

MISS RILEY

She seems to feel that it was immoral
and that I singlehandedly am the
cause of a general moral collapse
in the student body.

MR. BERNARD (Goes Back To Desk).

Miss Ingersoll gets unduly ruffled,
Miss Riley. The poem is hardly immoral ... if you would care to read
it ... (HE HOLDS OUT PAPER) _____ 3

MISS RILEY (TAKING IT)

Has it ever occurred to you and Miss
Ingersoll that if Hawkins has a desire to express himself in verse, he
has a perfect right to, without the
entire school faculty passing judgment on him? _____ 2

HAWKINS

Miss Riley!

-11-

MISS RILEY

Mr. Bernard, in the midst of the
oppressive atmosphere of this dreary
school, you should thank your stars
that there is at least one young man
with imagination and a soul. Instead
of punishing him, you should reward
him!

HAWKINS (DESPERATELY) *(Goes To Miss Riley)*

Miss Riley! I'm not being punished!

MISS RILEY

What's that?

HAWKINS

I'm not being punished! Mr. Bernard
is on our side!

MISS RILEY

How do you mean?

3

HAWKINS

(GRABBING MR. BERNARD'S POEM OFF DESK)
Here. Here's the proof. He wrote
this poem this morning ... to you.
He's in love with you, too, Miss
Riley!

(MISS RILEY STARES DOWN AT POEM, READS
IT, THEN TURNS SLOWLY TO MR. BERNARD)

MR. BERNARD

Now, Hawkins! I hardly think we
need lay all our cards on the table
at once. I, uh ... things seem to
have gotten a little out of hand,

-12-

MR. BERNARD (Cont'd)

don't they! The truth is, that
Hawkins and I discovered a while
ago that we had a number of interests
in common.

HAWKINS

And you're most of them, Miss Riley.

MISS RILEY

May I sit down?

MR. BERNARD

Certainly. **2**

MISS RILEY (*sits*)

I'm sorry, Mr. Bernard. It begins to
look as though Miss Ingersoll is right
....I am a trouble-maker. **3**

MR. BERNARD

You forget that Miss Ingersoll started
the whole thing.

HAWKINS *(goes To other side of Principal)*

I guess you'll just have to choose
between us, Miss Riley.

MISS RILEY

Must I?

HAWKINS

It's what they always do in the movies.

MR. BERNARD

Forgive my friend, Hawkins, Miss
Riley. He speaks with the impetu-
osity of youth. Contrary to popular

(MORE)

-13-

        MR. BERNARD (Cont'd)

tradition, it's when we are old

that we are willing to wait. ———————————— *1*

        MISS RILEY *(Goes Between them)*

(RISING, LOOKING AT ONE, THEN THE

OTHER)

Dear Hawkins, dear Mr. Bernard,

believe me when I say that I am

deeply touched by these evidences

of your regard. ~~However~~ *But*, in the

interest of fairness, I must confess

that I cannot choose between ~~either~~

~~of~~ you, because I have already chosen.

(BOTH LOOK TO HER HOPEFULLY)

On this coming Saturday, at eight

P.M. my engagement will be announced

to Mr. Horace Braisted.

        HAWKINS

You mean, Mr. Braisted, the chemistry

teacher?

        MISS RILEY

Yes, Hawkins.

(~~HAWKINS MAKES AN UNHAPPY FACE~~)

Since Mr. Braisted doesn't care for

me to continue as a teacher, I shall

be relinquishing my post this June. ———————————— *3*

        MR. BERNARD

MR. Braisted is a Lucky Man

~~Congratulations, Miss Riley~~! We'll

miss you. ————————————————— *1*

-14-

MISS RILEY

And I shall miss you.

(HOLDING UP POEMS)

May I keep these?

MR. BERNARD

Certainly. If Mr. Braisted won't

mind.

MISS RILEY

I'll not be engaged until Saturday,

Mr. Bernard. Good afternoon.   **3**

(SHE THROWS A KISS TO THEM BOTH,

LEAVES) *(Sound: Door Open + Close)*

MR. BERNARD

Well, Hawkins, that's that.

HAWKINS

Mr. Braisted is a dope.

MR. BERNARD *(Going Toward Door)*

There is no accounting for tastes.

HAWKINS

And I had ideas of becoming a poet.

DL

(D.I.: dolly in)

MR. BERNARD

Don't give up, Hawkins. The world's

finest poems have been written by re-

jected suitors.

HAWKINS

Gee, I never thought of that.

MR. BERNARD

The Cavalier poets made a specialty

of unrequited love ... Robert Herrick,

Richard Lovelace...How do you feel?   **2**

-15-

HAWKINS

(THINKING FOR A MOMENT)

Hungry!   *1*

MR. BERNARD *(Goes To Hat Rack)*

You're recovering already. I wish

I could say the same of myself.

HAWKINS

Cheer up, Mr. Bernard. I guess she

isn't the only pebble on the beach.

MR. BERNARD

I'm no longer at my best in a bath-

ing suit. Come Hawkins, let's take

a stroll and sublimate our feelings

in the miracle of spring's return.   *3*

HAWKINS

O.K., Mr. Bernard.

MR. BERNARD

Perhaps we'll stop at the drug store

and drown our sorrows in an ice cream

soda.

(THEY GO OFF ARM IN ARM)

(FADE OUT)

DIS
↓
on Kate Smith   *2*

THE   END

Part III

FULL-LENGTH SCRIPTS

11. A Documentary

"CONTROL OF CLIMATE" * from *AMERICAN INVENTORY*

INTRODUCTORY NOTES, SUGGESTIONS AND
PRODUCTION ORDERS

(By WILLIAM HODAPP, executive director, Teleprograms, Inc., and
producer, *American Inventory*, NBC-TV, New York)

"Control of Climate" has been selected from the Alfred P. Sloan
Foundation, NBC-TV experimental adult education series, *American
Inventory*, for study as exemplifying techniques by which a seemingly
impossible television subject can be made interesting and effective
television material.

This royalty-free, public affairs program can be done with a minimum of equipment and a maximum of local ingenuity. New to the
medium in this script is the featuring of an on-the-air animated cartoon technique, possible because of a modified usage by Charles
Luchsinger of the so-called N-B-See Box—a device by which a clever
artist draws on paper (behind glass) on-the-air cartoons which give
the effect of expensive animated moving pictures.

"Control of Climate," a vital subject in the public interest, exploited
revolutionary aspects of the subject, its legal ramifications, its human
interest drama—all done with a touch of suitable humor.

Employed in this program of *American Inventory* were:

1. Dramatized sequences.
2. Scientific demonstration with guest expert.

3. Use of free and available film clips and the integration of these into other sequences.

4. The unique visual gimmick of the N-B-See Box.

5. Use of the narrator as connective tissue for the seemingly complicated and disconnected subject.

6. Integration of the narrator himself as a character in dramatized sequences.

7. Use of the courtroom format.

The program is easy to stage, having few characters and simple sets. The visuals are easy to improvise or obtain, including the film. The TV visualization of this challenging theme provides an example of new and exciting subjects which are available in the expanding world around us. It should be noted that the trick of how to do a successful program about any topic is to find the method, or combined formats, which may present it in original, simple and unexpected ways.

Ordinarily, such a subject as "Control of Climate" is only suitable for the "illustrated lecture" type of TV presentation. This script, upon study, will perhaps act as a guide to thinking about other similar topics which can be effectively dramatized for this new medium.

Production Suggestions

The talent and the production materials needed for a production of "Control of Climate" can be obtained or readily simulated by the college group. The national expert used in the laboratory demonstration sequence has his local counterpart on nearly every college campus. An up-to-date film on cloud-seeding experiments can probably be obtained from Munitalp Atmospheric Research Project, R.D. No. 3, Schermerhorn Road, Schenectady, New York. Miscellaneous film clips on floods, storms, etc., may be found locally in college motion picture departments, or local television station newsreel libraries. The script may have to be altered, however, to fit the available film shots. Of course, still pictures can be substituted as illustrational matter during this last sequence. Stock shots may be obtained commercially from Tele-News and United World in New York as well as the theatrical newsreel services. The former two companies retain rights to permit actual television broadcast of their film material. An inexpensive way to obtain this film is to rent a film containing the desired material and use only a portion of it.

When first produced, "Control of Climate" originated from NBC's Hudson Theater in New York, on a stage of irregular proportions,

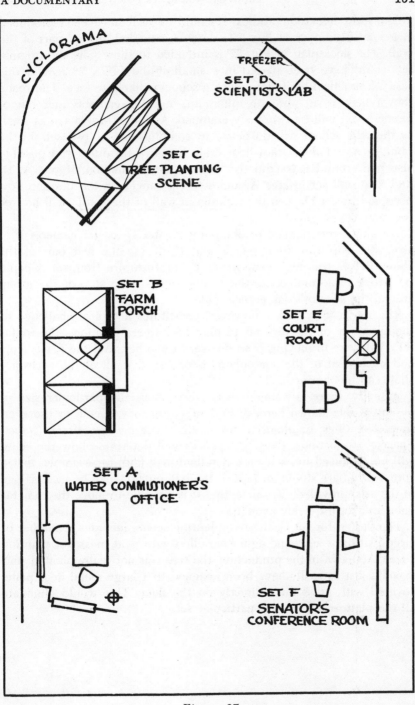

Figure 37.

unlike most television studios. It could as well have been produced in a small studio, providing a cyclorama extended around part of the wall. The floor plan in Fig. 37 is intended to show how the original sets could have been placed in a small studio (18 x 28 feet in this case), a practical limitation which a school is likely to face. The space shown here is an absolute minimum, and the cameras and microphone boom will be extremely cramped. Actually, in a space as small as this, the school will do better to combine one or two sets in the same area and delegate a floor crew to move furniture and possibly also background flats (quietly) during the production. If sets A, D, and F are all set in area A, and set E is moved to the position now occupied by set D, then the right-hand wall of the studio will be free for camera movement.

An alternative method of obtaining greater space for cameras is to strike the furniture from sets E and F, during the first part of the show. Before the final scene in set F, the furniture from set A could be struck to accommodate the camera for a wide shot of the group around the senator's conference table.

The set as it is drawn, however, constitutes a typical challenge to the ingenuity of the director to plan his camera positions, the routes they will take in moving from one set to another, and the placements and movement of the microphone boom, so that all of the necessary shots can be obtained.

Actually, there is nothing mandatory about the particular size or design of sets shown here. A student group may decide to use even simpler settings, or almost none at all in the manner of the *Cameo Theatre* productions. Existing facilities will determine how the show will be produced in each case. A school may find, for example, that a corner of a bare studio, or part of the hall outside, can be used as one of the sets, provided, of course, that it is possible to move the cameras back and forth quickly enough.

The design for set C, the tree-planting scene, includes a number of large platforms surrounding a hole filled with peat moss, for planting a tree. Actually, in the production, the tree was not really planted, and it could just as easily have been fastened to a large metal floor plate, covered with grass mats directly on the floor. This would eliminate all the platforms from this particular set.

PRODUCTION ORDERS FOR AMERICAN INVENTORY
of September 30, 1951
CONTROL OF CLIMATE
Rehearsal Schedule—Day of Show

7:00 A.M.—Set-up
. 8:00–10:00 A.M.—Camera Rehearsal
10:00–11:00   —Eat
11:00–11:25   —Film Facilities Rehearsal (Cameras Available)
11:30–12:30 P.M.—Camera Rehearsal
12:30– 1:00   —Dress Rehearsal
 1:00– 1:30   —T.P. (Lining up cameras on test pattern)
 1:30– 2:00   —Telecast
 2:00– 4:00   ⟶Breakdown

NOTE: Technical Director to be scheduled to attend dry rehearsal,
either 10:00 A.M. to 1:00 P.M. or 2:00 to 5:00 P.M., Friday,
Sept. 28th.
Floor Manager to be scheduled to attend dry rehearsal from
10 A.M. to 1 P.M *and* from 2 P.M. to 5 P.M., at rehearsal hall.

Engineering Facilities Requrements

Regular engineering equipment
 3 pedestal cameras
 1 dolly camera (Fearless Panoram)
 2 microphone booms
In addition to the regular engineering equipment, we will need the
following:
 1 extra boom mike
 1 extra camera on pedestal base
Additional Personnel:
 1 extra boom man
 1 extra cameraman

Preliminary Film Requirement Sheet

1. Orchard—orange grove with people working in it
2. Rain—rainstorm in Florida
3. Snow and ice—snow on orange grove in California, RR stuck in
 snow, skiers
4. Reservoir—empty reservoir bottom and empty spills
5. Flooded area—houses under water, people in boats
6. Forest fire

7. Desert—desolation, dry countryside
8. Tornado—Florida hurricane, rainswept scenery, palms swinging in storm
9. Impoverished people—starving people, old and young (Burmese, Chinese)
10. People in more ideal circumstances—people enjoying themselves in U. S.—handicrafts, dancing, sports

Film operations routine—for projectionist

Open in Studio—approx. 8 min.
Film, 16 mm positive, silent—approx. 5 min.
Studio—until approx. 1:55:00
Film—16 mm positive silent
Studio to fade-out

Set list—to designer

A. Office of the Water Commissioner
    1. An office three-fold with a window section and backing or Venetian blind
    2. A good-looking office desk
    3. 6 cradle type telephones on desk
    4. A swivel chair
    5. An office chair
    6. Hat rack

    In addition for a split-screen shot we shall require:

    1. 2 pieces of black velour (10′x5′) to be hung on a batten nearby
    2. 2 platforms about 30″ high
    3. 4 handpieces *only* of telephones

B. The Front Porch of a farm with pillars—painted front door— railing and—
    1. Farm-type chair
    2. Farm-type rocker

C. A small exterior set to be set in front of the cyclorama including:
    1. A suggestion of the edge of a house
    2. A small live tree
    3. Three platforms arranged to make a hole in which to plant the tree
    4. Earth and small ground cloth
    5. Grass mats to cover platforms
    6. Large can of paint marked "green"

D. A small laboratory consisting of:
  1. A two-fold
  2. A table, 4′ x 2½′, with a dark covering (drapes)
  3. A shelf on the two-fold with rack of test tubes, glass jars, etc.
  4. All other scientific equipment supplied by Dr. Schaeffer
  5. A barometer and thermometer hanging on a wall

E. A small section of a courtroom—consisting of:
  1. Three 5′ 9″ solid panelled flats—held from Westinghouse football kick-off
  2. Judge's bench
  3. Two large easels—with very firm bases
  4. Four chairs—courtroom type
  5. A small table—courtroom type—4′ x 2½′

F. A Senator's conference room, consisting of:
  1. A two-fold—discreetly pompous type
  2. A small mahogany table
  3. Four mahogany chairs
  4. Dressing as required

Hand Prop List—to Prop Department

Desk dressing	including blotter, pen-set, paper box, calendar, etc.
1 Pipe	practical
tobacco	for pipe
1 bushel basket	for unshelled peas
unshelled peas	enough to cover about 3″ of basket, which will have paper in the bottom
1 pan	to put peas in
1 paint brush	house painting size
1 toy balloon	on hand as alternate materials for scientist
1 soda-pop bottle	
1 pop-gun	child's toy type
6 pads	for taking notes
6 pencils	ordinary
1 gavel	for judge
desk dressing	for judge's bench
1 American flag	on a stand
desk dressing	for Senator's desk
2 pointers	about 3′ long
1 tube rubber cement	

CONTROL OF CLIMATE*

TEASER:

FADE IN: WATER COMMISSIONER'S OFFICE
IT CAN BE KEPT PLAIN, SMALL AND
SIMPLE. BESIDE THE USUAL DESK DRESSING,
THERE ARE ABOUT SIX TO EIGHT PHONES ON
HIS DESK.

(THERE IS, UNDER AND IN BG, AN
INCESSANT RINGING OF THE PHONES --
IN DIFFERENT TONES AND PITCH)

A SIGN ON THE DESK PROCLAIMS THE FACT
THAT THE MAN BEHIND IT IS THE WATER
COMMISSIONER. THE LATTER, A STOUT,
BALDISH, AMIABLE LOOKING MAN, IS
HARRASSEDLY PICKING UP ONE PHONE, THEN
ANOTHER, AND TALKING INTO THEM.

S.EFF:
PHONE
BELLS

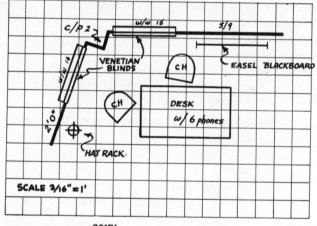

COMM:

UNDER

(SOMEWHAT HEATEDLY) Well, what do you

want me to do about it? I'm only the

Water Commissioner in this city.

(IMPATIENT PAUSE) I can't help it if

you're in the car washing business --

this is an emergency! You'll just have

to curtail your operations.

(SLAMS DOWN RECEIVER, PICKS UP ANOTHER)

Yes?

(LISTENS A BREATH, THEN WITH AN
IMPATIENT TWIST OF HIS BODY)
                                    -1-

* Written by Thomas J. Adams
  Reproduced through courtesy of Teleprograms, Inc. and Sloan Foundation

No -- you can't turn on the air-

conditioning in your movie house! It

uses water, doesn't it?

(PUTS RECEIVER DOWN, PICKS UP ANOTHER)

Water Commissioner...

       COMM: (CONT'D)

(LISTENS A MOMENT AS HE RUNS HIS HAND
OVER HIS BALD HEAD. THEN)

No -- you can't sprinkle your lawn!

(START FADING HIM SLOWLY AND SLOWLY
BRINGING SOUND OF PHONE BELLS UP AND
OVER)

There's a water shortage! There hasn't

been enough rain! Did I order the

weather? Do I control the climate?

(HIS MOUTH KEEPS MOVING AS BELLS COME
FULL UP)

*UP &
X TO
MUSIC-
THEME
FULL*

*1 CU
BOOKS
&
BACK ON
CUE*

0:30 (MUSIC: THEME)

(DISSOLVE TO BOOKCASE. NARRATOR TAKES
OUT TITLE BOOK AND HOLDS IT TO CAMERA.)

(AFTER ESTABLISHING, DOLLY BACK AS
NARRATOR STEPS IN FRONT OF BOOKCASE
HE TURNS THE BOOK TO LOOK AT TITLE,
THEN OPENS IT TO A SPOT TO READ.)

       NARR:

UNDER

0:45 The control of climate .. the ability

to fashion climatic and weather

conditions that best suit our welfare

and economic development...

(LOOKS UP AT CAMERA) What an idea...

if it works.

(SLIGHT PAUSE) (CLOSES BOOK, HOLDS
IT AGAINST HIS BODY WITH HIS ARMS
CROSSED)

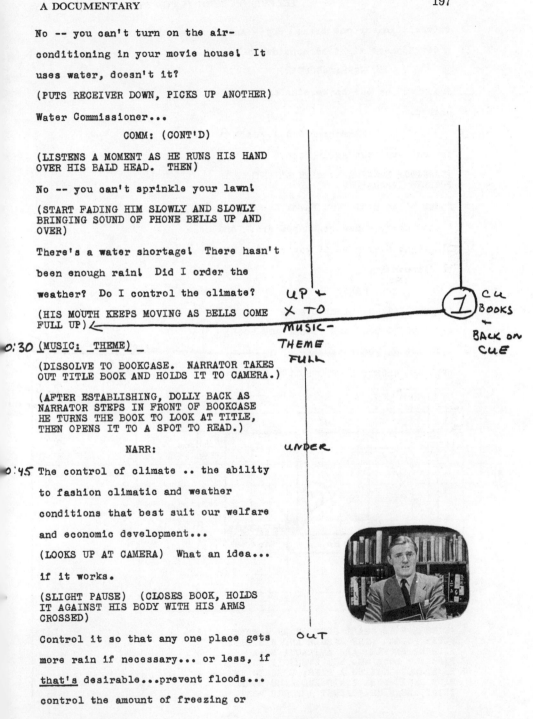

OUT

Control it so that any one place gets

more rain if necessary... or less, if

that's desirable...prevent floods...

control the amount of freezing or

snowfall in any one area. Why-- such

a development might be considered as

                NARR: (CONT'D)

important as the harnessing of atomic

energy...

01:10   FARMER: (O.S.) Boom A

You can say that again, son..

(NARRATOR LOOKS O.S. WITH SLIGHTLY
PUZZLED EXPRESSION)

Speakin' as a man who farms for a livin'

I know exactly how right you are. And

I'm right over here if you're of a mind

to discuss it...

                NARR:

(NODS) I'll be right over..

(TURNING TO BOOKCASE TO REPLACE BOOK)

01:25 Just let me put this away... ←   WIPE TO →   ③
                                                  MUSIC
(MUSIC: SHORT, LIGHT, BOUNCY BRIDGE)   IN FULL

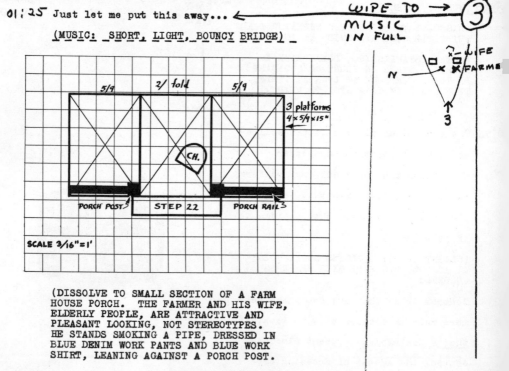

(DISSOLVE TO SMALL SECTION OF A FARM
HOUSE PORCH. THE FARMER AND HIS WIFE,
ELDERLY PEOPLE, ARE ATTRACTIVE AND
PLEASANT LOOKING, NOT STEREOTYPES.
HE STANDS SMOKING A PIPE, DRESSED IN
BLUE DENIM WORK PANTS AND BLUE WORK
SHIRT, LEANING AGAINST A PORCH POST.

                -3-

SHE, DRESSED IN A PRETTY COTTON DRESS,
SITS WITH A BUSHEL OF UNSHELLED PEAS
AT HER FEET UNSHELLING THEM IN A PAN
WHICH RESTS IN HER LAP. AN EMPTY FARM
CHAIR WHICH THE NARRATOR WILL OCCUPY
IS NEAR HERS)

UNDER

                    FARMER:

You made a pretty big statement for a

young feller. Just want you to

realize how important what you said

is to a farmer.

OUT

(LOOKS O.S. IN DIRECTION FROM WHICH
NARRATOR WILL ENTER)

(NARRATOR ENTERS NEAR VACANT CHAIR)

                    NARR:

Hello. You wanted to talk to me?

                    WIFE:

(LOOKS UP, SMILES)

Won't you sit down?

(NARRATOR LOOKS FROM CHAIR TO FARMER.

LATTER GESTURES WITH HIS PIPE)

                    FARMER:

Don't worry 'bout me -- just set.

(NARRATOR SITS)

Were you serious just now when you

got talkin' 'bout really controllin'

weather and climate? 'Cause weather's

never a joke to anyone in the farmin'

business...seems to be a joke to   *4*

everyone else, though. For instance..   1. CARTOON: Cloud drenching

Take those radio and TV fellows,   farmer - *BOARD (A)*

FARMER: (CONT'D)

laughin' about the drought over in   2. CARTOON: Radio   **PAN TO (B)**

one part of the country -- kiddin'   --smog, fog, drizzle

about the smog over another -- or   **(B)**

havin' themselves a time 'bout a

rainy spell in some other place   **PAN TO (C)**

T'ain't funny at all, my boy --

hundreds of people are probably   3. CARTOON: TV - dry spell,

losin' their livelihoods, bein'   drought **(C)**

wiped out...   **③ 3 SHC**

NARR: ~~WIPE BACK TO LIVE~~

Well, -- everybody kids about the

weather, I guess. No one means any

harm by it.

WIFE:

Tell the young man about Cousin George,

Andy...   **①**

FARMER: **2 SHOT**

(NODDING) Relative of mine...lived in   **FARMER &**

what came to be called the dust bowl   **WIFE &**

back in the '30's. You must be old   **INTO CU**

enough to remember that, young fellow.   **FARMER**

(NARRATOR NODS)   **ON CUE**

Sand and grit gettin' into everybody's

lives -- Ruinin' everything. Hundreds,

maybe thousands, of people bein'

driven from their homes like from a

plague. Cousin George was one of 'em...

-5-

                              WIFE:

It was terrible...
                              FARMER: *IN TO CU*
                                                               FARMER
George saved what he could and took

it with him -- to California. Took

him ten years o' hirin' out before

he could get himself another farm.

Went into raisin' oranges. Did

pretty well.

(PAUSES TO KNOCK ASHES OUT OF HIS PIPE)
(BOTH NARRATOR AND WIFE WAIT EXPECTANTLY)

33:00 Last year they had one o' them sudden

cold spells in his section...the kind

them fellers I mentioned joke about.

Cleaned George out of every nickel he

had. He's waitin' till I sell my crop

this fall so's he can borrow money to

get started again.   ③ 3 SHOT
                              WIFE:

Got to take the weather seriously

when your life and living depends on

it....
                              NARR:

How have *you* been doing?
                              FARMER:

(TURNS TO HIM)

Not bad this year. The summer's been

kinda dry. I raise bing cherries and

they like it dry, sorta. Should do

pretty well financially 'round market-

ing time.   -6-

                    WIFE:

'Less there's an early frost....

                    FARMER:

Or heavy rains and winds just around

pickin' season...

                    NARR:

(RISING)

No wonder you're so interested in

the subject of weather control.

You're constantly at the mercy of

the elements, aren't you?

                    FARMER:

It's not just myself I'm thinkin' about.   WIPE TO CARTOON BOX

It's a matter of economics -- big   CARTOON: Farmer and

economics. Farmers like me make up at   City fellow --   CARTOON

least half the country's economy --   dollars which are   BOX

maybe more. When we're hit hard by   scratched out   "BAD CROP

bad climate conditions, we ain't the   ROUTINE"

only ones that lose money. Crops we

have to sell are scarce. The farmer,

having less to sell, makes less money

even when he charges more. That means

he has less to spend on the things he

wants to buy from the city folks. That

means they get less from the farmer.

And once that business starts -- then

everybody's in trouble. Nobody's

making any money and business all

over the country comes to a standstill

                        -7-

                                                                                3 SH

                    COMM: (O.S.)

Send that fellow to me -- I'll tell   ~~WIPE~~ BACK TO LIVE

him some more things about trouble

with weather -- in the city.

                    FARMER:

That's the water commissioner. Might

be interestin' for you to hear what

he has to say...

                    NARR:

Sure....←—————————————————————————— WIPE TO ——→ ②

(MUSIC: SAME SHORT, LIGHT, BOUNCY   MUSIC IN   MCU ON
BRIDGE AS BEFORE)   FULL   COMM. AT
                                                             DESK. D.B.
(AS NARRATOR LEAVES FRAME, FARMER SITS   ON CUE
DOWN BESIDE HIS WIFE, DISSOLVE TO
WATER COMMISSIONER AT HIS DESK.)

(SOUND: PHONE RINGS)
(HE IS MUCH MORE RELAXED AS HE PICKS
UP THE PHONE, PUTS HIS FEET UP ON THE
DESK AND SPEAKS INTO MOUTHPIECE)

                    COMM:

Yes, Mayor..? (SLIGHT PAUSE) According   UNDER

to latest reports we're holding our own.   OUT

(SLIGHT PAUSE. NARRATOR ENTERS MEANWHILE
AND IS GESTURED TO TAKE THE CHAIR NEXT TO
THE DESK)

05:00 Yes - should have the answer in about an   D.B. TO
                                                            INCLUDE NAR.
hour from now.

(COMM. HANGS UP PHONE, SITS UP STRAIGHT
AT DESK)

By George, have I been having a summer!

Everything was fine until it looked as

if the reservoirs were going to run

dry, then everybody got panicky.

                         -8-

COMM: (CONT'D)

Can you imagine a city the size of mine
suddenly having to do without water?

NARR:

I can imagine the terrific health problem
there would be -- no water to drink, to
use for washing, cleaning and all the
other things. I don't see how the city
could exist.

COMM:

It couldn't. But fortunately things
haven't gone quite that far around here.
Apart from having to ask everyone to cut
down on the amount of water they used,
one of the worst things we've had to
face was the economic angle... no car
washing...no commercial laundries...
some business wiped out by the drought.
Nature can literally wipe you out...
unless you can get nature to work for
you.

NARR:

Can it be done?

COMM:

(TAKES HAT FROM HATRACK WHICH IS CLOSE
BY AND PUTS IT ON) I'm going over to
see a man who thinks so right now.
Professor Schaefer of the G.E. Lab.
06:00 Like to come along? We'll stop for a
minute at another place on the way over.

-9-

COMM: (CONT'D)

Want to show you another little

experiment in weather control.... ← WIPE TO →

MUSIC IN
FULL

(DISSOLVE AS NARRATOR RISES AND COMM.
TAKES HIM BY THE ARM TO LEAD HIM OFF)

(MUSIC:_ BRIGHT_BRIDGE_AGAIN)

①

C.U. TREE
BASE. BACK
TO SHOW
PAINT CAN.
BACK TO
2 SHOT

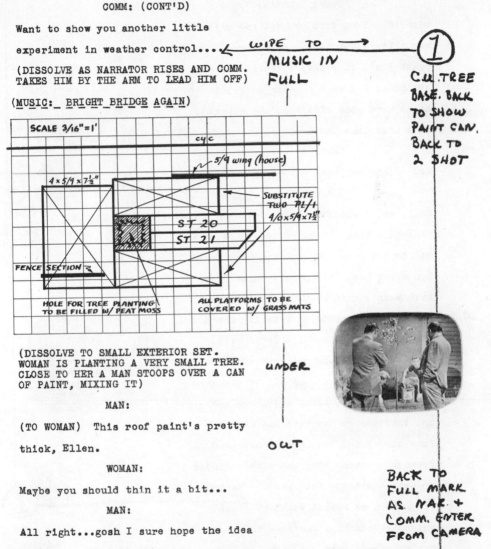

SCALE 3/16"=1'

c/c

5/9 wing (house)

4 x 5/9 x 7½"

SUBSTITUTE
TWO PL/1
4/0 x 5/9 x 7½"

ST 20
ST 21

FENCE SECTION

HOLE FOR TREE PLANTING
TO BE FILLED W/ PEAT MOSS

ALL PLATFORMS TO BE
COVERED W/ GRASS MATS

(DISSOLVE TO SMALL EXTERIOR SET.
WOMAN IS PLANTING A VERY SMALL TREE.
CLOSE TO HER A MAN STOOPS OVER A CAN
OF PAINT, MIXING IT)

UNDER

        MAN:

(TO WOMAN) This roof paint's pretty

thick, Ellen.   OUT

        WOMAN:

Maybe you should thin it a bit...

        MAN:

All right...gosh I sure hope the idea

works.

(NARR. AND COMM. ENTER OPPOSITE SIDE
OF FRAME. COMM. STOPS NARRATOR)

        COMM:

This is a little experiment we've

just put into operation around here --

BACK TO
FULL MARK
AS. NAR. +
COMM. ENTER
FROM CAMERA

COMM: (CONT'D)

kind of a long term project you might

say. The Mayor heard that if you

plant trees in a city wherever you can

and paint houses a certain color, it

might have some effect on the climate.

Ever hear that yourself?

NARR:

No. Can't say that I have...

COMM:

Well, as he explains it, rain doesn't   WIPE TO CARTOON BOX   CARTOON B

fall on a desert because the white sand   "REFLECTION

reflects the heat of the sun back into   ROUTINE"

the air. Now, it's a well-known fact

that when air is heated it expands,

07:00 and when it expands it gets lighter and

rises. Over a desert it could rise

with such force and pressure as to keep

any rain or rain clouds out of the area.

Whereas you take trees and grass and so

on, they absorb the heat and keep the

free air around that area cooler and

fresher. Clouds come and stay -- under

proper conditions they rain -- making

for much more normal weather. That's

why we're planting trees -- to help

mother nature bring us rain.   WIPE TO LIVE

(CALLS TO MAN WHO IS STILL MIXING
PAINT)

What you got there, John?

-11-

          MAN:

Roof paint, Commissioner. Green

paint -- green as grass...

          COMM:

(TO NARRATOR) All part of the same

idea. Now let's go see Dr. Schaefer.. *WIPE TO →* ③ *ON MARK*

(THEY EXIT)   *MUSIC IN FULL*

(MUSIC: SAME HAPPY, CAREFREE BRIDGE)

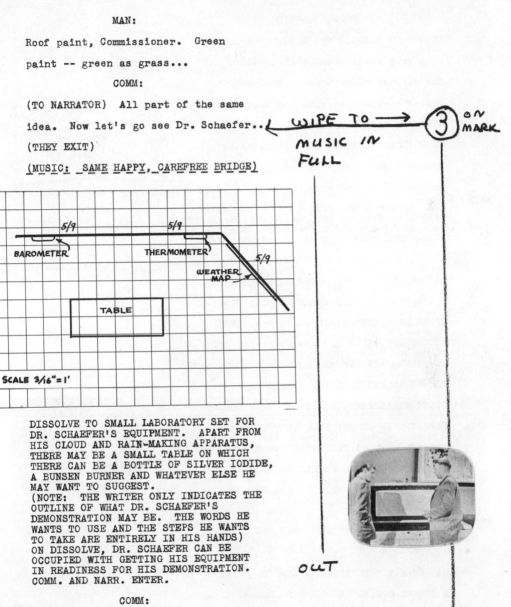

BAROMETER   5/9   THERMOMETER   5/9

                              WEATHER MAP   5/9

          TABLE

SCALE 3/16"=1'

OUT

DISSOLVE TO SMALL LABORATORY SET FOR
DR. SCHAEFER'S EQUIPMENT. APART FROM
HIS CLOUD AND RAIN-MAKING APPARATUS,
THERE MAY BE A SMALL TABLE ON WHICH
THERE CAN BE A BOTTLE OF SILVER IODIDE,
A BUNSEN BURNER AND WHATEVER ELSE HE
MAY WANT TO SUGGEST.
(NOTE: THE WRITER ONLY INDICATES THE
OUTLINE OF WHAT DR. SCHAEFER'S
DEMONSTRATION MAY BE. THE WORDS HE
WANTS TO USE AND THE STEPS HE WANTS
TO TAKE ARE ENTIRELY IN HIS HANDS)
ON DISSOLVE, DR. SCHAEFER CAN BE
OCCUPIED WITH GETTING HIS EQUIPMENT
IN READINESS FOR HIS DEMONSTRATION.
COMM. AND NARR. ENTER.

          COMM:

07:30
Dr. Schaefer -- I'd like you to meet

a friend of mine --

COMM: (CONT'D)

(TURNS TO NARR.) Dr. Schaefer has made

some very significant contributions to

the subject of weather control as a

research scientist with the General

Electric Research Laboratory... (TURNS

TO DOCTOR) Now, sir, if you will be

good enough to show me how rain can be

produced when and where we might need it..

08:00

(DR. SCHAEFER MAY PICK THIS UP BY SAYING
THAT RAIN MAY, AS YET, ONLY BE MADE IN THE
LABORATORY "ON ORDER," BUT NOT NECESSARILY
EVERYWHERE ELSE. HE MAY POINT OUT THAT:

1. RAIN-MAKING ON A BROAD BASIS IS STILL

LARGELY IN THE EXPERIMENTAL STAGES. THAT

WHILE SOME RESULTS UNDER CERTAIN CONDI-

TIONS HAVE BEEN ACHIEVED IN THE FREE

ATMOSPHERE, MUCH REMAINS TO BE LEARNED.

2. THERE ARE CERTAIN PHENOMENA WHICH CAN

BE DEMONSTRATED IN THE LAB, HOWEVER.

USING HIS APPARATUS, HE MAY SHOW CLOUD

FORMATION. HE MAY THEN ILLUSTRATE AND

EXPLAIN WHAT HAPPENS WHEN THE TEMPERATURE

OF THE CLOUD HE'S FASHIONED IS REDUCED

BY THE EXPANSION OF AIR RELEASED FROM A:

A) TOY BALLOON

B) COCA COLA BOTTLE

C) POP-GUN

3. HE MAY THEN EXPLAIN WHAT IS MEANT BY

A "SUPER-COOLED" CLOUD AND ICE-NUCLEI AND

WHAT IS THE RESULT UNDER CERTAIN CONDITIONS.

Roll FILM

SCHAEFER moves ~~FILM~~ *TO DEEP FREEZE*

WHEN UP ⟶ Ⓕ

-13-

HE MAY RELATE HOW HE HAPPENED TO LEARN

THE EFFECT DRY-ICE HAD UPON A "SUPER-

COOLED" CLOUD AND HOW THIS LED TO THE

"SEEDING" OF CLOUDS BY AIRCRAFT.

OPTIONAL: G.E. FILM SHOWING EFFECT OF
CLOUD SEEDING MAY BE USED TO ILLUSTRATE
REMARKS.

4. HE MAY THEN EXPLAIN HIS ASSOCIATE'S

(DR. VONNEGUT'S) CONTRIBUTION -- "RAIN

BY FIRE" -- WHICH YIELDED SIMILAR BUT

MORE EFFECTIVE RESULTS. FIRST WITH

CHARCOAL, THEN WITH THE SILVER IODIDE

BURNED IN A HYDROGEN FLAME.

5. AND, IN CONCLUSION, HE MAY EXPLAIN

BRIEFLY HOW DR. LANGMUIR SUCCEEDED IN

"PROJECT CIRRUS" IN NEW MEXICO AND HOW

OTHERS HAVE SUCCEEDED ELSEWHERE ALSO.

HIS CONCLUSION MAY BE THAT WHILE PROGRESS

HAS BEEN MADE MUCH HAS YET TO BE LEARNED

IN THE CONTROL OF WEATHER AND CLIMATE)

LAST SCENE:
EXPANDING
CLOUDS (20 SEC)

       COMM:

(AT END OF DR. SCHAEFER'S REMARKS.   LIVE
PULLS OUT PAPER AND PENCIL AND STANDS
READY TO TAKE NOTES)

② TIGHT
2 SHOT
OF
SCHAEF
+ COMM.

#5:00 Thanks, Dr. Schaefer -- ~~now there are~~ BUT AREN'T THERE a

few problems which can come out of any

organized control of climate... some

law suits, for example.

① MCU
JUDGE

       JUDGE: (O.S.)

Matter of fact, we have a sample case

based on a problem like that just about

ready to start right now..

② AS
ABOVE

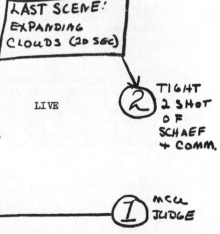

COMM:

(TO NARR) Why not go over and see

what the judge is talking about...? ← *WIPE TO →* ①*MCU*
                                                      JUDGE
(MUSIC:_ HAPPY,_CAREFREE BRIDGE)   *MUSIC IN*   *D.B TO*
                                         FULL   *INCLUDE*
                                                      NAR.

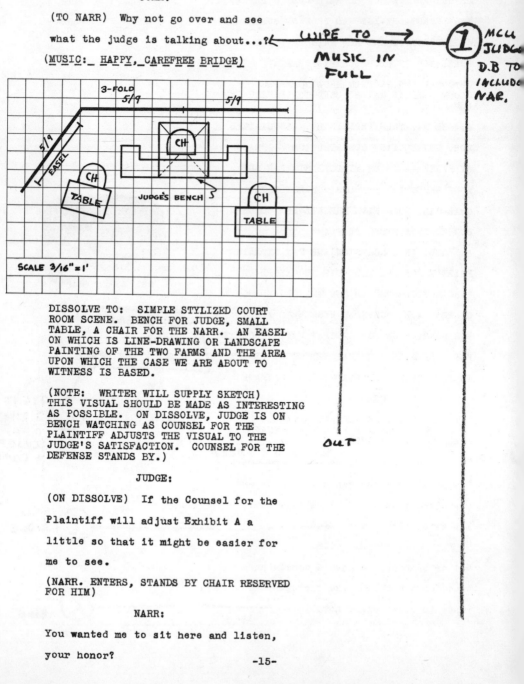

DISSOLVE TO: SIMPLE STYLIZED COURT
ROOM SCENE. BENCH FOR JUDGE, SMALL
TABLE, A CHAIR FOR THE NARR. AN EASEL
ON WHICH IS LINE-DRAWING OR LANDSCAPE
PAINTING OF THE TWO FARMS AND THE AREA
UPON WHICH THE CASE WE ARE ABOUT TO
WITNESS IS BASED.

(NOTE: WRITER WILL SUPPLY SKETCH)
THIS VISUAL SHOULD BE MADE AS INTERESTING
AS POSSIBLE. ON DISSOLVE, JUDGE IS ON
BENCH WATCHING AS COUNSEL FOR THE
PLAINTIFF ADJUSTS THE VISUAL TO THE   *OUT*
JUDGE'S SATISFACTION. COUNSEL FOR THE
DEFENSE STANDS BY.)

            JUDGE:

(ON DISSOLVE) If the Counsel for the

Plaintiff will adjust Exhibit A a

little so that it might be easier for

me to see.

(NARR. ENTERS, STANDS BY CHAIR RESERVED
FOR HIM)

            NARR:

You wanted me to sit here and listen,

your honor?
                                    -15-

JUDGE:

As a member of the American public, you
might be vitally interested and
concerned, I should imagine. Have a
seat, young man.

NARR:

(SITTING) Thank you, Judge.

JUDGE:

We are about to demonstrate by means
of a purely hypothetical case the age-old
axiom that when man learns to solve one
problem, he generally finds he has
created others.... (TO PLAINTIFF'S
LAWYER) Now if the Counsel for the
Plaintiff will proceed.

(NOTE: BOTH COUNSELS WILL USE THE
VISUAL PROVIDED TO ILLUSTRATE THEIR
ARGUMENTS. CAMERA WILL CONCERN ITSELF
PRIMARILY WITH THE VISUAL)

PLAIN:

Your honor -- as the briefs submitted
will indicate, my client, Mr. Fayerweather
has a hundred thousand acre farm which
adjoins the defendant's, Mr. Wetmore's
60,000 acre farm here on the east. It
should be noted for the record that the
plaintiff, Mr. Fayerweather, is primarily
engaged in the raising of stock and farm
products which he sells on the market for
a profit. Mr. Wetmore, on the other hand,
is engaged in the business of raising

④

CARTOON BOX

~~WIPE TO~~ CARTOON BOX

16:00

                              PLAIN: (CONT'D)

sapling pine, a tree which, upon
reaching maturity -- is generally sold
for lumber. Referring to Exhibit A
again, we can see there is on the
western boundary of the defendant's
property a body of water called, The
Great Lake. Now normally and naturally
clouds rise on the eastern shore of
Great Lake, travel eastward over the
low-land of Mr. Wetmore's farm and are
trapped by the hills which bound Mr.
Fayerweather's land here on the east.
Not being able to pass over these hills
without giving up some of their water,
they quite naturally spill a good deal
of it down on my client's land. In
fact, your honor, there are records to
show that before the illegal inter-
17:00 ference of Mr. Wetmore and his rain-
making devices, my client's land
enjoyed an average yearly rainfall
of 29.73 inches while that over
Wetmore's land was a mere 18.22 inches!

                              DEF: ~~WIPE~~ TO LIVE   3 SHOT

Your honor, we admit that the facts
submitted are still correct, but we
take exception to Counsel's use of the
term, illegal in regard to our client!

                              -17-

A DOCUMENTARY   213

             PLAIN:

How else could one define an act which

has not only deprived a man of his

normal business profits, but turned his

entire business into a loss!

             JUDGE:

(RAPS GAVEL ONCE LIGHTLY)

Gentlemen. (TO PLAIN) Please go on

with the facts...   ① MCU. PLAIN,

             PLAIN:

Up until a year ago, sir, my client's

farm had an adequate supply of rainfall,

while it is evident from Mr. Wetmore's

actions that his did not. In an effort   WIPE TO CARTOON BOX   ④ CARTOON BOX

to improve this situation, the defendant

proceeded to contract the services of

Rain Control, Incorporated -- a rain-

making organization -- to intercept the

clouds that passed over his property --

clouds that normally spilled their

rainfall on Mr. Fayerweather's property

-- and had them seeded with dry-ice

18:00   from above and silver iodide from below.

The net result, your honor, was that the

average annual rainfall on my client's

land has been cut in half, and because

of this he has personally suffered losses

in farm crops and farm stock amounting

to the sum of $16,000! That is the sum   ① 3 SHOT

for which we are suing the defendant,

                        -18-

PLAIN: (CONT'D)

and we are asking the court to enjoin
the defendant from continuing to deny
my client his legal and natural rights!   ~~WIPE TO LIVE~~

    DEF:

Your honor...!

    JUDGE:

Let Counsel for the Plaintiff continue
with the arguments upon which he bases
his suit...

    PLAIN:

We base our case on two legal contentions:
the doctrine of prior appropriation and
the doctrine of natural rights. As the   ④ CARTOON BOX
court well knows, the doctrine of prior
appropriation -- which is the common   ~~WIPE~~ TO CARTOON BOX:
law in most states and the enacted law
in many -- states that the first party
19:00   to put a source of water to beneficial

use thereby acquires a legally protected
right to the continued use of that water.
Our contention is that rainfall is
definitely a source of water --(PAUSE)
agricultural water in this instance --
and the plaintiff, Mr. Fayerweather, has
definitely put the water his land has
been receiving to a beneficial use --
farming and the breeding of stock.

    -19-

① 2 SHOT JUDGE + PLAINTIFF

                    JUDGE:

(TO NARR) Clear so far?   ~~WIPE TO LIVE~~

                    NARR:

Thank you, your honor, very clear...

                    JUDGE:

(TO PLAIN) Proceed...   ③ MCU PLAIN.

                    PLAIN:

Your honor -- ~~let us~~ turn to an

appraisal of a doctrine which has

influenced the thought and action of

free men everywhere -- the doctrine

of "natural rights." One of these --

recognized in this country from its

very inception -- is the right of a

landowner to freely enjoy the use of

his land without the interference of

his neighbor. And who, in this case,

has interfered? Mr. Wetmore has

interfered to the extent of a $16,000

loss to the plaintiff! He has

interfered until now the plaintiff's

property is threatened with tragic

20:00 devaluation! The court must intervene!   ④   CARTOON BOX

The court must stop this cloud-seeding,   CARTOON BOX

this cloud-stealing, this selfish

destruction of one man by another!

Not just bankruptcy to my client, Mr.

Fayerweather, but disruption of the

entire farming industry! The complete

destruction of land values everywhere!   ① 3 SHOT JUDGE + LAWYERS

(STOPS, PAUSE. THEN QUIETLY)

                    -20-

PLAIN: (CONT'D)

If it please the court, we ask that it be

ordered, judged, and decreed that John

Fayerweather recover of Henry Wetmore

the sum of $16,000 damages, together with

costs; and that Henry Wetmore be per-

manently enjoined and restrained from   ~~LIVE~~

interfering with any clouds which pass

over his land.

(HE SITS DOWN. THE JUDGE TURNS TO NARR)

JUDGE:

Since this is simply a hypothetical case,

I can dispense with the rules of procedure

and ask if you have any questions up to

this point.

NARR:

What's the other side of the story, your

honor?

JUDGE:

(TO DEF) Will the Counsel for the

Defense begin...?

DEF:

Your honor -- may I say that I am not a

little surprised at Counsel's ignorance

21'00 of the law, of his distortion of the

true application of the Doctrine of

Prior Appropriation. Certainly it has

been accepted -- at least until a

law is enacted that states otherwise --

that the first man to take water and put

**IN TO MCU
DEF. ATTY.**

-21-

                    DEF: (CONT'D)

it to beneficial use has prior claim

to that water. We don't deny that.

But what kind of water? Where? Doesn't

plaintiff's counsel know -- or is he

purposely forgetting -- that the

doctrine is only applied to water in

streams...water flowing in a definite

channel...a watercourse such as a

creek with banks? Does he argue that

cumulus clouds, which produce most of   ④ CARTOON

our rainfall, fall into that category?   BOX

How naive can he be? For he has

implied in his arguments that his

client, Mr. Fayerweather, has an

ownership in certain clouds -- an

ownership which he is asking this

court to protect. On what legal basis?

And which clouds? Who anywhere can say

which clouds are his and which are not?

                                                              BIG CLOUD --

22:00   Mr. Fayerweather also claims that he   BIRD AND AIRPLANE

has been deprived of a benefit to

which he has a legal right -- natural

rainfall. And he asks that the court

protect him in this right. I'd like

to ask Mr. Fayerweather what he intends

doing when a stray airplane or a flock

of birds disturb his precious clouds --

these, too, could affect rainfall and

could very possibly affect his annual

                          -22-

DEF: (CONT'D)

average. Does he intend bringing suit

against every plane and bird that passes

over his land? And as to the argument

WIPE TO LIVE

about beneficial use, your honor, may I

point out the act that <u>my</u> client is

engaged in the production of trees for

lumber -- a scarce commodity -- with a

war in Korea and defense preparations

here, an important commodity -- a vital

commodity!

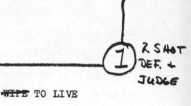

(DEF. MOVES TO EXHIBIT A TO ILLUSTRATE
HIS REMARKS)

Your honor -- no one can live in an

organized society without <u>legally</u>

suffering or doing some injury to his

own or another's rights! If I own a

building, does that mean no one can

build one next to mine because it may

mean shutting off some of my light?

23:00 If I have a business, can't someone

else open the same business because it

may be the harm or even ruin of mine?

Can't I dig a well which may dry up all

the others in the neighborhood and still

not suffer legally? The court knows I

can. And if I can legally do this

underground, why can't I legally do it

above the ground -- with the clouds?

(CHANGE OF PACE. BRISKLY)

-23-

                    DEF: (CONT'D)

If it please the court -- the defense

asks that plaintiff's complaint be

dismissed on the grounds that the

facts do not constitute a claim upon

which relief can be granted.

(DEF. SITS. JUDGE RAPS GAVEL, RISES)

                    JUDGE:

Court stands adjourned until further

notice...

(PLAIN. AND DEF. RISE)

Gentlemen, I think you both have done

very well...good-day...

(THEY NOD AND EXIT. JUDGE IS ABOUT
TO EXIT WHEN HE NOTICES NARR. WAITING)

That's all there is, young man... the

trial is over....

                    NARR:

But I don't understand, sir. Don't

you normally render a verdict?

                    JUDGE:

Normally, yes. But this business of

controlling weather and climate is

much too new for me to follow normal

24:00 procedure. Suppose I sustained the

plaintiff's claims? Suppose I said

he had a right to the clouds which

normally came over his property? I'd

be establishing a precedent of far --

far-reaching importance. I might be

JUDGE: (CONT'D)

interpreted as saying in effect that
no man has the right to improve himself
or the condition of his land. My
verdict might lead to a million suits
all based on vague and insoluble claims.
No. Rain-making is a problem that
ultimately will have to be handled by
the state and federal legislatures, I'm
afraid. You see, as judge I only
interpret the law. It is up to the
legislatures to write them.

NARR:

I see. Anyone in the process of doing
that right now?

JUDGE:

Senator West, down the hall, is
exploring the matter. You might ask
him...

NARR:

25:00 Thank you, Judge. And it's been a
pleasure ...

(AS NARR. TURNS AND EXITS, HOLD ON
JUDGE SMILING AND NODDING)

WIPE TO ⟶ ④ M S.
MUSIC IN   SENATO
FULL   + GUES
            NAR. W
            IN.

(MUSIC: _ BRIDGE) _

(DISSOLVE TO SMALL CONFERENCE ROOM
WITH SMALL TABLE FOR SENATOR, CHAIR
FOR HIM AND THREE VISITORS. FARMER
AND HIS WIFE ARE ALREADY SEATED,
BACKS TO CAMERA AND FACING SENATOR
WEST. LATTER LOOKS UP)

OUT

WEST:

Come in, young man, I've been

WEST: (CONT'D)

expecting you.... You know these two

constituents of mine? We're all

vitally interested in weather control

now....

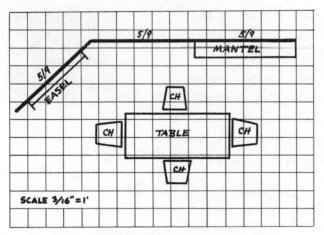

SCALE 3/16"=1'

NARR:

To tell you the truth, what I'm

interested in learning is how we are

going to control the controllers? ⟵——————————————————③ MCU FARMER

FARMER:

That's right. What happens to me if

that Water Commissioner, for example,

gets it raining good and hard over

my cherry orchards? What do I do --

sit back and take it? ⟵——————————————————④ CU SENATOR

WEST:

For the present, I'm afraid yes.

Legislatures won't act, probably,

until weather-making is practiced on

a larger scale than it is now.

WEST: (CONT'D)

But new developments in science always
bring benefits to the many and injury
to some. Legislators try to protect
the rights of the few, but it is the
vast benefits to the vast majority that
must be given the strongest consideration.

(BEGIN SLOW DOLLY IN ON HIM FOR CU)

26:00 For example, when and if atomic energy
is ever applied as power for automobiles,
producers of gasoline will undoubtedly be
affected. Talking pictures and television
had their effects on related means of
entertainment and communication. Thus
weather-making will have its effects.
But just think of the impact weather and
climate control will have on the
American and world economy! Visualize
with me the tremendous results we may
be able to accomplish!

ROLL FILM

(F)

(DISSOLVE TO FILM)

(1. SHOT OF ORCHARD)

Where for economic reasons it is to our
advantage to keep an area dry, we may
be able, with further knowledge and
technological development, to keep
rainfall away.

(2. RAINFALL FALLING ON AN AREA)

And where, for other economic reasons
it will be advantageous to induce more

-27-

                        WEST: (CONT'D)
rainfall -- even excessive rainfall --
we already have indications that we may
be able to do that.
(3. SHOT OF RESERVOIR)
We may be able to solve water shortage
problems for every village, town and
city in the country.
(4. WINTER SPORTS, SNOW AND ICE)
There will be certain places where we
will want to dispel ice, snow and
frost. There also will be others
where we will want to induce it. Using
our new knowledge and with techniques
that will grow with the years, we
should be able to prevent this....
(5. FLOODED AREA)
And this...
(6. FOREST FIRE)
This...
(7. DESERT)
As well as this....
(8. TORNADO, HURRICANE DAMAGE)
(9. SHOTS OF IMPOVERISHED PEOPLE OF
27:00 THE WORLD -- EQUATORIAL, ESKIMO, ETC...)
We should be able to provide more food
and better living conditions for
millions -- everywhere. Modern research
has established the existence of a
strong tie between medicine and meteorology --
                        -28-

(10. PEOPLE IN MUCH MORE IDEAL
CIRCUMSTANCES AND CONDITION)

        WEST: (CONT'D)

Knowing this, and knowing how to
control these conditions, we may be
able to promote only that type of
climate which contributes to the
fertility of man's mind and body,
his happiness, and to the length of
his life. No wonder it has been said
that the new yet undeveloped capacity
of man to control climate is as
important a step forward as the
harnessing of atomic energy.

(DISSOLVE BACK TO SENATOR)

I have purposely omitted the military
aspects of this subject -- such
things as creating floods to hamper
enemy troops, promoting icing
conditions to divert enemy aircraft
and the like. All of these carry
their own problems and are a separate
subject. But the total aspect of
climate control is a picture of a
better, fuller, richer life -- for
everyone.

(MUSIC: THEME)

TELOP: BOOKCASE, AMERICAN INVENTORY.
(DISSOLVE TO MORGAN, LIVE, ON SET)

        MORGAN:

28:00

This is Ray Morgan, to tell you about

// -29-

[handwritten annotations: 4 CU SENATOR; ROLL RECORD CLOSE; UNDER; UP FULL + OUT; TO BLACK; 2 MCU RAY]

MORGAN: (CONT'D)

some of the things you saw in today's
American Inventory program. Our cast
included Bob Middleton, Franklin Fox,
Will Hussung, Charles Eggleston; Myrtle
Ferguson, Nelson Olmstead, James Russo,
Bob Lansing and Vera Massey. Our
special guest this afternoon was Dr.
Vincent Schaefer of the General
Electric Laboratories in Schenectady,
New York. We are indebted for the
film used in this program to the Hayden
Planetarium, New York City. We are
also indebted to the General Electric
Company, and to Dr. Henry G. Houghton
of the Massachusetts Institute of
Technology. The case used in this
afternoon's American Inventory was
based on research furnished us by the
Junior Committee of the Association of
the Bar of the City of New York. Next
week at this same time American
Inventory will bring you _____

28:30

DISSOLVE TO:

> TELOP: TELEPROGRAMS, INC.
>
> TELOP: ALFRED P. SLOAN
>   FOUNDATION
>
> TELOP: IN COOPERATION WITH
>   NBC-TV

29:25

-o-o-o-o-o-o-o-o-

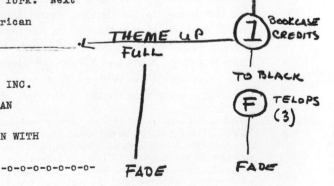

THEME UP
FULL

① BOOKCASE
CREDITS

TO BLACK

Ⓕ TELOPS
(3)

FADE   FADE

-30-

12. A Family Drama

"THE NIGHT THE ANIMALS TALKED" * from *MAMA*

Production Suggestions

By

Ralph Nelson

"The Night the Animals Talked" was selected by the authors of this book from more than 150 scripts of the *Mama* series to date. Aside from its excellence as a script, it provides a good example of directorial problems. It was first performed Christmas, 1950. Audience response was so great, and the demands for a repeat so numerous, that it was performed again the following Christmas. Only minor shooting changes were made the second time, and we learned, among other things, that in the dimness of a barn a Holstein cow is much better photographically than a Guernsey.

This script demands that greatest problem to a director: animals important to the plot. He is helpless and can only tear out his hair in anguish if the cow should moo at the wrong time, or if the donkey should refuse to remain docile in his stall. The script also presents numerous audio problems, intricate camera movements, and a number of special effects: falling snow, as we first see the exterior of the house in Norway, and again as we find the thieves spying from outside the house on the dancing about the tree; deep snow, for Papa and Dagmar to trudge through; a roaring fire, for the huge fireplace; smooth recorded transitions, to match Mama's "live" voice as she starts to tell the story; and a thorough identification of the actor's voice who plays the thief. Without that, we would lose the effect of the mysterious voice that speaks at the end of the barn scene, and could

226

not join in the wonder of Mama and Papa as they speculate on who did give Dagmar the warning.

Most important, in production preparation, Mama's story should be recreated through Dagmar's eyes. Dagmar, of course, plays her own great grandmother, and her family is the same, but the house in Norway must look like the basic *Mama* set, with cutout panels of Norwegian design covering identifiable sections of the kitchen—so that the end illusion in Dagmar's mind, recreating this legend for herself, is that Mama's house and the house in Norway a hundred years ago are alike, and yet different.

The opening camerawork depends heavily upon the excellence of the technical crew. Camera 2 (the only camera mounted on a Fearless panorama dolly) must be pre-set, cranked very high at the top of the Christmas tree; and Camera 1 must be pre-set for an intricate dolly shot, its cable threaded through the stalls of the barn to pick up Papa and Dagmar making their way through the snow from the back porch. Thus the first scene must be shot entirely on Camera 3. Five people are involved in the scene. Playing it wide would lose the values, so there is a constant regrouping of the actors as they carry the camera in a pan from one to the other, so that seldom is it necessary to pull wider than a two- or three-shot, except in the final grouping as they sit to hear Mama's story.

As Mama tells it, the transition is made to a recording of "Outside the Wind Was Howling"—the sound effect helping to cover the slight change in audio from the live pickup. Meanwhile, visually, Camera 1 frames up on an 11" by 14" blowup of a farmhouse and dollies slowly in, with "snow" falling on a fir bough in the foreground to give dimension to the photograph.

Dissolving to the star atop the tree on the indicated cue, the camera cranks very slowly down the tree, following the description of the Christmas decorations until it finally alights on Dagmar's "great grandmama." The recording, the exterior shot, and the slow pan down the tree have given the actors time to strip to their Norwegian costumes which they had overdressed for the first scene. Again, this scene must be carried by one camera, panning Dagmar from one character to another, until she and Papa are picked up at the back door by Camera 1.

At the close of the script, with Mama's narration, the same technique is used in reverse. As Papa says "I wonder," he looks to Dagmar, the camera panning with his look, moving to Dagmar, then slowly up the tree as Mama's recorded voice finishes the story; meanwhile the actors scurry back to their original positions in the parlor, and the camera dissolves through to them grouped around Mama in time to hear her say, live, "And that is the tree your great grandmama is looking at tonight."

One shot may need further explanation than appears: On Pape 26 of the script, we dissolve to a clock in the kitchen chiming the hour of midnight, then the camera arcs around a "wild" ladder; Dagmar's slippered feet appear, and she climbs down in closeup, moves to the fireplace for a light for her lantern, then into the barn. Once there, all cameras are required, covering basically the thieves, Dagmar and the donkey, and Dagmar and the cow.

Our animals proved wonderful troopers. On air, the donkey, busily chewing a cud, actually appeared to be talking to Dagmar, and I could have blessed the cow when, as Dagmar entered the barn and said, "Merry Christmas, Hilda!" the cow mooed her reply.

At the dress rehearsal, however, she proved more temperamental. She mooed loudly and raised a fuss in her stall until a technician with a bucolic background suggested that the dress rehearsal might be coinciding with Bossy's normal milking time. Rehearsal was held up while the technician did the honors with the cast grouped around, uproarious with laughter. I fretted, drumming my fingers over the console board, impatient at the delay that was costing me time. But I can say in all admiration for a bovine actress, Bossy truly "milked" that laugh.

M A M A

"The Night the Animals Talked"

by Frank Gabrielson

CBS-TV, December 22, 1950

Producer — Carol Irwin
Director — Ralph Nelson
Cast   — Mama   — Peggy Wood
           Papa   — Judson Laire
           Katrin   — Rosemary Rice
           Nels   — Dick Patten
           Dagmar   — Robin Morgan
           Jenny   — Ruth Gates
           Robber   — Santos Ortega
           Robber's wife   — Enid Markey

<u>"MAMA"</u>

<u>"THE NIGHT THE ANIMALS TALKED"</u> *

WIDE ON ALBUM ①

MOVE IN

OPEN ALBUM

HIT NARRATION

(FADE IN ALBUM)

      KATRIN:

   (OVER SCENE)

I remember the Christmases when I was

a girl.

   (TURN TO ALBUM, PICTURES OF
   KATRIN'S FRIENDS)

Across the years I can still hear

our shots when school was out and

Christmas vacation began.  TURN PAGE

   (TURN TO PICTURES OF STORES)

* Courtesy of CBS Television and Carol Irwin, Producer

-2-

KATRIN:(CTD)

I can still see the wonderful windows
of the stores downtown. And I can
still smell the Christmas cookies
Aunt Jenny and Aunt Trina used to
make.

  (TURN TO PICTURES OF AUNTS
  INCLUDING ONE OF JENNY
  HOLDING PLATE OF COOKIES)

And how I remember our   house on
Christmas Eve!   The tree, the holly
wreaths, the Christmas Carols.

  (TURN TO PICTURE OF HOUSE.
  DISSOLVE THROUGH TO LIVE
  SHOT OF DAGMAR HANGING STOCKING
  ON MANTEL.   DRESSED IN
  BATHROBE. BESIDE HER IS
  THE CHRISTMAS TREE)

I remember my little sister Dagmar
in her bathrobe, hanging her
stocking up for Santa Claus.

  (KATRIN AND NELS HANG THEIRS
  UP, NELS VERY BLASE ABOUT IT
  ALL. BOTH ALSO WEAR BATHROBES.

I remember Nels and I hanging our
stockings too, and how bored we
tried to be and how much we loved
it.

XMAS TREE ③
IN PARLOR

SLOW PAN AROUND
ROOM AND PULL
BACK TO DAGMAR
AT FIREPLACE

MOVE TO KATRIN
AND NELS

MOVE TO PAPA

-3-

(CAMERA MOVES TO PAPA BY
KITCHEN DOOR, SMOKING AND
SMILING AT THEM)

(PAPA WEARS COAT AND PANTS)

    KATRIN:

And I remember Papa smiling at us.

    (CAMERA MOVES TO MAMA AT STOVE.
    SHE IS WEARING HER COVERALL
    APRON)

But most of all when I remember the

Christmasses when I was a girl, most

of all I remember Mama.

    (COMMERCIAL)

PULL BACK FOR
GROUP

C.U. MAMA
AT STOVE

②

(COMMERCIAL)

GROUP
AS BEFORE ③

-4-

DAGMAR:

(CALLING FROM FIREPLACE)

Mama!   We've got our stockings
hung!

MAMA:

(ENTERING FROM KITCHEN)

Oh my!

DAGMAR:

Nels' and Katrin's and mine are all
hung.

NELS:

I don't know whether it's any use
hanging them up, though.

DAGMAR:

What do you mean?

NELS:

Our chimney's pretty small and I
hear Santa Claus has put on weight.

DAGMAR:

You're silly.

NELS:

Just don't be surprised if there's
nothing in your stocking.

PAN DAGMAR TO
MAMA AT ARCHWAY

PAN THEM TO
NELS AT MANTLE

-5-

DAGMAR:

(KNOWINGLY)

Don't worry, Nels.   Santa Claus
will get down that chimney as
long as he's got Papa here to help
him.   Won't he, papa?

PAPA:

(LAUGHING WITH THE OTHERS)

Ja, sure.

MAMA:

Well, now that the stockings are hung,
I think it is time for bed.

DAGMAR:

We haven't put out the glass of milk
for Santa Claus yet.

MAMA:

(HANDING HER A GLASS OF
MILK ON A SAUCER)

Here it is.

DAGMAR:

And we have to have a carrot for
his reindeer.

MAMA:

(GIVING CARROT WITH OTHER
HAND)

Here is that.

PAN DAGMAR TO PAPA AT TABLE

MAMA IN

PAN DAGMAR TO KATRIN AT MANTLE

MAMA IN

-6-

DAGMAR:

If every child in the world leaves
out a carrot for the reindeer, how
many do you suppose they eat?

PAPA:

Quite a big bunch, Lilliven.

DAGMAR:

(SUDDENLY)

Oh!   We almost forgot the cigar!

PAPA:

(HANDING HER A CIGAR)

Here it is.

(DAGMAR PUTS IT BESIDE THE
CARROT AND THE MILK)

KATRIN:

I hope Santa Claus likes that kind.

DAGMAR:

(WINKING AT PAPA)

Oh, he'll like it, won't he, Papa?

PAPA:

Ja, sure.

(LAUGHS)

MAMA:

Now bedtime.

PAPA IN.

-7-

DAGMAR:

Just a little longer, Mama?

MAMA:

We have got to give Santa Claus

time to get here.

DAGMAR:

Couldn't we sing just one more

Christmas carol?

MAMA:

No, Dagmar we have sung carols,

we have played games. The Aunts and

Uncles have been here and given us

wonderful presents.   We have had a

fine Christmas Eve.

DAGMAR:

But I don't want it to stop.

MAMA:

If Christmas Eve does not stop,

Christmas cannot come.   And you

want that, don't you?

DAGMAR:

But you haven't told the story of

Great Grandmother and the animals

yet.

PAN DAGMAR AS SHE
SLIPS FROM MAMA AND
RUNS AROUND THE
TREE TO BE CAUGHT
BY PAPA
MAMA IN.

-8-

MAMA:

I know, but it is getting late,
Dagmar.

DAGMAR:

But you always tell that Christmas
Eve.

PAPA:

She is right, Marta.

DAGMAR:

Tell us, Mama.

MAMA:

You children know it as well as
I do.

DAGMAR:

Go on. Tell it. It wouldn't be
Christmas Eve without it.

(MAMA LOOKS AROUND AT THE
OTHERS)   KATRIN-NELS IN

PAPA:

(NODDING)

Ja.

KATRIN:

Please, Mama.

-9-

NELS:

Might as well get it over with,

Mama.

MAMA:

    (SETTING HERSELF IN A
    CHAIR)

It is just an excuse to stay up

late.

DAGMAR:

    (CLIMBING INTO HER LAP)

Oh no, Mama. It's my very favorite

story in the whole world.

MAMA:

Well, once upon a time there was

a little girl named Dagmar.

DAGMAR:

This isn't me.   This is my Great

Grandmother. I was named after

her.

KATRIN:

We know.

MAMA:

And when your Great Grandmother was

a little girl she lived on a farm.

DAGMAR:

In Norway.

PAN THEM TO CHAIRS

TIGHTEN ON GROUP

-10-

NELS:

Let Mama tell it.

MAMA:

It was not a very big farm. There
was just a kitchen.

DAGMAR:

Just like ours.

MAMA:

And a loft where the family slept.
And next to the house a small barn
where the animals were.

DAGMAR:

They had a cow named Hilda and a
donkey named Olaf.

KATRIN:

We know.

NELS:

(AT THE SAME TIME)

Let Mama tell it.

PAPA:

(AT THE SAME TIME)

Dagmar!

    (CAMERA MOVES CLOSE TO MAMA'S
    FACE, SNEAK MUSIC UNDER)

DOLLY IN SLOWLY TO MAMA - DAGMAR

-11-

MAMA:

As I was saying, it was not a big

farm but on Christmas Eve it was

a very nice place to be. ⎤Outside

the wind was howling and the snow

was falling down.

> (CROSS FADE TO EITHER
> MINIATURE OF FARM IN SNOW
> STORM OR, IF THIS IS TOO
> ELABORATE, TO KITCHEN WINDOW,
> SNOW BEATING AGAINST IT.
> SOUND OF WIND.)

MAMA'S VOICE:

(RECORDED)

But inside, it was warm and cozy

and right in the middle of the

kitchen, was a great tall Christmas

tree with a straw Star of Bethlehem

on top.

> (DISSOLVE TO SHOT OF STAR ON
> TOP OF TREE)

> (CAMERA MOVES SLOWLY DOWN
> TREE)

Oh, that was a tree to see!

And what do you think was at the

bottom of the tree, so long ago?

I'll tell you.   There, standing

looking up was your own Great

Grandmamma, who was also called

Dagmar.

HIT NARRATION

WIDE ON PHOTO MURAL (1)

CLOSE UP STAR COME DOWN TREE SLOWLY (2)

-more-

-- 11 A --   (REVISED)

MAMA:(CONTINUED)

And all over the tree wonderful things
were hanging. Little gold and silver
angeles, candy pigs, brightly colored
paper chains linking all the boughs.
And there were apples, little baskets
filled with candy and fourteen
different kinds of Christmas cookies.
Oh, that was a tree to see! And
what do you think was at the bottom
of the tree, so long ago? I'll
tell you. There, standing looking
up was your own Great Grandmama,
who was also called Dagmar.

PAN DOWN TO
DAGMAR

                              -12-

        (CAMERA MOVES TO BOTTOM OF
        TREE SHOWING DAGMAR, NOW IN
        NORWEGIAN PEASANT COSTUME,
        LOOKING UP AT IT.)

            DAGMAR'S VOICE:

        (RECORDED)

    And she looked just like me!

        (KATRIN, ALSO IN NORWEIGAN   PAN HER TO
        COSTUME, APPEARS BEHIND DAGMAR.
        SHE PUTS HER HANDS OVER HER   KATRIN
        EYES. DAGMAR PULLS THE HANDS
        DOWN AND TURNS TO SEE KATRIN.
        BOTH LAUGH)

            MAMA'S VOICE:

        (RECORDED)

    Ja, and she had an older sister like

    you have.

        (NELS, LIKE HIS SISTER, IN   — TO NELS
        NORWEIGAN DRESS, COMES TO
        THE TREE, TAKES COOKIE OFF
        AND EATS IT.)

            MAMA'S VOICE:

    And a big brother, too.

            DAGMAR'S VOICE:

        (RECORDED)   —TO MAMA

    What else did Dagmar have, Mama?

        (MAMA, IN NORWEIGAN DRESS,
        AS WILL BE PAPA, APPEARS,
        KISSES DAGMAR ON THE TOP OF
        THE HEAD)

-13-

            MAMA'S VOICE:

        (RECORDED)

Well, she had a mama like yours.

            DAGMAR'S VOICE:

        (RECORDED)

What else?

        (DAGMAR RUNS TO PAPA)   — TO PAPA

            MAMA'S VOICE:

        (RECORDED)

And of course she had a Papa like

yours.

        (DAGMAR WHISPERS IN PAPA'S
        EAR. HE NODS)

            DAGMAR'S VOICE:

        (RECORDED)

And what else?

        (DAGMAR TURNS TO PLATE OF   MOVE IN TIGHT
        COOKIES, QUICKLY PUTS ONE
        IN HER MOUTH, AND ANOTHER IN   ON THEM
        EACH HAND)

            MAMA'S VOICE:

        (RECORDED)

Well, she had a good appetite like

yours.

            DAGMAR'S VOICE:

        (RECORDED, EXASPERATED)

Not that, Mama.   What else did she have?   FOLLOW THEM
                                              TO STAIRS

-14-

(PAPA RISES, THROWS SHAWL
AROUND DAGMAR'S SHOULDERS,
PICKS UP LANTERN, AND HE AND
SHE START FOR THE BARN DOOR
(PANTRY)

      MAMA'S VOICE:

(RECORDED)

She had a nice, warm shawl.

      DAGMAR'S VOICE:

(RECORDED)

No, Mama!   What else?

      MAMA:

Well, she had a lantern that

belonged to her Papa.

      DAGMAR:

Oh please, Mama, what else?

      MAMA:

Well --

      DAGMAR:

Oh, please, please, please.

      MAMA:

Well she had deep snow to play

in.

(DAGMAR AND PAPA OPEN THE
DOOR THAT SEPARATES THE KITCHEN
FROM THE LITTLE BARN, ENTER
THE BARN, CAMERA MOVING WITH
THEM.)

⌐THRU BARN DOOR TO ⌐
BACK PORCH

PULL BACK WITH
DAGMAR - PAPA

-15-

        MAMA'S VOICE:

     (RECORDED)

Well, what do you want Dagmar to
have?

        DAGMAR'S VOICE:

     (RECORDED)

I want her to have a cow named Hilda

and a donkey named Olaf.

        (IN THE BARN, IN THE LIGHT
        OF PAPA'S LANTERN, WE SEE
        A DONKEY AND A COW.)

        DAGMAR:

     (LIVE)

Merry Christmas, Hilda. Merry

Christmas, Olaf!

        (SHE OFFERS EACH OF THEM A
        COOKIE WHICH NEITHER OF
        THEM ARE INTERESTED IN)

        PAPA:

     (DIGGING OUT GRAIN)

I don't think they like cookies.

        (FEEDS THEM)

        DAGMAR:

Papa.

ARC RIGHT AROUND STALL

335 SEE COW AND DONKEY

PULL BACK AND ARC LEFT AROUND HAYLOFT WITH PAPA

-16-

PAPA:

Ja, Dagmar?

DAGMAR:

Tonight at midnight will you come

out to the barn with me?

PAPA:

My goodness, why?

DAGMAR:

I'm afraid to come alone.   The trolls

might get me.

PAPA:

But why do you want to come here

at all?

DAGMAR:

I want to hear the animals talk.

PAPA:

Oh, my goodness!

(LAUGHS)

DAGMAR:

They always do on Christmas Eve.

Don't you know that, Papa?

PAPA:

(SMILING)

It is Christmas Eve and I do not

hear them talking.

DOLLY IN TO
C.U. DAGMAR

-16A-

          DAGMAR:

But it doesn't happen 'til midnight,
Papa.

          PAPA:

So?

          DAGMAR:

But then they talk, Papa. Honest.
That's because there were animals
in the manger when Lord Jesus was
born.   So forever after on Christmas
Eve animals can talk all they want.

          PAPA:

Ja, Lillivan?

          DAGMAR:

They sing, too. They sing hymns of
praise to the Lord Jesus.   And if
you don't believe me, ask the witch
woman.

          PAPA:

She is just full of talk, that
one.

          DAGMAR:

Oh no, Papa. She once heard her
cow singing.

-16B-

PAPA:

She saw her too?

DAGMAR:

Well, not exactly. By the time she
got to the barn the cow got shy and
stopped singing.

PAPA:

Then I think it was some person
she heard singing.

DAGMAR:

Oh no, Papa. You ask the witch
woman.

MOVE AROUND
HAYLOFT WITH
THEM TO COW

PAPA:

(PICKING UP HIS LANTERN)

Well, we better get back with the
others, now.

DAGMAR:

Can we come out to the barn at
midnight, Papa?

PAPA:

This is awfully late for a little
girl to be up.

DAGMAR:

Can we ask Mama?

-16 C -

PAPA:

(HOLDING OUT NO HOPE)

Well, you can ask her.

DAGMAR:

Gosh, Papa. I bet Hilda and Olaf

have interesting things to say.

(THERE IS A SUDDEN SCURRYING
SOUND)

DAGMAR:

(GRABBING PAPA)

What's that?

PAPA:

Just a rat, I think.

DAGMAR:

Maybe it's a troll.

PAPA:

A troll would make more noise than

that.

MOVE UP WITH
DAGMAR TO
PAPA

17

                    DAGMAR

Maybe this is one of the troll's children.

                    PAPA

I think more likely it is one of the

rat's children. Come on, now.

          (DAGMAR STARTS AFTER HIM, THEN
          STOPS SUDDENLY)

                    DAGMAR

Excuse me a second.

          (RUNS BACK TO THE DONKEY AND
          THE COW AND SPEAKS TO THEM
          ·IN A LOW VOICE)

Don't say anything 'til I get back.

          (TURNS AND RUNS AFTER PAPA.
          THEY REENTER THE HOUSE,
          CAMERA MOVING WITH THEM)

                    MAMA

We were wondering what kept you.

                    DAGMAR

Mama, can I do something please,

please, please, please?

                    MAMA

Four pleases. This must be something

you should not do.

                    DAGMAR

Oh no, Mama. All I want to do is stay

up a little later.

PAN DAGMAR TO
COW

PAN HER TO PAPA
MAMA THRU FIREPLACE 2
KITCHEN DOOR B.G.
LOW ELEVATION
SEE KATRIN · NELS
AT TABLE
PAPA - DAGMAR IN
DAGMAR COMES
TO MAMA

18

MAMA

Ja?

DAGMAR

Just 'til midnight. Papa said he'd
take me to the barn.

KATRIN-NELS 1
(FROM STOVE)

KATRIN (CONTEMPTUOUSLY)

And here the animals talk!

NELS

Is she starting that again?

SAME 2

MAMA

I told you earlier today, Dagmar,
midnight was too late for a little
girl.

DAGMAR

But I want to hear what Hilda and
Olaf say.

SAME 1

KATRIN

They won't talk.

DAGMAR IN

DAGMAR

They will so.

NELS

Sure, Hilda will say moo and Olaf
will say hee-haw.

SAME 2

(A LAUGH FROM ALL)

19

          DAGMAR

They will not either. They'll talk
as good as you and me. You ask the   SAME   1
witch woman.

          NELS

The witch woman! She's ———
                                                  SAME   2
     (ROTATES A HAND BY HIS HEAD TO
     INDICATE SCRAMBLED BRAINS)

          DAGMAR

You shouldn't talk like that about her.
She'll cast a spell on you.

          NELS

I'd like to see her try it.

     (THERE IS A KNOCK ON THE DOOR)

          PAPA

Who is that?

          KATRIN (LOOKING OUT WINDOW)

Gosh, it's the witch woman.

          JENNY (OFF)

Yoo. Hoo.

          MAMA
                                               MED. NELS   3
     (TO NELS WHO IS CLOSEST TO THE DOOR)
                                               (THRU ARCH)
Well, let her in Nels. She will not
                                               PAN HIM TO BACK DOOR
hurt you.
                                               JENNY IN

20

(NELS OPENS THE DOOR. THE
WITCH WOMAN (AUNT JENNY) ENTERS
IN A WEIRD NORWEIGAN OUTFIT
OF THE PERIOD)

MAMA

Well, Merry Christmas!

JENNY

Merry Christmas to you.

DAGMAR

Tell them the animals talk on Christmas
Eve.

JENNY

Of course they do. Everybody knows
that.

DAGMAR (TO NELS AND
KATRIN)

See?

JENNY

Of course folks growing up now do not
always believe things like that. But
we know better, don't we, Dagmar?

DAGMAR

I want Papa to take me out to the
barn at midnight. Can I do it, Mama?

[handwritten margin notes: PAN JENNY TO DAGMAR]

[handwritten margin notes: SAME / JENNY COMES TO FIRE]

21

MAMA

I am afraid midnight is too late,

Dagmar.

DAGMAR

Please, Mama. I want to hear them

talk.

MAMA

We are not sure they will talk.

DAGMAR (TO WITCH WOMAN)

They will, won't they?

JENNY

Ja, but it is not good to go in the

barn at midnight. The trolls might

get you.

DAGMAR

Not with Papa there.

JENNY

Some of the trolls are much bigger

than your Papa.

DAGMAR

They are?

JENNY

Bigger than this house.

22

DAGMAR (FRIGHTENED)

Are they, Mama?

MAMA

I do not know. I have never seen a
troll, even this big.

    (HOLDS HER HANDS ABOUT A FOOT
    APART)

DAGMAR

I don't care if there are trolls.
I want to hear Hilda and Olaf talk.
Can't I, Mama?

MAMA

Maybe sometime when you are bigger,
Dagmar.

JENNY

It is not only trolls you have to
be afraid of. There is robbers around.

DAGMAR

Robbers!

MAMA

Now, now. Don't frighten the child.

JENNY

I am telling only the truth. I heard
it from Mistress Johnsrud. There are
two bad, wicked robbers around. I
have come especially to tell you so you
will keep everything locked up?

TIGHTEN 3 SHOT

23

            MAMA

Who would steal on Christmas Eve?

            JENNY

Anytime these two would steal. They

do worse. They are wicked, bad.

            DAGMAR

I still want to go to the barn at

midnight. I'm not afraid of any

old robbers or trolls. I want to

hear the animals talk. Can't I

Mama? Please?

            MAMA

That is just a story people tell,

Dagmar. It is not true.

            DAGMAR

Can't I find out, Mama?

            MAMA

No. Papa and I do not want you up

so late.

            DAGMAR

Please, please.

            MAMA

No means no, Dagmar. Even on Christmas

Eve.

24

DAGMAR

Aw heck.

MAMA (TEASING HER)

What kind of a face is that for

Christmas Eve?

NELS

Gosh, you look just like the

wi -- (STOPS HIMSELF IN TIME,

GIGGLES) You look terrible.

PAPA

Come on, Lilliven. Smile.

KATRIN

Come on, Dagmar. We're all going to

sing carols.

    (MAMA BEGINS TO SING, JOINED
    BY THE OTHERS INCLUDING JENNY.
    THEY JOIN HANDS AND MOVE IN A
    RING AROUND THE CHRISTMAS TREE,
    SINGING.

    (CUT TO WINDOW OUTSIDE THE HOUSE,
    THERE IN THE DRIVING SNOW THE
    ROBBER AND HIS WIFE ARE PEERING
    IN THE WINDOW)

ROBBER (SNARLING)

Look at them singing and dancing

around. Well, they'll sing another

tune before morning.

NELS IN

WIDEN FOR GROUP

PAN THEM TO TRE

OUTSIDE WINDOW

ESTABLISH WINDOW
SEE DANCING
PULL BACK FOR THIE
KNEELING

25

ROBBER WIFE

They look like nice folks. I'll bet
you if we was to knock on their door
and tell them we was cold and hungry
they'd take us in.

ROBBER

They'd take us in and send for the
sheriff. COME ON.

ROBBER WIFE

Where to?

ROBBER

To find us a place where we can hide
'til they're asleep. There ought to
be fat pickin's here.

ROBBER WIFE

Couldn't we ask them to take us in?

ROBBER

We'll ask for nothing. Later we'll
take what we want.

ROBBER WIFE

It don't seem right on Christmas
Eve somehow.

ROBBER (SNEERING)

You think some Angels are going to
mind?

THEY RISE
PAN UP

THEY CROSS FROM
WINDOW

26

ROBBER WIFE

Don't talk like that.

ROBBER

If they mind, just let them watch

this house tonight. They're going

to need it. Come on.

(DISSOLVE TO INTERIOR DARKENED
KITCHEN. DAGMAR CREEPS
SILENTLY DOWN THE LITTLE LADDER
FROM THE LOFT. SHE IS MOVING
CAREFULLY SO AS NOT TO AWAKE THE
SLEEPING HOUSEHOLD. SHE CROSSES
IN THE DARK TO WHERE THE LANTERN
IS, PUTS A STICK IN THE STOVE,
GETS A LITTLE FLAME FROM THE
BANKED COALS AND LIGHTS THE
LANTERN.

(CUT TO BARN..WE SEE HILDA AND
OLAF. NEARBY THEIR STALLS THE
ROBBER AND HIS WIFE APPEAR FROM
THEIR HIDING PLACES)

ROBBER (IN A WHISPER)

Come on. It's time.

ROBBER WIFE

Do you think they're asleep?

ROBBER

They ought to be. I heard a church

bell strike eleven almost an hour

ago.

Handwritten margin notes:

C.U. CLOCK ③
PULL BACK SLOWLY
PAST TREE TO
LADDER. DAGMAR IN
PAN HER TO FIREPLA

THIEVES
BEHIND HAYLOFT ②
PAN THEM TO DOOR
TIGHT THIEVES
AT DOOR

27

                ROBBER WIFE

I wish you wouldn't keep talking about

churches.

        (ROBBER GIVES HER A WITHERING
        LOOK)

                ROBBER

Come on. Let's be about it.

        (HEARS A NOISE FROM THE KITCHEN)

Sh!

        (FREEZES A MOMENT, THEN ALARMED)

Someone's coming!

        (THEY QUICKLY RETURN TO THEIR
        HIDING PLACE NEAR THE ANIMALS.

        DAGMAR ENTERS TIMOROUSLY. SHE
        TAKES A FEW TIMID STEPS TOWARD
        THE ANIMALS. THERE IS A SOUND
        OF A RAT SCURRING. SHE STOPS,
        FRIGHTENED. AN OWL HOOTS.
        DAGMAR RUNS BACK INTO THE HOUSE.

        CUT TO ROBBERS LOOKING AFTER HER.
        THE ROBBER IS ABOUT TO ARISE
        CAUTIOUSLY FROM HIS PLACE OF
        HIDING WHEN HE HEARS DAGMAR
        COMING BACK TO THE BARN. HIDES
        AGAIN.

        CUT TO DAGMAR REENTERING BARN.
        THIS TIME SHE HAS WITH HER THE
        LANTERN, BUT FOR COMPANIONSHIP
        AND SECURITY, HER DOLL. SHE
        CROSSES TO THE ANIMALS.)

[handwritten annotations in right margin:]

SAME 2

PAN THIEVES BEHIND
HAYLOFT — SEE THEM
HIDE — PAN UP TO
DOOR

DAGMAR AT DOOR 3

PAN HER TO COW
THEN TO DONKEY

28

DAGMAR (IN HARDLY MORE
THAN A WHISPER)

Merry Christmas, Hilda. Merry Christmas,

Olaf.

> THIEVES F.G.   2
> DAGMAR B.G.

(CUT TO ROBBER REACTING, BORED,
WONDERING WHAT HIS NEXT STEP
SHOULD BE, AND ALSO ANNOYED...
FAR OFF, A CHURCH BELL STRIKES
TWELVE)

> SAME   3

DAGMAR

It's midnight, Olaf and Hilda. It's

when Jesus was born. You can talk

now.

> C.U. COW   2
> C.U. DONKEY   3

(CUT TO SHOTS OF THE PLACID
ANIMALS)

(CUT TO DAGMAR)

> TIGHT - DAGMAR AND   1
> DONKEY

DAGMAR

Please say something.

(CUT TO ROBBERS)

> THIEVES F.G.   2
> DAGMAR B.G.

ROBBER WIFE

(MOUTHING THE WORDS BUT HARDLY
WHISPERING THEM)

Is she talking to us?

(POINTS TO HERSELF AND HER
HUSBAND)

ROBBER (CLAPPING A HAND OVER
HER MOUTH)

Sh-h-h!

> SAME   1

(CUT TO DAGMAR)

29

                    DAGMAR
Golly, other animals are talking
tonight. I don't know why you two
aren't. Please say something. Say   SAME   2
anything.

     (CUT TO ROBBERS)

                    ROBBER (SUDDENLY)   SAME   1

Merry Christmas!

     (HIS WIFE LOOKS AT HIM
     THUNDERSTRUCK)

     (CUT TO DAGMAR, OVERJOYED)

                    DAGMAR   SAME   2

Olaf! You talked!

     (CUT TO ROBBER)

                    ROBBER
                                        DAGMAR ACROSS COW   3
Nothing to it.

     (HIS WIFE IS MORE BAFFLED THAN
     EVER)

                    DAGMAR (PLEADING WITH COW)   SAME   2

Now you say something, Hilda.

     (CUT TO ROBBER AND WIFE. ROBBER
     PRODS WIFE. HIS LIPS FORM THE
     SILENT WORDS "SAY SOMETHING")

                    ROBBER WIFE (TAKING THE
                              PLUNGE)   SAME   3

Merry Christmas!

     (CUT TO DAGMAR)

30

                    DAGMAR

You're the most beautiful old cow   SAME   2

in the world, Hilda.

        (CUT TO ROBBER WIFE)

                ROBBER WIFE (INDIGNANTLY)

Who me?

        (ROBBER NUDGES HER VICIOUSLY)   SAME   3

Why, thanks!

        (CUT TO DAGMAR)

                    DAGMAR

Oh, I knew you could talk! I'm so   SAME   2

happy. I'm going to get Mama and Papa.

        (CUT TO ROBBER, ALARMED)

                    ROBBER

No, no. Stop!

        (CUT TO DAGMAR)

                DAGMAR (STOPPING)

What's the matter, Olaf?

        (CUT TO ROBBER)

                    ROBBER   SAME   1

Don't get your folks.

        (CUT TO DAGMAR)

31

DAGMAR

I want them to hear you. They didn't
believe you could talk. SAME 2

(CUT TO ROBBER) ~~NOTE: FROM THIS~~
~~TIME ON WE WILL~~
~~STOP INDICATING~~
~~THE CUTS)~~

ROBBER

We never do in front of grown-ups.

DAGMAR

Oh.

ROBBER

You just stay here and us three will
have a nice talk. SAME 1

DAGMAR (RETURNING TO THE
ANIMALS)

Is it fun to be a donkey, Olaf?

ROBBER

It is when you belong to a nice rich
farmer like your father (ADDING CURIOUSLY)
he is rich, isn't he?

DAGMAR

Oh yes, he has a whole sack of money
hidden away.

32

ROBBER:

Gold?

DAGMAR:

I'm not sure whether there's
any gold but there's silver and
lots of nice pennies.

SAME 2

ROBBER:

I'd love to know where he hides
it, wouldn't you, old cow?

(CUT TO ROBBER WIFE GLARING
AT HIM)

ROBBER WIFE:

Why yes.

ROBBER:

Do you know where he keeps it,
little one?

DAGMAR:

Yes, but I'm not allowed to tell.

SAME 1

ROBBER:

You can tell us. We're in the
family.

DAGMAR:

I'd have to ask Papa first.

ROBBER:

You're being just as stubborn as
a mule.

SAME 3

33

DAGMAR:

Is it fun to be a cow, Hilda?

ROBBER WIFE:

Well, yes and no.

DAGMAR:

Thanks for all the lovely milk.

ROBBER WIFE:

Oh, that's all right.

DAGMAR:

When are you and Olaf going to sing?   SAME   2

ROBBER WIFE:

Sing?

ROBBER: SAME   3

Us?

DAGMAR:

The witch woman says that on   SAME

Christmas Eve you animals not

only talk, but you sing hymns

in praise of Lord Jesus.

ROBBER:

Oh yes, but we won't do that

'til later tonight when we go to

see him?

DAGMAR:

See who?

34

ROBBER:

Lord Jesus.

DAGMAR:

You're going to see Lord Jesus
tonight?

ROBBER:

Every Christmas we animals are
allowed to gallop right up through
the sky and visit him.

DAGMAR:

Oh, my golly.

ROBBER:

Would you like to go with us?

DAGMAR:

Could I?

ROBBER:

If you've got a present for him.

DAGMAR:

Do you think Lord Jesus would
like my doll?

ROBBER:

(CONTEMPTUOUSLY)

Your doll?

35

DAGMAR:

I like it better than anything
in the world and I'd like Lord
Jesus to have it.

SAME   2

ROBBER:

I guess you haven't read your
Bible very carefully. Remember the
story of the Wise Men? For
presents they brought frankincense,
myhrr and gold. That's what's
right for Lord Jesus.

DAGMAR:

But I don't have any frankincense
or myhrr or gold.

SAME   1

ROBBER:

Your father's got silver. That's   (#3 C.U. DONKEY TO
just as good.   BE TAKEN AT WILL)

DAGMAR:

It is?

ROBBER:

Why don't you go right now and
get it.

DAGMAR:

You think Papa will let me have it?

ROBBER:

Don't even ask him.

36

            DAGMAR:

Oh, I couldn't just take it.

            ROBBER:

Your Papa would want Lord Jesus

to have it.

            DAGMAR:

Why can't I ask him then?

            ROBBER:

He's grown-up. He wouldn't believe

where we're going.

            DAGMAR:

I guess he wouldn't. Golly, what'll

I do?

            ROBBER:

Just take the money.

            DAGMAR:

But Papa might need it.

            ROBBER:

If you give a present to Lord

Jesus he'll watch out for you and

this house forever after that.

            DAGMAR:

Gosh, I don't know what to do. SAME

37

ROBBER:

Don't you want to see Lord Jesus'
house? He's got the biggest
Christmas tree there is and it's
trimmed with every star in the
sky.

SAME   1

DAGMAR: (EAGERLY)
Is the Star of Bethlehem on top?

ROBBER:

Oh yes.

DAGMAR:

DAGMAR ACROSS COW 3

Oh, I want to see it.

ROBBER:

Get the silver.

DAGMAR:

SAME   2

Do you think I should, Hilda?

ROBBER WIFE:

(HESITATINGLY)
Well, I don't know.

ROBBER: (FURIOUSLY)
What do you mean you don't know,
old cow?

(TWISTS HER ARM)
Of course she should get it,
shouldn't she?

38

             ROBBER WIFE:

Oh yes, yes.

             ROBBER:

Get it quick, little one. We

have to hurry.

             DAGMAR:

Don't go without me.

        (RUNS OFF)

             ROBBER:

        (VICIOUSLY TO WIFE)

You don't know, huh? I'd like

to bust you in half.

             ROBBER WIFE:

I don't like this. It's

blasphemy.

        (ROBBER LAUGHS)

Something will happen using the

name of the Lord like this.

             ROBBER:

We'll get the money. That's what

will happen.

        (LOOKS AT THE COW, AT HIS
        WIFE, BACK AT THE COW)

Quite a likeness at that.

DAGMAR OUT

IN TIGHT ON THIEVES

PAN THEM TO DOOR

C.U. COW   1

TIGHT THIEVES   3

ACROSS COW

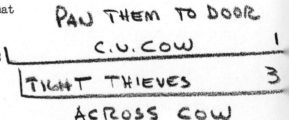

39

ROBBER WIFE:

Ain't you got no decent feelings?

ROBBER: (MOCKINGLY)

Don't you like to be called old

cow?

ROBBER WIFE:

I ain't talking about that. But

it ain't right to be speaking

of God's Christmas tree with stars

on it.

ROBBER:

I thought that was kind of pretty?

ROBBER WIFE:

I don't see nothing pretty fooling

a child.

ROBBER:

Would you rather starve?

(START SUDDENLY)

Sh!

SAME   2

(THEY GO QUICKLY TO THEIR
HIDING PLACES. DAGMAR RE-ENTERS
WITH A LITTLE CHEST OF MONEY)

PAN THEM TO
HIDING PLACE
PAN UP TO DAGMAR
ENTERING

ROBBER:

(FROM HIDING PLACE)

Did you get the silver, little one?

DAGMAR ACROSS   1
DONKEY

40

DAGMAR:

Yes, but I don't know if it's
right. Are you sure Lord Jesus
wouldn't like my doll?

ROBBER:

Absolutely not, little one.

DAGMAR:

Well, shall we go then? ⌊_____ SAME   2

ROBBER:

You can't go like that.

DAGMAR:

What do you mean?

ROBBER:

In just your shawl. Where we're
going it's so cold the stars have
icicles on them. you will need
your warm coat.

DAGMAR:

I'll go get it.

     (TAKES A STEP OUT WITH BOX)

ROBBER:

But leave the box here. The old
cow and I will watch that for   SAME   1
you. ⌊_____

     (DAGMAR STARTS TO PUT THE
     BOX DOWN)   HIT NARRATION

41

ROBBER'S VOICE: (RECORDED)

No, Dagmar. Keep that money.

DAGMAR:

What Olaf?   C.U. DONKEY   3

ROBBER'S VOICE: (RECORDED)

Keep the chest and tell your father,   SAME   2

(CUT TO ROBBER BEWILDERED AT
SOUND OF HIS OWN VOICE)

that there are two thieves hidden   SAME   1

here behind my stall.

DAGMAR: (SHOUTING)   PULL BACK AND

Papa, Papa!   ARC RIGHT WITH

PAPA'S VOICE: DAGMAR BEHIND

Don't worry, Dagmar. We'll catch   HAY LOFT.

them.   PAPA - NELS IN

(CAMERA SWINGS TO SHOW PAPA
COMING INTO DOORWAY FOLLOWED
BY NELS. PAPA HAS AN OLD
FASHIONED GUN WITH HIM.
HURRIES TOWARD THIEVES WITH
THE GUN)

PAPA:

Up, you.

(ROBBER AND HIS WIFE RISE)

(DISSOLVE TO KITCHEN, MAMA   BLACK
AND KATRIN)

KATRIN: 2

Golly it was lucky Papa and Nels   MAMA-KATRIN

got there in time, wasn't it?   IN KITCHEN

42

MAMA:

It is a good thing the "animals"
talked so loud. That is what
woke us up.

KATRIN:

I think the most wonderful thing
of all was Papa pretending to be
Olaf. Nels was standing right
behind him and said Papa changed
his voice so he could hardly
recognize it.

MAMA:

Don't tell Dagmar it was Papa,
though. She feels bad enough
without finding out that even that
wasn't Olaf.

      (CAMERA PULLS BACK TO SHOW
      THE REST OF THE KITCHEN. THE
      ROBBER AND HIS WIFE ARE SEATED
      SOLEMNLY, NELS STANDING
      NEARBY GUARDING THEM WITH A
      GUN. PAPA PUTTING MITTENS ON
      ETC. DAGMAR NEARBY DEEPLY
      THOUBLED. SHE IS WATCHING
      THE ROBBERS)

PAPA:

Well Nels. I think we should get
these two over to the sheriff.

PAN MAMA AND
PULL BACK TO
SEE THIEVES F.G.
PAPA - NELS B.G.

43

                    NELS:

Yes, Papa.

                    DAGMAR:

Mama.

                    MAMA:

Ja, Dagmar?

TIGHT MAMA-DAGMAR 3
(THRU ARCH)

          (DAGMAR WHISPERS TO HER)

Well, we would have to talk to

Papa about that.

                    PAPA:

          (STOPPING ON THE WAY OUT
          NEAR THE DOOR)

What about?

                    MAMA:

Dagmar does not like it we have

to arrest anyone at Christmas time.

                    PAPA:

But Marta. They tried to rob us.

SAME   2

                    MAMA:

Maybe they had reasons.

                    ROBBER WIFE:

We were hungry and cold. That's why.

MAMA FORWARD

                    MAMA:

Why did you not come and knock on

the door and ask? We would have

given you food and a place to stay.

44

ROBBER WIFE:

That's what I wanted to do, but
he's proud. He don't trust no one.

ROBBER:

Why should I?

MAMA:

Have you had your supper?

ROBBER WIFE:

We ain't eaten since yesterday
morning.

MAMA:

Then right now we are going to
eat. I think maybe my little girl
is right. Christmas is no time
for arresting.

ROBBER WIFE:

God bless you.

MAMA:

It is Dagmar you should thank.

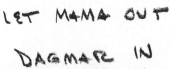

ROBBER WIFE: (TO DAGMAR)

The Lord Jesus will watch over
you always, like he did tonight.

(DAGMAR BURSTS INTO TEARS)

ROBBER WIFE:

Have I said something?

45

DAGMAR:

But I wanted to give him a present.

ROBBER:

You have given the Lord Jesus
the best present of all, little
one. You have forgiven someone who
needed it.

DAGMAR:

But you said he only wanted
frankincense and myhrr and gold.

ROBBER:

Yes, but I know better.

(PATS HER GENTLY ON THE HEAD)

MAMA: (ASIDE TO PAPA)

I am glad you pretended you were
Olaf talking. Dagmar liked that.

PAPA:

I pretended? It was Nels.

MAMA:

Nels said you did.

PAPA:

No, Marta. I swear it.

MAMA:

If it was not you and it was not
Nels, who was it?

IN TO ROBBER
DAGMAR

AS PAPA CROSSES
IN B.G. PAN HIM
TO MAMA AND
DOLLY IN ON
THEM

46

PAPA:

I wonder.

    (CAMERA SWINGS FROM THEM
    TO DAGMAR LOOKING AGAIN
    AT THE CHRISTMAS TREE)

    MAMA'S VOICE: (RECORDED)

And that is how your Great Grandmama

one night long ago heard the animals

talk on Christmas Eve.

    (THE CAMERA BEGINS TO MOVE
    SLOWLY UP THE TREE)

In her life after that, she had

almost seventy more Christmas

trees and always when she saw

them, she thought of the time in

the little barn when Olaf and Hilda

told her of Lord Jesus and his

tree that was hung with all of the

stars of heaven, and had a Star of

Bethlehem on top.

    (BY THIS TIME THE CAMERA IS
    ON THE TOP OF THE TREE)

    (CROSS FADE TO MAMA IN CHAIR,
    DAGMAR IN HER LAP, THE OTHERS
    GROUPED AROUND HER AS IN
    OPENING)

[Handwritten margin notes:]

PAN WITH THEIR LOOK
TO DAGMAR AT TREE
HIT NARRATION

START UP TREE
LOSE DAGMAR

CRANK UP SLOWLY
TO STAR

TIGHT
GROUP IN
LIVING ROOM
AS IN OPENING.

③

47

MAMA:

And that is the tree your Great
Grandmama is looking at tonight.

(KISSES DAGMAR)

F A D E   O U T

PULL BACK SLOWLY

RACK OUT OF FOCUS

↓

BLACK

13. A Serious Drama

"THE LINE OF DUTY" * from *CAMEO THEATRE*

PRODUCTION SUGGESTIONS

BY

ALBERT McCLEERY

I am particularly pleased that the authors of this volume have chosen "The Line of Duty" to represent *Cameo Theatre*—it is so admirably suited to our requirements. For *Cameo* is not merely a name but a succinct description of a technique. We concentrate on the faces of human beings rather than on their surroundings. There is no scenery save a dark gray or purple cyclorama which encircles the studio and brings the light of the human face sharply into focus, an intimate focus. Consequently, character becomes our emphasis . . . and a story whose motivations are rooted so firmly in character as in "The Line of Duty"—is ideal.

Casting "The Line of Duty" presents no serious problems. The producer would do well to look around his community and seek real-life replicas of the characters. They certainly exist. It is entirely possible to use amateurs with no dramatic experience; sometimes it is even an advantage. If the producer casts to type, the man will fit the part because he is not acting; he is simply being himself.

As for the mood of this play—it is not so far removed from our experience as we would like to think. Many army veterans have witnessed a court-martial, or a board of inquiry. If your cast is unfamiliar with

---

such matters, find an articulate army man to describe his feelings to them. Or better still, take them to night court. Let them see what happens when human beings are caught in circumstances from which they cannot escape except by "due process of law."

The student-director should study the play thoroughly until he is sure of the motivating relationships and the underlying theme. The relationship of each character to the colonel is the keynote of the play. At one time the colonel was a private and doubtless acted much like the private does in the play. Coming up through the ranks, he was a sergeant and thought like a sergeant. Then he was an arrogant major. Just like each of his subordinates, he had followed the line of duty without question or thought. Now, he comes face to face with his Maker and questions in his heart for the first time the morality of the totalitarian way. No one else in the play has done any thinking at all, it's not safe to think. Even the prisoner chose not to think. Actually, he is as guilty as anyone else for the tragedy of these events. Presumably, he put this tyranny into power, or at least did nothing to oppose it. If he had to die, he might have died much more gallantly. His meekness and acquiescence ended in his being caught like a rat in a trap of his own making. These are thoughts not so much explicit as *implicit* in the play. The director must think this out and discuss it with the actors if the real meaning and depth of this play is to come across.

Physical action in this play is very simple and comes naturally from the characters. If an actor correctly grasps the role, he will probably move in character just as he speaks in character. The major walks and stands with assurance, the captain swaggers, the sergeant struts, the private merely perambulates. Let each actor do what comes naturally. In directing this play for television, I built the composition of the shots out of the faces and bodies of the actors, with very little empty space left between them. In this kind of play it will probably be found that the actors naturally work close together. However, the director may find it necessary to remind them of the need for playing it tight—that "if you ain't touching, you ain't in"—so the cameras can hold to the close shots so necessary to this style of production.

For economic reasons, I produced this play with four and a half hours of camera rehearsal. Six would have been better. Although the student-producer may find more time available to him, I doubt very strongly the wisdom of using more. The television medium, like anything else, has its limitations; and one universal limitation is short rehearsal time. Until the day arrives when a student can move into professional television and find dramatic shows rehearsing with more comfortable schedules, he will be well advised to learn the techniques of pre-planning, clear thinking and quick decision which make for efficient use of limited studio time.

The entire rehearsal schedule was as follows:

1 hr.—Reading Rehearsal
Delineation and analysis of character—discuss symbolism and implicit thoughts of play.
3-4 hrs.—Blocking (dry rehearsal outside studio)
Move people around—visualize shots—probe for angles—have actors do what is natural.
3 hrs.—Dry Rehearsal
Smoothing, tightening.
Action and position—conquering memory work so action is effortless and authentic.
3-4 hrs. Final Dry Rehearsal
More tightening—final decisions on camera shots—which cameras were available for each shot—where cables would lie along floor— each shot was picked and put down in black and white.

Rehearsal scripts were then prepared for TD, audio man (with directions and cues for moving microphone boom) cameramen's cue sheets, sound effects, etc.

4½ hrs. Camera Rehearsal in Studio
½ hr. Dry-Run
On set with actors only, who simply walked through for action, not bothering to say all the lines.
2 hrs. 15 min. Camera Blocking
Each scene was taken individually—first the actors played the scene as the technical crew grouped around to watch; then to the control room and cameras to work out the shots.
45 min. Run-Thru
Stop and start when necessary (expected to be a little sloppy)— actors speed up and cameras are caught not quite ready, etc.
1 hr. Dress Rehearsal

The craft of television directing requires that the director so master his medium that he can plan every detail before the day of studio rehearsal. Above all, he must be able to visualize what his cameras are going to show him. He should do this so well that he will be neither surprised nor chagrined at the shots he finally gets. Out of a script such as this containing some 75 shots, he should lose no more than five shots due to unforeseen conditions. In other words, he should come into the studio knowing *exactly what he wants.* The director who vacillates, who listens to too many people, will make so many changes that his pre-planning will be of little value and his camera blocking will run way over into run-through or dress rehearsal time. The cameraman, for his part, should give the director what he wants, but should not presume to tell the director what he should have. He should never have to say "I have a better shot." He may contribute a better or an easier way to the director's objective, or he may improve on the shot the director has planned. The best cameraman not only gives the director what he wants but makes it better.

Since the setting for "The Line of Duty" is so extremely simple, it was not necessary here to include a floor plan of the studio. The small sketches of the set that I have made along the margins of the script, which were sufficient for me at the time of production, will serve to guide the student-designer in laying out his studio.

A word about my illustrations. I believe there is no better way to record one's visualization of a camera shot than to draw a picture of it. As the reader can readily see, I am no artist. Yet I can with a few strokes record the essentials of a shot as I have planned it—information which, if made verbal, would take a great many words. Furthermore, on the next day's rehearsal, it takes only a glance to refresh my memory completely on each shot. I add these sketches to the technical director's script and to the cameramen's cue sheets so they will know what I am after and a minimum of explanation is required. Any television director or student-director can draw well enough for this purpose. If he can visualize a shot and hold this picture in his mind until he directs a camera to form it, he can also sketch the picture in a few simple lines. However, if he cannot visualize the picture until he sees it on camera, he belongs in some other, less visual, field. Incidentally, these drawings are not made directly on the script but on gummed labels which are then fixed to the script. Shot changes made during the early rehearsals may be recorded simply by drawing the new shot on another label and sticking it down on top of the first.

CAMEO THEATRE

DEVISED AND DIRECTED BY ALBERT McCLEERY

Presents
"THE LINE OF DUTY"
by
Guy de Vry
on
NBC — TV
July 26, 1950
<u>Cast</u>

THE COLONEL	William Post, Jr.
THE SERGEANT	James Little
THE LIEUTENANT	Douglas Kennedy
THE PRISONER	Robert Crozier
HIS WIFE	Jane Murray
THE MAJOR	Ed Begley
THE PRIVATE	Richard McMurray

THE LINE OF DUTY [*]

(FADE IN ON A LONG SHOT OF A
VERY BARE SUGGESTED COURTROOM.
THERE ARE FOUR CHAIRS ... WOODEN,
STRAIGHTBACK, UNCOMFORTABLE. THREE
ARE OCCUPIED. TO ONE SIDE STANDS A
WOODEN PLATFORM, TWO STEPS LEADING
UP TO IT. ON IT, A LARGER CHAIR
WITH ARMRESTS. THE SCENE IS LIT
SHARPLY WITH PIN SPOTS. ON THE
FLOOR, BETWEEN THE CHAIRS AND THE
PLATFORM, WE SEE THE ELONGATED
SHADOW OF A BARRED WINDOW WHICH
WE CAN IMAGINE BEING ABOVE AND
BEHIND THE WITNESS CHAIR.)

(SITTING IN THE THREE CHAIRS ARE
THE SERGEANT, THE MAJOR, AND THE
PRIVATE. STANDING BY THE WITNESS
CHAIR, BESIDE THE PLATFORM, LOOKING
UP AT THE INVISIBLE BARRED WINDOW
STANDS THE COLONEL. ALL ARE IN
UNIFORMS, WHICH ARE DARK, SEVERE.
THE SHINY BELTS AND BOOTS GIVE THEM
A TOTALITARIAN APPEARANCE AND THIS
WILL SERVE AS OUR ONLY CLUE AS TO
THE MILITARY NATURE OF THE UNIFORMS.
NOW, VERY SLOWLY, THE CAMERA TRUCKS
FORWARD TOWARDS THE COLONEL. AS
THIS HAPPENS.........

........TITLE CARDS ARE SUPERIMPOSED
OVER THE PICTURE. THE LETTERING IS
BOLD, CRISP, OFFICIAL AND COLD.
WITH THE LAST TITLE CARD.....

.....THE COLONEL IS HELD IN A ~~MEDIUM~~ _LONG_
SHOT, PROFILE. WE CAN SEE THE OTHER
BEYOND HIM. OVER THIS PICTURE, WE
NOW HEAR THE ANNOUNCER'S VOICE. HE
SPEAKS SLOWLY, CLEARLY ... VERY CLOSE
ON MIKE.....ALMOST WHISPERING, GIVING
THE IMPRESSION THAT IF HE WERE TO
SPEAK LOUDER, HE WOULD DISRUPT THE
GATHERING.)

ANNCR:

(OFF SHOT) It isn't necessary to

give the characters names. Neither

is it necessary to place the action

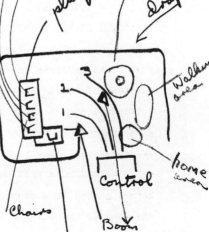

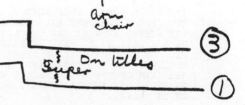

-1-

ANNCR: (CONT.)

in any particular locality. Perhaps

it happened yesterday .... perhaps

it happened today. That doesn't matter.

What matters very much is that it won't

happen here. .....ever!

(THE COLONEL TURNS, FACING THE SEATED

MEN. HE'S A SHARP, INTELLIGENT MAN

OF SIXTY, ACCUSTOMED TO AUTHORITY ...

A MAN OF SOME DIGNITY, TOLERANCE, AND

QUIET WISDOM)

COLONEL:

(A LITTLE TIRED, WEARY, DISILLUSIONED)

Gentlemen ... I have asked you here so

that I can discover the truth about the

incident of the prisoner. Two days ago,

I issued a simple order requesting that

a certain man be brought to me here at

headquarters. As a result of that ...

well, we all know what happened. But

before I turn in a complete report to

the Commanding General, I have decided

to ...

(HE STOPS FOR AT THIS MOMENT, EMERGING
OUT OF THE DARKNESS AND STEPPING INTO
THE ACTING AREA WE SEE THE LIEUTENANT.
HE'S A TALL YOUNG MAN, IMPRESSED WITH
HIS OWN IMPORTANCE. HE TAKES PRIDE IN
BOTH UNIFORM AND RANK, AND IS A PERFECT
SPECIMEN OF THE WELL TRAINED MILITARY
MACHINE. AS THE LIEUTENANT GOES TO THE
EMPTY CHAIR....)

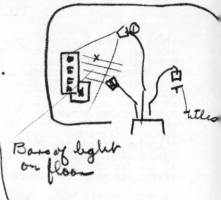

Bars of light on floor

titles

③ moves to center when released from titles

②

tight med of II high rack shot

-2-

                    COLONEL:

(SHARPLY) You're late, lieutenant.

                    LIEUTENANT:

(VERY CALMLY) Yes sir.

                    COLONEL:

(SLOWLY) No explanation?

                    LIEUTENANT:

(WITH A HALF SMILE) Do you want one,

sir?

                    COLONEL:

Yes.

                    LIEUTENANT:

(CALMLY) I was detained, sir.

                    COLONEL:

Detained?

                    LIEUTENANT:

Yes sir.

                    COLONEL:

By whom?

                    LIEUTENANT:

The General.

                    COLONEL:

I see. (LOOKS AT THE LIEUTENANT,

AND WE RECEIVE THE IMPRESSION THAT

THE COLONEL IS WELL AWARE OF WHAT

MUST HAVE TRANSPIRED BETWEEN THE

TWO) Please take your seat,

Lieutenant!

(THE LIEUTENANT SITS, HIS BEARING

STIFF, FORMAL, ALERT)

In order to turn in a satisfactory

report about the incident of the

prisoner ... my nature compels me to

go into the entire matter in detail.

I therefore demand complete coopera-

tion from all of you.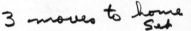

(CALLS OUT) Sergeant?

(THE SERGEANT, A MAN OF FORTY AND A

WELL DISCIPLINED SOLDIER, IS A TRIFLE

ILL AT EASE)

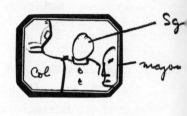

       COLONEL:

Sergeant, you were the very first one

to come in direct contact with the

prisoner. Isn't that so?

       SERGEANT:

Yes sir.

       COLONEL:

Will you tell me how?

       SERGEANT:

(THE QUESTIONING PUZZLES HIM) Well,

sir, I .... I received written orders

from you to arrest the man.

       COLONEL:

(SLOWLY) Are you sure of that,

Sergeant?

       SERGEANT:

(PUZZLED) Sir?

-4-

> COLONEL:

(PATIENTLY) Sure that the order said
arrest?

> SERGEANT:

Oh! (BRIGHTENING) Well ... of
course! I have it right here!
(HE DIGS INTO HIS POCKET AND BRINGS
FORTH A SHABBY, WELL WORN PIECE OF
PAPER) I always keep documents like
this! (PROUDLY) After twenty five
years in the service ... I know
what's what!

> COLONEL:

(SLYLY) I'm sure you do, Sergeant.
(DOES NOT LOOK AT THE ORDER OR TAKE
IT) Does the order say to arrest
the man?

> SERGEANT:

Here, sir, you can see for yourself!
(STILL THE COLONEL MAKES NO MOVE, SO
THE SERGEANT UNFOLDS IT WITH ALMOST
LOVING PRIDE) It says right here
that ...

> COLONEL:

Well, sergeant?

> SERGEANT:

Well ... it doesn't say arrest ...
but it says pick up! And that's
the same thing!

COLONEL:

Since when?

SERGEANT:

Sir ... I don't see why all these
questions are ...

COLONEL:

Since when, Sergeant?

SERGEANT:

Since I've been in the service!
I can show you a stack of other
orders ... they say either pick up
or arrest .. but they all mean
arrest!   2:30

COLONEL:

You may lower the pitch of your
voice, Sergeant. I can hear you
quite well!

SERGEANT:

I have lots of orders I can show,
sir!

COLONEL:

(WEARILY) Continue with your story,
Sergeant.

SERGEANT:

(HESITATES, THEN SPEAKS A TRIFLE
SULKILY) Well, I went to the
prisoner's home. As you know, he's
a laborer and lives in a little
house in ....

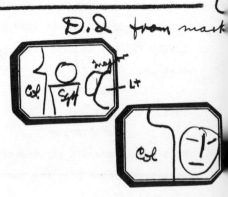

            COLONEL:

(IMPATIENTLY) Just tell me what you

did, sergeant! I can fill in details

of local color myself!

            SERGEANT:

I knocked on the door. At the second   300

knock, it opened and a woman looked out.   3

            WIFE:

Yes? What is it?

            SERGEANT:

(OFF SHOT) Does this man live here?

            WIFE:

Yes. He lives here. He's my husband.

(WITH FEAR) But what do you ....

            PRISONER:

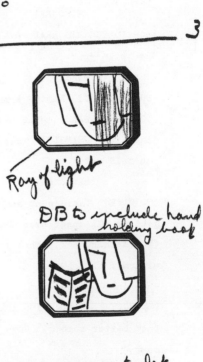

Ray of light

DB to include hand
holding book

(OFF SHOT) Who is it?

            SERGEANT:

Tell your husband I must see him.

            WIFE:

But why? Why must you see him? Why ...

(NOW THE PRISONER ENTERS THE PICTURE.

HE'S A SMALL, LEAN, ORDINARY LITTLE

MAN IN HIS SIXTIES, IN NEED OF A SHAVE

AND HAVING OBVIOUSLY JUST RISEN FROM

A NAP.)

            PRISONER:

Who wants to see me? Who ...

(SEES THE SERGEANT AND STOPS)

DB move to let
in Prisoner

Sgt

                  -7-

SERGEANT:

(TAKES THE PHOTOGRAPH BACK FROM THE
WIFE, LOOKS AT IT, THEN AT THE
PRISONER, THEN PUTS IT INTO HIS
POCKET) You will come with me.

PRISONER:

(SCRATCHING HIS HEAD, WAKING UP NOW)
Come with you?

WIFE:

(TO SERGEANT) What's wrong?
(TO HER HUSBAND) What have you
done? (ACCUSINGLY) What haven't
you told me?

PRISONER:

(TO WIFE) There's no sense in your
getting all upset over nothing.
(TO THE SERGEANT) What do you want
with me?

SERGEANT: 3:30

(WITHOUT FEELING) You must know
that better than I. Come along,
now!

WIFE:

(TO SERGEANT) Please ... tell me
.... what has he done? Where are
you taking him?

SERGEANT:

(WEARILY) He'll find out at
headquarters!

-8-

WIFE:

At headquarters!! You must have
done something!

PRISONER:

Don't you have any faith in me?

WIFE:

In you ... yes, of course! But not
in headquarters!

PRISONER:

(TO SERGEANT) There ... there must
be some mistake. Only political
enemies are ever taken to headquarters!

SERGEANT:

I don't know anything about that. 4:00
I've got my orders and I'm obeying
them. That's all!

PRISONER:

You ... you have the wrong man!

WIFE:

(TO SERGEANT) Sure ... that's it.
The wrong man! Don't you see,
sergeant? It's possible to make
mistakes! The wrong name on a
piece of paper ... the wrong
address ... It is possible to make
mistakes.

PRISONER:

Oh, come, I have nothing to fear.

WIFE:

Headquarters! Have you ever seen
anyone come <u>back</u> from headquarters?
Ever?

PRISONER:

(TRYING TO CONVINCE HIMSELF) But
I ... this is different!

WIFE:

<u>IS</u> it different? Is it different
only because it's happening to you
and not to somebody else?

PRISONER:

I have a clear conscience. *4:30*

WIFE:

That's wonderful. Tell that to
the Colonel! <u>That</u> should settle
everything!

PRISONER:

What have I to be afraid of? I've
lived here for twenty years. I've
worked for the Party ... I've made
friends with no one ... I ...

SERGEANT:

(COLDLY) Say goodbye to her and
let's go.   *4:45*

WIFE:

(TO PRISONER) I'll never see you
again!

-10-

PRISONER:

But of course you will! Why ... in
a day or so .... I'll be back.
They'll discover the mistake ...
and ... why, they'll even apologize,
you'll see! I'll be back and we'll
laugh about this and ... (STOPS,
BECAUSE HE DOESN'T, AND CAN'T,
BELIEVE IT HIMSELF) I'll be back.

WIFE:

(LOW) I'll never see you again!

SERGEANT:

I took the prisoner to headquarters
and there I turned him over to the
Major.
(THE CAMERA TRUCKS BACK FOR A
MEDIUM TWO SHOT, INCLUDING THE
COLONEL)
The Major dismissed me ... and
that was the last time I saw the
prisoner.

COLONEL:

I see. (HE PAUSES, PURSING HIS
LIPS, WONDERING HOW TO PHRASE THE
NEXT QUESTION)
Now sergeant, you admit, then,
being the first ever to use the
word ... arrest?

-11-

SERGEANT:

(HEDGING) Well, sir, I only ...

COLONEL:

(SHARPLY) Answer my question!

SERGEANT:

(CRUSHED) Yes sir. I was!

COLONEL:

You may go back to your chair.

Major? Will you please step up

here?

(THE MAJOR RISES. HE'S A SMALL,
HEAVY SET MAN, AND QUITE BALD. HE'S
A PATRONIZING MAN WITH A SLIMY AIR
... IMPRESSED BY HIGHER RANK ...
HUMBLE IN THE PRESENCE OF SUPERIORS
... AND A TYRANT TO THOSE UNDER HIS
IMMEDIATE COMMAND. HE SITS DOWN
VERY SELF CONSCIOUSLY, SMILING
NERVOUSLY AT THE COLONEL. HE CROSSES
HIS LEGS BUT A LOOK FROM THE COLONEL
MAKES HIM SIT UP STRAIGHT, THE SMILE
GONE FROM HIS FACE)

COLONEL:

Well, Major, we meet again!

MAJOR:

(UNSURE, DOESN'T KNOW WHAT LINE OF
ATTACK THE COLONEL WILL TAKE,
PLAYING IT VERY SAFELY)

Yes sir, It's...it's been quite

some time hasn't it, sir?

COLONEL:

Almost four years. You were only a

second lieutenant then. You've come

a long way!

MAJOR:

(SMILING) Yes sir.

-12-

                COLONEL:

My congratulations.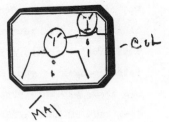

                MAJOR:

(VERY UNSURE, BUT WILL PLEASE THE
COLONEL AT ALL COSTS)

I....I had some fortunate breaks,

Colonel. There was a local uprising

and ...

                COLONEL:

....and ten suspects were shot. I

remember it well!

                MAJOR:

I was under orders, sir.

                COLONEL:

And you carried them out exceedingly

well. You and the sergeant have a

lot in common, Major!

                MAJOR:

(SLIGHTLY OFFENDED, BUT STILL
PLAYING IT SAFELY)

Our backgrounds are different, sir.

                COLONEL:

And your principles? Yes, Major,

you've come a long way!

                MAJOR:

Why, sir....you...you speak as if

I were on trial <u>myself</u>!

                COLONEL:

It's difficult to determine <u>who's</u>

on trial, isn't it, Major!

                        -13-

MAJOR:

(WITH AN EMBARASSED SMILE) I'm ...
I'm afraid, sir, I don't quite see
what you're getting at!

COLONEL:

No, no, I guess you don't. (ALMOST
SADLY NOW) Yes, you've come a long
way! You've pushed a lot of things
into the back of your mind. (SHAKES
HIS HEAD, AND THEN FORCES HIMSELF TO
COME BACK TO THE PRESENT MOMENT)
Now then...the prisoner was brought
directly to your office?

MAJOR:

(VERY SUBSERVIENT) Yes, Colonel.
That's right, sir. To my office!
Yes sir!

COLONEL:

Tell us what happened.

MAJOR:

Er ... yes sir. (RUNS A FINGER
UNDER THE EDGE OF HIS TIGHT COLLAR)
Well, sir, I told the sergeant he
could leave and then I left the
prisoner alone for a moment. (SMILING)
To collect his thoughts! My personal
feelings play no part in matters of
this sort. I was completely impersonal
to the prisoner at all times, sir.

-14-

                COLONEL:

(FINDING THE MAJOR OBNOXIOUS) Yes,

Major. I have no doubts as to what

your attitude must have been!

(THE MAJOR SMILES, PLEASED, THEN
SUDDENLY THE SMILE FREEZES. HE
REALIZES THERE ARE TWO POSSIBLE
INTERPRETATIONS. HE BECOMES SERIOUS)

                MAJOR:

(FLUSHING SLIGHTLY) You're being

unfair, sir!

                COLONEL:

Your story, Major.

                MAJOR:

Yes, of course! Well, I left the

prisoner alone a few minutes and then

I walked into my office.

(DISSOLVE QUICKLY INTO A MEDIUM SHOT
OF THE PRISONER STANDING IN FRONT OF
A DESK, FACING THE CAMERA. BLACK
BACKGROUND. HE IS ALONE. HE IS
LOOKING AROUND NERVOUSLY, THEN, HEAR-
ING FOOTSTEPS, HE TURNS, AND THE
MAJOR WALKS INTO THE PICTURE. HE
IGNORES THE PRISONER, SITS BEHIND
THE DESK, PICKS UP A SHEET OF PAPER,
LOOKS AT IT, PUTS IT DOWN SLOWLY,
THEN GLANCES UP AT THE PRISONER.)

                MAJOR:

(HIS ATTITUDE HAS CHANGED FROM WHAT
IT WAS WITH THE COLONEL. NOW HE'S
IN CHARGE ... THE MAN IN LOVE WITH
POWER AND AUTHORITY, THE DANGEROUS
SADIST)

So ... you are the notorious prisoner,

eh? Do you know why you've been

arrested?

                        -15-

PRISONER:

No sir. I think it's all a terrible
mistake.

MAJOR:

(SHARPLY) Mistake? (SNEERING) Be
careful what you say, my good man.
To accuse the party of mistakes is   D. I.
to voice political doubt! That can
be both unwise and dangerous! (HOLDS
UP THE SHEET OF PAPER) Can you read? 8:00

PRISONER:

Yes sir.

MAJOR:

(SARCASTIC) A splendid accomplishment
for a man of your class. As you can
see ... it comes from main headquarters and is signed by the Colonel.
You've heard of the Colonel, haven't
you?

PRISONER:

Yes sir.

MAJOR:

(WITH FINALITY) The Colonel doesn't
make mistakes. There's no doubt in
my mind that you're guilty. (WITH A 8:15
SIGH) After all the party has done   D.I.
for this country ... still there are   tighter
those who aren't satisfied!
(SHAKES HIS HEAD)

-16-

                    PRISONER:

(HESITANTLY) Sir ... does that ...
that order say <u>why</u> the Colonel wants
to see me?

                    MAJOR:

(ANGRILY) Of course it doesn't! You
know what you have done and the
<u>Colonel</u> knows. Nobody else <u>has</u> to   8:30
know!

                    PRISONER:

(SLIGHT PLEADING) But sir ... I
haven't done <u>anything</u>! I've not been
disloyal ... not even in my thoughts!
Why, I pay my taxes and I ...

                    MAJOR:

Taxes? (LAUGHS UPROARIOUSLY) Do
you think the Colonel would bother
himself with so insignificant a thing
as <u>taxes</u>? Oh, my good man, really!
You will be taken to Junction K where
you will be turned over to the Lieutenant. (HE STOPS, LOOKS UP, GRINS
AS HE GETS A NEW THOUGHT. HE WRITES,
BLOTS THE PAPER WITH SATISFACTION)
And you shall be placed in handcuffs!

(CAMERA TRUCKS IN FOR AN EXTREME
CLOSE UP OF THE PRISONER'S FACE,
FILLED WITH ASTONISHMENT. HOLD THIS
CLOSE UP UNTIL END OF SCENE)

                    PRISONER:

(AGHAST) Handcuffs?   9:00

                    -17-

                    MAJOR: (OFF SHOT)

(COLDLY) Handcuffs.

                    PRISONER:

But I won't try to escape! I'll go   *D. d.*

peacefully! Don't you understand,

sir, I <u>want</u> to see the Colonel now!

A mistake has been made and I must

be cleared of all suspicion. The

handcuffs aren't necessary. I'm not

a dangerous man!

                    MAJOR: (OFF SHOT)

(SMUGLY) Those who appear <u>most</u>   *Dolly sharply into*

harmless are. always <u>most</u> dangerous.   *Prisoner's face —*

You shall be put in handcuffs and   *Extreme C.U.*

if I were you ... I'd say nothing

more about a ... <u>mistake!</u>

(THE PRISONER WANTS TO SAY SOME-
THING, BUT HE THINKS BETTER OF IT.
NOW A LOOK OF GRIM DETERMINATION
COMES ACROSS HIS FACE. HE STILL
HAS A BIT OF HOPE)

(DISSOLVE THE CLOSE UP INTO AN   *3 moves into*
EXTREME CLOSE UP OF THE MAJOR'S   *center of set*
FACE, HE IS BACK IN THE WITNESS   *to take Lt. & Major*
CHAIR. HIS ATTITUDE HAS REVERTED
BACK AGAIN TO THE HUMBLE, SUB-
SERVIENT MAN)

                    COLONEL:

(OFF SHOT) And is that all, Major?

                    MAJOR:

(SMILING) Yes sir, it is, sir.

(CAMERA TRUCKS BACK FOR A MEDIUM
SHOT OF THE TWO)

                          -18-

> COLONEL:

Then it was <u>you</u>, and you <u>alone</u> who
authorized the handcuffs?

> MAJOR:

I ... er ... well, sir, I ... yes
sir, I did.

> COLONEL:

(SOFTLY) Why?

> MAJOR:

Well, sir ... it's a long way to
Junction K. I knew nothing about
the man ... nothing about the nature
of his crime. The last revolution
taught us to beware of the apparently
innocent. Even now, there are underground forces at work, trying to
destroy the glorious work which the
party has ...

> COLONEL:

(INTERRUPTING) Spare me your
opinions, Major.

> MAJOR:

It wasn't wise or prudent of me to
take unnecessary chances. I was only
acting in the line of duty!

> COLONEL:

The line of duty? I see. Is that
going to be your line of defense?

-19-

MAJOR:

I don't think a defense is
necessary, sir! It's a fact! There
are existing regulations one can
adhere to in <u>all</u> situations! After
all, sir, I think you'll agree ...
the safety of the party is <u>more</u>
important than the physical
discomfort of one insignificant
individual!

2

COLONEL:

Insignificant? Is <u>that</u> your new
opinion of people, Major?
Insignificant?

MAJOR:

Well, Colonel, sir..you....you
know that to be true yourself!
Compared to the party....what <u>is</u>
the individual <u>but</u> insignificant?

COLONEL:

And that includes yourself, too,
Major?

MAJOR:

(HESITATES SLIGHTLY. IT TAKES AN
EFFORT FOR HIM TO UTTER THE NEXT
LINE, BUT HE DOES IT)

Yes sir....that includes me too.

COLONEL:

You've come a long way, Major.
That's all, Major.

*on Lt & Major
as they exchange looks* *3*

DB

(CAMERA TRUCKS BACK FOR A LONG SHOT
AS THE MAJOR STEPS DOWN AND RETURNS
TO HIS CHAIR. ONCE AGAIN, THE
LIEUTENANT GLANCES TOWARDS THE MAJOR.
ONCE AGAIN HIS IMPRESSION IS ONE OF
CONVEYING FULL CONFIDENCE AND A
TOUCH OF OPEN REBELLION AGAINST THE
COLONEL)

            COLONEL:

Lieutenant?

You're a stickler for military

courtesy, aren't you?

            LIEUTENANT:

I have respect for higher <u>rank</u>, sir.

            COLONEL:

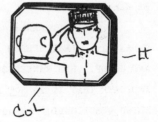

Only the rank?

            LIEUTENANT:

(KNOWS DAMN WELL WHAT THE COLONEL
MEANS, BUT PLAYS DUMB)

Sir?

            COLONEL:

Can you separate the rank from the

individual?

            LIEUTENANT:

(CAREFULLY) I don't understand

your question, sir.

            COLONEL:

You don't understand it...or you

don't <u>want</u> to understand it?

            LIEUTENANT:

(DELIBERATELY CHANGING THE SUBJECT)

May I sit down, sir?

                    COLONEL:

By all means, Lieutenant.

                    LIEUTENANT:

Thank you.

(HE SITS, HIS ENTIRE MANNER
EXTREMELY ALERT)

                    COLONEL:

Suppose you tell me what happened

at Junction K.

                    LIEUTENANT:

Certainly. (HIS SPEECH IS PRECISE

AND SHARP. HIS MANNER SEEMS TO

INDICATE THAT IT IS NOT HE WHO IS

BEING QUESTIONED) I had received my

instructions from the Major earlier

in the day, and so I was fully

prepared.

(CAMERA SLOWLY TRUCKS IN FOR AN
EXTREME CLOSE UP OF THE LIEUTENANT)

I was to guard the prisoner and

deliver him to you, sir, the following

day. He came into my office, dragging

his feet. He could have been tired

... (SMUGLY SUPERIOR) ...or he could

have been doing it for effect. A lot

of political prisoners try to use age

as a defensive weapon. (A SLY SMILE)

I'm hardly a gullible type of man.

(NOW THE CLOSE UP OF THE LIEUTENANT
DISSOLVES INTO AN EXTREME CLOSE UP
OF THE PRISONER'S HANDS, HANDCUFFED
BEHIND HIS BACK. AS THIS PICTURE IS

-22-

ESTABLISHED, THE CAMERA SLOWLY TRUCKS
BACK TO GIVE US A LONG SHOT OF THE
PRISONER. HE STANDS (HIS BACK TO THE
CAMERA) DRAWN AND TIRED. THERE IS A
CHAIR SOME DISTANCE AWAY FROM HIM,
LIT BY A VERY BRIGHT SPOTLIGHT. IN
IT SITS THE LIEUTENANT LOOKING UP AT
THE PRISONER WITH DISDAIN)

    LIEUTENANT:

You're much older than I expected.

One would suppose that a man of your

age had learned discretion and gratitude

by now. What have you done?

    PRISONER:

Sir ... my arrest is a ...

    LIEUTENANT:

(INTERRUPTING QUICKLY AND CALMLY) ...

a mistake. (SMILING) Was that what

you were going to say? (HIS SMILE

FADES) I could hardly expect you to

say anything else. When the enemy is

caught, it is <u>always</u> a mistake.

    PRISONER:

(DESPERATELY) But it really is, sir.

<u>Someone</u> has to believe me. They have

the wrong man, I'm sure of it!

    LIEUTENANT:

(WITH GREAT WEARINESS) Yes, yes, yes.

You conspire against the party and

then when you're caught ... it's a

mistake. (LAUGHS) You're right. It

<u>is</u> a mistake. For <u>you</u>! There's no

doubt that your crime is a political one.

Dd
slow
to
Elbow
Shot

LIEUTENANT: (CONT'D)

It always seems to begin with the old
people nowadays. They remember the
old and dead world; they can't gear
their minds to accept the new. It
leads to confusion and ...to treason!

PRISONER:

Sir, I'm only a little man. I've
always done what I was told.

LIEUTENANT:

Did you do everything willingly?

PRISONER:

I've never disobeyed an order ...
never! I don't even bother myself
with politics. If the party says do
this ... I do it....All I want is peace
and to be left alone.

LIEUTENANT:

You'll have your chance for that
tonight. You'll spend the night here.
Our prison cells may not be the clean-
est ... but they are the loneliest.
The experience will do you a world of
good. You'll have a chance to search
your conscience ... give yourself a
much needed self examination ... and
see precisely where and how you have
failed the party!

(CAMERA NOW come TO AN EXTREME CLOSE
UP OF THE PRISONER'S FACE. HOPE HAS
DRAINED OUT OF IT. DESPAIR HAS
REPLACED IT. HE LOWERS HIS HEAD
SLOWLY AND CONSIDERS HIS SITUATION
USELESS)

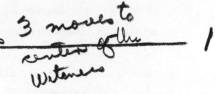

(CAMERA NOW DISSOLVES INTO AN
EXTREME CLOSE UP OF THE COLONEL,
LOOKING DIRECTLY INTO THE CAMERA, A
LOOK OF INTENSE DISPLEASURE ON HIS
FACE)

            COLONEL:

(BRISKLY) Is that all, Lieutenant?

(SLOWLY THE CAMERA TRUCKS BACK, AND
NOW AGAIN WE FIND THE LIEUTENANT IN
THE WITNESS CHAIR, SITTING CALMLY,
THE TIPS OF HIS FINGERS TOUCHING,
SMILING SLYLY AT THE COLONEL)

            LIEUTENANT:

At reveille the following morning, I

turned the prisoner over to the private.

(HE LOOKS TOWARDS THE OTHER CHAIRS, AND

THEN NODS AT THE PRIVATE SITTING THERE)

I told him that the prisoner was

dangerous and that his attitude of

confused innocence might be nothing

but a sham. He would have to be watched

every step of the way. I gave further

instructions for the prisoner to be

walked to headquarters! (SMUGLY)

That's in accordance with regulation

274, issued last Monday ... aimed at

the necessary conservation of gasoline

due to our armament policy and the

anticipated northern maneuvers.

COLONEL:

(SHARPLY) I'm acquainted with the
regulation, Lieutenant.

LIEUTENANT:

(UNRUFFLED) Quite so, sir.

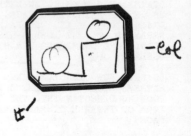

COLONEL:

Lieutenant ... by what strange method
of reasoning did you assume the man
to be a political prisoner?

LIEUTENANT:

(SLIGHT RESENTMENT TO THE TONE OF THE
QUESTION) It was quite obvious, sir.
He showed an open hostility to the
party. He claimed that headquarters
had made a mistake. A man loyal to
the party hardly permits himself so
absurd an assumption. It is paramount
to have faith in the party, even in
the face of seeming contradictions.
His entire attitude was proof of his
treasonous nature!

COLONEL:

(BITTERLY) Your party logic is
commendable! Only your conclusions
leave a lot to be desired. That's
all, Lieutenant.

(THE LIEUTENANT STEPS DOWN, AND
AGAIN SALUTES THE COLONEL. BUT
THIS TIME IT'S ONLY A MOCK SALUTE,
THE COLONEL REFUSES TO RETURN IT,
AND WITH A CAUSTIC SHRUG OF HIS
SHOULDERS, THE LIEUTENANT RETURNS

TO HIS CHAIR. IT IS OBVIOUS THAT
THE COLONEL HAS MADE A DANGEROUS
ENEMY. THE COLONEL TURNS)

          COLONEL:

Private!

(THE CAMERA TRUCKS BACK FOR A LONG
SHOT AS THE PRIVATE RISES AND COMES
TOWARDS THE PLATFORM. HE TAKES HIS
SEAT, CLEARS HIS THROAT. CAMERA
TRUCKS FORWARD FOR A TWO SHOT. THE
PRIVATE IS A YOUNG MAN IN HIS EARLY
TWENTIES. HIS APPEARANCE IMPLIES
THAT HE'S A DREAMER, AND PROBABLY A
VERY BAD SOLDIER. HIS ENTIRE MANNER
IS MOST UNMILITARY)

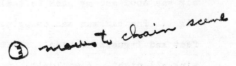

          COLONEL:

And now we come to you. (SMILES

DOURLY) Ironic ... the lowest rank

commands the highest attention. You

may sit down, Private. How long

have you been in the service?

          PRIVATE:

Two years, sir.

          COLONEL:

Volunteered?

          PRIVATE:

No sir.

          COLONEL:

Why not?

          PRIVATE:

I didn't think I was cut out for

military service.

          COLONEL:

To judge by what happened ... that

appears to be true. What did the

-27-

COLONEL: (CONT.)

party's compulsory aptitude test

reveal about you?

PRIVATE:

(SHYLY) I was rated politically

immature .... and unstable.

COLONEL:

I suppose army life has helped?

PRIVATE:

I don't know, sir.

COLONEL:

Suppose you begin?

PRIVATE:

(TAKING A DEEP BREATH) The prisoner

was turned over to me at ten minutes

after six, and we began our walk to

headquarters. It was a day. The

air was cool and my pack felt almost

light. The old man was dragging his

feet and I guess he hadn't slept a

wink all night. I wouldn't have if

I had been in his fix. So at about

nine, I called for the first rest.

(PICTURE DISSOLVES INTO A MEDIUM
SHOT OF THE PRISONER, STILL HAND-
CUFFED, MUCH MORE TIRED, SINKING
EXHAUSTEDLY TO THE GROUND. A PACK
APPEARS IN THE PICTURE AND IS
DROPPED TO THE GROUND, THE CAMERA
TRUCKS BACK AND THEN THE PRIVATE
STEPS INTO THE PICTURE, SITTING
DOWN AND RESTING A RIFLE ON HIS
LAP. UNDER THIS WE HEAR THE
DISTANT SOUND OF BIRDS.)

on feet
extreme C U.

① gets in position

-28-

PRIVATE:

(SYMPATHETICALLY) You look tired,
old man.

PRISONER:

I'm not so strong any more. I run
out of breath easily.

PRIVATE:

Had this happened last week, you'd
have got to go by car.
(SHAKING HIS HEAD) But now, with
all those new regulations...
(CHANGES THE SUBJECT, AND LEANS
AGAINST THE PACK) Why do they want
you at headquarters?

PRISONER:

(MISERABLY) I don't know. And I
don't care any more. It's like a
horrible nightmare. (WITH REGRET)
Things weren't like this in the old
days.

PRIVATE:

(DISMISSING THE MATTER) Well, you'll
find out soon enough. (LOOKS AROUND
AND SIGHS) What a day.

PRISONER:

(SADLY) When I was your age, I used
to go fishing on a day like this.
That was before the revolution.

                    PRISONER: (CONT.)
(REMEMBERING) I can't even remember
if things were any worse then. I <u>do</u>
remember that a man once had some
privacy ... some life of his own.
                    PRIVATE:
You must be older than I thought.
When I was born there was only the
party. (CURIOUSLY) Tell me, what
was it like <u>before</u> the party?
                    PRISONER:
(QUICKLY, A BIT FRIGHTENED) I...I
don't remember!
                    PRIVATE:
(REALIZING THAT HE ASKED A TABOO
QUESTION) I forgot. It's against
the law to ask that question. Well,
it doesn't matter. I read the books
in school. It was called democracy,
wasn't it? The exploitation of
labor ... freedom of competition ...
(SHAKES HIS HEAD) ... it must have
been rough. I never could understand
what it all meant.
                    PRISONER:
(SLOWLY) I guess it's hard for you
to imagine a world different from this.

                    13 -30-

PRIVATE:

Sometimes I get curious. Especially
when there are questions in my head
which the textbooks don't answer.
9SHRUGS HIS SHOULDERS AGAIN) As long
as one makes the best of things, *1830*
nothing is too bad.

PRISONER:

(HESITANTLY) Sir? Could I ... could
I have a drink of water?

PRIVATE:

(SLOWLY) It's not permitted. I only
have one canteen.

PRISONER:

I'll drink very little, just enough
to get the dust out of my mouth.

PRIVATE:

Do you know what it would mean if I
were caught? (THEN HE SMILES) It
wouldn't be the first time I did
something on my own ... against
regulations. (BITTERLY) It seems
that no matter what one does, it's
always in violation of some regulation
anyway! (TURNS TO HIS PACK AND
REMOVES THE CANTEEN) Here ...I'll hold
it for you. (HE FEEDS SOME WATER TO
THE OLD MAN AND THEN RETURNS IT TO
HIS PACK)

-31-

PRISONER:

(SINCERELY) Thank you. Thank you
very much. (HE RUBS THE SWEAT OFF
HIS FACE WITH HIS SHOULDER) The sun
is so hot. Everything is so bright. 1900
I...I can almost see the trees
dancing in the waves of the heat.

PRIVATE:

(LOOKING CAREFULLY AT THE PRISONER)
You know, I can't see anything
dangerous about you. But then ...
like they say ... it's what a man
thinks. Independent thinking ...
that's a man's worst enemy.

PRISONER:

Haven't you ever been guilty of
that?

PRIVATE:

Me? (HE STOPS, CONFUSED) You're
confusing me. I suppose everyone
has ... really. No wonder they said
I was politically immature ... that
I would never fit into any responsible
party position. I guess my trouble
is ... I ask too many questions.

PRISONER:

And their answers don't satisfy you?

PRIVATE:

There can't be answers for everything.

-32-

PRIVATE: (CONT.)

(CHANGING THE SUBJECT) Do you have

any kids?

PRISONER:

(SHAKING HIS HEAD) I wanted to

raise children for the state. There

was a child, a little girl. She

died and my wife couldn't have

another.

PRIVATE:

(SERIOUSLY) Why didn't you get

another wife? That's what the state

encourages a man to do in a case

like that.

PRISONER:

(SOFTLY) I happen to love my wife!

PRIVATE:

You know what they teach in school

about love? "Love is a selfish

emotion ..and selfishness can lead

to the destruction of the state."

PRISONER:

(GENTLY) It has great values.

PRIVATE:

(SERIOUSLY) I've wondered about it

.. often. This idea that we don't

exist for ourselves, but just for the

state...does that really make sense?

PRISONER:

Does it make sense to you?

PRIVATE:

It confuses me. They say a man should
only take a wife so that he can have
strong, healthy children to make a
strong, healthy state. Well, when I
questioned that in school.. they told
me I lacked faith ... that I didn't
understand.

PRISONER:

Then you've never been in love?

PRIVATE:

Not in the way I think you mean. Oh,
I've been to accepted camps. I've
looked around for somebody. I must
marry sooner or later; not to marry
is treason. If I can't find anybody,
the medics will help me pick a suitable
mate...someone who will be a good
mother.   3

PRISONER:

(SHAKING HIS HEAD SLOWLY) Everything
is very scientific now, isn't it.
From birth to death...it's the state
and always the state. It's hard to
remember that once there was something
called happiness. The revolution
brought us the party, and the party
told us to accept reality. And what
have they given us? Despair!   1

PRIVATE:

There's no sense in your moaning about
the old world. It's dead. You might
as well face it.

PRISONER:

Yes. It's dead, because no one ever
thought it could die!

PRIVATE:

(GENTLY) Take it easy, old man.
Things won't get any different by
crying about them.

(CAMERA MOVES IN FOR AN EXTREME
CLOSE UP OF THE PRISONER)

PRISONER:

The old world is dea. So is love ..
pity .. compassion! I was innocent
when all this began....innocent even
in thought. But now I __am__ guilty of
treason. The very little faith I
had in the state.. even that has now
been taken away from me. Only despair
remains. There is no longer anything
to live for! My thoughts can only
contaminate. They have contaminated
you, soldier. They will contaminate
my wife. I will bring nothing but
destruction upon the innocent. That
__should__ not be. That __cannot__ be!

(SLOWLY, THE CLOSE UP OF THE PRISONER
DISSOLVES INTO AN EXTREME CLOSE UP OF
THE PRIVATE, SITTING IN THE WITNESS
CHAIR, LOOKING INTO THE CAMERA)

-35-

PRIVATE:

I can remember a lot of things now.

It was warm and I started to feel

comfortable -- I didn't fall asleep --

I just felt -- well, you know -- a

little lazy, I guess.

(HE STOPS, LOOKS DOWN. CAMERA TRUCKS
BACK SLIGHTLY, GIVING US A MEDIUM
SHOT OF THE PRIVATE. HE CONTINUES,
LOOKS UP, HIS FACE GRIM)

When I turned my head to look at the

prisoner.. he was gone! I jumped to

my feet and then I saw him.. hobbling

over a field .. running...

(QUITE EMOTIONAL NOW AS HE RELIVES

THE EXPERIENCE) He was a good thirty

yards away. I shouted: "Come back,

you fool!" but he either didn't ...

or wouldn't.. hear. I put the rifle

to my shoulder, shouted again, but

it only made him run faster. (ALMOST

WITH DESPERATION) I became sore ..

at him .. at myself .. at... (STOPS,

FOR HE WAS AT THE POINT OF SAYING

"AT THE STATE.") I took careful aim

and then I fired.

(HE STOPS, TAKES A DEEP BREATH. WHEN
HE CONTINUES, HIS VOICE IS VERY SOFT)

The old man stopped, his head thrown

back. Then his legs buckled as if

hinges had come loose.

-36-

PRIVATE: (CONTD)

By the time I got to him, he was dead
... his blood looked bright red ...
dripping into the brown stubble of
the field. He was such a poor old man.
I couldn't help feeling that he had
run away <u>not</u> because he wanted to
escape ... but because he wanted to
die! (LOOKS UP INTO THE CAMERA)
That bothers me a little. They say
we have a perfect state. Why should
anyone want to die ..deliberately?

(CAMERA TRUCKS BACK, INCLUDING THE
COLONEL IN THE SHOT. THE COLONEL IS
OBVIOUSLY MOVED. HE HESITATES)

COLONEL:

(VERY WARMLY) Thank you, Private.
You .. you may go back to your chair.

(CAMERA TRUCKS BACK FOR A LONG SHOT
AS THE PRIVATE STEPS DOWN AND RETURNS
TO HIS CHAIR. NOW THE COLONEL SLOWLY
WALKS TOWARDS THE SEATED MEN, CAMERA
KEEPING HIM IN FRONT AND TRUCKING
FORWARD WITH HIM)

So now we know the whole story, don't
we... the whole story except <u>why</u> I
wanted this man brought to me here at
headquarters!

(HE STANDS BEFORE THEM NOW, QUIET,
RESERVED, ARMS BEHIND HIS BACK, A
CHALLENGER)

Well, gentlemen, I shall tell you.
There was a <u>slight</u> error in our
official records.. a small oversight.

-37-

COLONEL: (CONTD)

I wanted this man merely for the

purpose of recording his finger-

prints on our citizen registration

cards!

Pan with Col   2

(HE STOPS. THE MAJOR IS A BIT
STARTLED, LOOKS AROUND NERVOUSLY,
THEN SLOUCHES IN HIS SEAT. THE
SERGEANT LOOKS UP, DUMBFOUNDED.
THE PRIVATE SLOWLY RISES IN HIS
SEAT, THEN SINKS BACK HEAVILY,
DUMBFOUNDED, ANGERED, CONFUSED.
ONLY THE LIEUTENANT SITS COMPLETELY
CALM, UNMOVED, UNTOUCHED)

Now the man is dead. The card in

our files will be destroyed.. and he

will be forgotten. But not by

everyone.

(CAMERA CUTS QUICKLY TO AN EXTREME
CLOSE UP OF THE SERGEANT'S
DUMBFOUNDED FACE)

Not by you, Major...

(CAMERA CUTS TO AN EXTREME CLOSE UP
OF THE MAJOR'S FACE.. STARTLED,
INSECURE, BEWILDERED)

... who placed him in handcuffs and

labelled him a criminal. Not by

you, Lieutenant...

(CAMERA CUTS TO AN EXTREME CLOSE UP
OF THE LIEUTENANT.. HIS FACE COLD,
ARROGANT, UNEMOTIONAL. THERE'S
EVEN A SLIGHT SMILE ON HIS LIPS)

...who assumed him a political

enemy. Who began the chain of

events by turning a simple order

into an arrest.

-38-

(CAMERA CUTS BACK TO A MEDIUM SHOT,
THE COLONEL -- BACK TO CAMERA -- IN
THE FOREGROUND, FACING THE OTHERS)

And not by <u>you</u>, private. <u>Especially</u>

not by you. Well, the old man is

dead ... as dead as a way of life.

But he had dignity .. a hidden

spark of righteous indignation. He

is dead but we .. the living .. we

are the poorer!   *on Lt*   3

(THE LIEUTENANT RISES SLOWLY FROM
HIS CHAIR AND ADVANCES TOWARDS THE
COLONEL)

LIEUTENANT:

(SMUGLY) Are you quite finished,

Colonel?

COLONEL:

(WITHOUT SURPRISE, ONLY WITH

FINALITY) I was waiting for you

to act!

LIEUTENANT:

I think we've heard enough of your

.. perverted philosophies!   2

COLONEL:

(SHARPLY) I hardly expected that

my philosophies would make an

impression on <u>you</u>, Lieutenant!

(SMILING) I congratulate you for

showing such admirable restraint

up to now. But then.. it's all in

the line of duty, isn't it?

COLONEL: (CONTD)

The longer I talked .. so much more

firmly did I place a noose around

my neck!

(THE LIEUTENANT LOOKS UP IN SURPRISE)

(CALMLY) Yes, Lieutenant. I know

quite well what transpired between

you and the General earlier today.

LIEUTENANT:

Well! (HE HAS RECOVERED HIS

COMPOSURE) Then this mock trial

was rather useless, wasn't it?

COLONEL:

Not entirely. I have sat through

enough mock trials conducted by the

party to make me anxious for one of

my own!

LIEUTENANT:

(TAKES AN OFFICIAL DOCUMENT OUT OF

HIS POCKET, OPENS IT, READS) By

order of the Commanding General ..

for political sympathies alien to

the state... for expressions of a

treasonable nature... you are

hereby placed under official

arrest pending a trial.

Match with ①
on Pvt

(HE LOOKS UP AT THE COLONEL, THEN
FOLDS THE LETTER AND REPLACES IT)

-40-

PRIVATE:

(STANDING UP) Why, this is...

C U
on Lt. 1

LIEUTENANT:

(TURNING ABRUPTLY, FACING THE
PRIVATE) This is <u>what</u>? (THE
PRIVATE REMAINS SILENT) Come now,
private, you were about to say
something. This is <u>what</u>???

C U 3

PRIVATE:

(LOWERING HIS HEAD) Nothing, sir.

same as above 1

LIEUTENANT:

(TO THE PRIVATE) I need not remind
you that you are pending trial yourself. It was your negligence which
caused the death of the prisoner!
(HE TURNS BACK TO THE COLONEL)
Are you finished now?

3 goes to titles

2

COLONEL:

Beware of growing old, Lieutenant.
There comes a time when the line of
duty is not enough of an answer for
everything.

LIEUTENANT:

(SMUGLY) For the time being it
will do.

Med 1

COLONEL:

Beware of wisdom, for it contains
the seeds of treason. Even in our
<u>perfect</u> state,...duty is hardly a
substitute for human decency.

COLONEL: (CONTD)

That's the one thing the party has

never been able to eradicate,

Lieutenant. Decency! It won't

take much more than _that_ to defeat

the state!

(SLOWLY THE CAMERA TRUCKS BACK. WE
SEE THE SCENE IN A LONG SHOT. THE
COLONEL WALKS FORWARD AND AS HE COMES
ALONGSIDE THE PRIVATE, HE HESITATES
FOR JUST A MOMENT.)

(INSERT A CLOSE UP OF THE COLONEL
AND THE PRIVATE. HE SMILES WARMLY,
AND THE PRIVATE SMILES BACK. THERE'S
A NEW DIMENSION IN HIS FACE NOW.. HE
SEEMS OLDER... WISER... SURER OF
HIMSELF. HE SEEMS ALMOST MATURE.)

(BACK TO THE LONG SHOT. THE COLONEL
LEAVES THE ROOM, FOLLOWED BY THE
LIEUTENANT. THEN THE MAJOR AND THE
SERGEANT FOLLOW.)

(THE PRIVATE HESITATES, LOOKING
AFTER THEM. THEN, WITH A DETERMINED
STEP, HE ALSO EXITS.)

(SLOWLY THE CAMERA PANS OVER TO THE
WITNESS CHAIR AND TRUCKS FORWARD.
WE SEE THE EMPTY CHAIR, THE PLATFORM,
AND THE SHADOW ON THE FLOOR OF THE
BARRED WINDOW. WHEN THIS PICTURE IS
ESTABLISHED, HOLD. OVER IT .. AS IN
THE BEGINNING.. WE ONCE MORE HEAR
THE WHISPERING VOICE OF THE ANNOUNCER)

ANNOUNCER:

(OFF SHOT) (WHISPERING) Perhaps it

happened yesterday. Perhaps it

happened today. _That_ doesn't matter. 27⁴⁰

What matters very much is that it

won't happen _here_.... ever!

(SLOWLY THE PICTURE FADES OUT) ᴍ _closing titles_ 3

THE END   -42-

Appendix. Design for Simple Viewing Box

The simple portable viewfinder described here has usually carried the name "Bretzbox." There are many variations on the same principle that have been built and used by directors, but this particular design has been found to be the simplest and the most practical.

The principle of the box is to confine the field-of-view of the eye so that it can see only the horizontal and vertical angle-of-view of the camera lens. The eye is placed at an opening at one side of the box, and views the scene through a window on the far side. The size of the peep-hole which is placed against the eye is of no importance: the only reason for a peep-hole at all—rather than simply holding up a two-dimensional frame to look through—is that the eye must be a certain distance from the window in order to see the correct angle-of-view.

The most critical factor is, of course, the size of the opening on the far side of the box. This is easily calculated, however, from the lens angles.

Since the "Bretzbox" is cubical in shape it has six sides, in which a maximum of six windows may be cut, to correspond with six different lenses. A lens window on one side of the box will then serve as a peep-hole for a window on the opposite side.

In building the box, start with six squares of cardboard each six inches on a side. Choose one as a templet and lay out all the lens angles on it. For this you will need a ten cent protractor. Imagine this templet to be the top of the box when laying out each angle. Start at the middle of the back where the eye will be placed, draw a center line from back to front, and lay out the first lens angle (say, the 50-mm. lens: 34 degrees) so it is centered on this line. There will be a 17-degree angle on either side of the middle line. The width of the window to be cut in the front of the box is then established. Lay this templet on one of the other squares and transfer this measurement to it. Since the television picture is three-quarters as high as it is wide (an aspect ratio of 3 to 4) it is then a simple matter to measure the width with a ruler, calculate three-quarters of it, and mark out the height of the window as well. Then it can be cut out with a razor blade. The lens angles of six television lenses are given below:

Standard lenses found on all cameras

50-mm.	(2-inch)	34°
90-mm.	(4-inch)	19°
135-mm.	(6-inch)	13°

Long lenses occasionally used

	(8½-inch)	8°
	(13-inch)	5°

Extreme wide angle occasionally used

35-mm.		51°

When all the windows have been cut, the parts should be painted black and the windows marked with white numerals so they can be read from the *inside* of the box. The six sides of the cube are then taped together with scotch cellulose tape. The box will be most convenient to use if the more commonly used lenses are placed side by side—the 90 in the middle, for example, with the 50 and the 135 on either side.

After the box is together, lens numbers should also be placed on the outside of the box above the proper peep-holes. This will indicate where to look for the view of each desired lens. Some directors have made this even more specific by adding "look here for 50-mm. lens." This will prevent someone from mistaking the labeling of the peep-hole to mean the same opening when it is used as a lens window from the other side of the box.

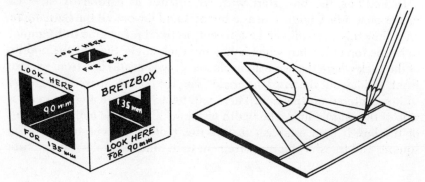

Index

RUDY BRETZ has been in television since 1939, when he started as a cameraman in what was then still a largely experimental field. Subsequently he was production manager of New York City's WPIX-TV. He is also television consultant to the Canadian Broadcasting Corporation and WOI-TV, the educational station at Iowa State College. Past experience includes teaching stints at the College of the City of New York, the American Theater Wing Professional Training Program, and the School of Radio Technique.

EDWARD STASHEFF is associate professor of speech at the University of Michigan, where he teaches radio and television courses. He is also a free-lance TV writer and director, whose recent assignments have included the direction of *I Cover Times Square* (ABC-TV) and the moderating of the panel show *It's Worth Knowing* (WCBS-TV). He was formerly director of television development for the New York City Board of Education and assistant program manager of WPIX-TV.

This is an exercise in poor composition. The white frames represent the field of view of a camera as it pans around the scene. In order to show what not to do, the authors have stopped the camera on six framings with the worst compositions they could find. What makes these compositions poor? The reasons are discussed in Chapter 2.